Antique Tins

IDENTIFICATION & VALUES

BOOK II

Fred Dodge

COLLECTOR BOOKS

A Division of Schroeder Publishing Co., Inc.

The current values in this book should be used only as a guide. They are not intended to set prices, which vary from one section of the country to another. Auction prices as well as dealer prices vary greatly and are affected by condition as well as demand. Neither the Author nor the Publisher assumes responsibility for any losses that might be incurred as a result of consulting this guide.

Searching For A Publisher?

We are always looking for knowledgeable people considered to be experts within their fields. If you feel that there is a real need for a book on your collectible subject and have a large comprehensive collection, contact Collector Books.

Photography: Fred Dodge

Cover Design: Michelle Dowling

Book Design: Mary Ann Dorris

...❖...

CONTENTS

...❖...

ACKNOWLEDGMENTS

I would like to give thanks to a wonderful group of family, friends, collectors, and dealers listed below. Without their contributions of time, tins, and knowledge, this book would not be possible. With great hospitality, many have opened their homes to share their remarkable collections for all to enjoy.

Grant Smith
(310) 545-5171

Alex & Marilyn Znaiden

Ken & Nancy Jones

Lehmann's Antique Advertising & Collectibles
Richard & Ann Lehmann (310) 253-3890
Dealers — All advertising (highest paid)

Dave Garland
(614) 376-0910
Collector — shaving memorabilia, specializing in Star

Schimpff's Confectionery
Jill & Warren Schimpff
347 Spring Street
Jefferson, IN 47120
(812) 283-8367
Collectors — candy memorabilia/museum open 1999

Michael & Sharon Hunt
(317) 271-5602
Dealers/Collectors — all advertising, specializing in popcorn

Bob & Correna Anderson
(706) 657-8465
Dealers/Collectors — all advertising, specializing in early soda

Roy & Lynne Mosemann
(706) 549-0749

Arnold & Cindy Richardson

Archie & Carol Ford

Ben Labudde

Bill & Amy Vehling

Bob & Sherri Copeland

Carol Dodge

Jason Dodge

Don & Mary Perkins
(317) 638-4519
Collectors — all shaving memorabilia

Tom & Mary Lou Slike
(216) 449-1913
Collectors — all advertising, specializing in typewriter ribbon tins

David Fry
P.O. Box 18085
Cleveland Heights, OH 44118-0085
(216) 371-8433
Collector — prophylactic tins

Edward Seidel & Patricia Kaler
319, JPM Rd.
Lewisburg, PA 17837
(717) 523-6435
Dealers/Collectors — all advertising

Hoby & Nancy Van Deusen
28 The Green
Watertown, CT 06795
(860) 945-3456
Editor of *Ribbon Tin News*

Bill & June Mason
(910) 738-1524

Allen & Judy Kimmel

Tom & Lynne Sankiewicz

Joan Bunte

INTRODUCTION

Because of the rapidly growing number of collectors, antique advertising tins have become one of the hottest collectibles on the market today. Do you remember the pocket tin in which your grandfather used to carry his tobacco, or the tin canister that sat on his smoke stand? Remember the coffee tin that grandmother reached for every morning, or the abundance of colorful tins that filled the shelves of the old country store? Those days are long gone, but when sitting down for a relaxed evening and looking up at such a tin, it warms the heart. Whatever your reason for purchasing an antique tin, whether it be simply to decorate your home or to stimulate fond memories, the presence of only a few tins may create an uncontrollable addiction. Today, collectors avidly scurry to antique auctions, flea markets, shows, shops, and malls, searching for these prize works from past artists. From a collector's view the possibilities are unlimited. There are thousands of collectible tins in all shapes and sizes suitable for any budget. Although the value of some tins are soaring to heights beyond the reach of the average collector, the largest percent remains very affordable. Over the past few decades, antique tins have been among the leaders of investment collectibles. From an investor's view, the market is very strong with enormous growth potential for the future. Seldom have I left an advertising show or auction that I did not meet new collectors. The increasing number of new collectors will lower supply, add to demand, and secure investments. Within this guide you will find helpful tips for purchasing and caring for tins, information on advertising collectible clubs, a descriptive and photo grading scale, and over 1,600 color photographs not seen in my previous book, *Antique Tins*. Along with photographs you will find distributors, locations, can makers, approximate sizes, and estimated average values. I derived the values from each tin's respective owner, several dealers, and countless hours of research. For identification and value, I hope this guide will be a great asset to both novice and advanced collectors.

PRICE AND CONDITION

The values within this guide were determined from countless hours of research and input from dealers, collectors, and owners of these tins. While viewing current market values from shows and auctions across the country please keep in mind this is only a guide, and to pinpoint an exact value of a tin would be impossible due to the many different opinions and varying conditions. To a collector, price and condition are of upmost importance when purchasing a tin. Condition, rarity, and artistic design play major roles in determining a tin's value, but condition sometimes arouses controversy.

Many collectors have adopted the numeric grading system 1 through 10, with "1" being poor condition and "10" being mint. One collector may determine a tin grade 8, while another may disagree and consider it only grade 7. To help eliminate this confusion and different grading standards, I have tried to illustrate examples of this system on pages 7, 8, and 9.

It's important to remember, if a tin merits a low grade its value will drop drastically, but if its condition is pristine it will most likely demand a higher price than that listed in this guide.

It has been my experience that very few collectors show interest in tins graded 6 or below. The majority of collectors would rather buy above grade 7 depending on its rarity, but many tins are scarce enough that collectors are overjoyed just to have an example of its kind added to their collection.

> NOTE: All values in this guide pertain to tins of grade 8 condition regardless of their appearance in these photographs. All containers are tin litho unless stated otherwise.

PRICING BRACKETS

Please understand, especially in the lower brackets, a tin valued at $10.00 will fall within the $1.00 – 25.00 bracket, but does not mean it will bring up to $25.00. A tin valued at $30.00 will fall within the $25.00 – 50.00 bracket, but does not mean it will or has ever commanded a $50.00 value. If a tin's condition is pristine, it may be worth the highest amount of the bracket or more, but not always.

Because of the many variables in condition and grading opinions, the purpose of these price brackets are to create flexibility and not pinpoint an exact value. Do not assume a $5.00 tin will sell for five times its value because it falls within the $1.00 – 25.00 price bracket.

$1.00 – 25.00	$300.00 – 350.00	$900.00 – 1,000.00
25.00 – 50.00	350.00 – 400.00	1,000.00 – 1,250.00
50.00 – 75.00	400.00 – 450.00	1,250.00 – 1,500.00
75.00 – 100.00	450.00 – 500.00	1,500.00 – 1,750.00
100.00 – 150.00	500.00 – 600.00	1,750.00 – 2,000.00
150.00 – 200.00	600.00 – 700.00	2,000.00 – 2,500.00
200.00 – 250.00	700.00 – 800.00	2,500.00 – 3,000.00
250.00 – 300.00	800.00 – 900.00	3,000.00+
		No Price Available

No Price Available — I regret using this phrase, but after searching all available resources, I was unsuccessful in finding history or sales of these items. Most tins falling within this category are rare and have never been openly offered for sale, making it extremely difficult to determine their values. If the owners are not sure and cannot comment on the value of such items, it would be unfair for me to render a sole opinion. If these tins are available for sale in the future, it will be the decision of those performing the transactions as to where the value trends will begin.

SIZE

All measurements are rounded to the nearest ¼" and follow the order of height, width, and depth. Flat tins were photographed standing on their side, but measurements reflect the position of normal use. Canister measurements consist of height, then width through their circumference.

GRADING EXAMPLES

Grade 10: Mint – flawless – unused perfect condition – absolutely no sign of wear – rare to find tins in this condition.

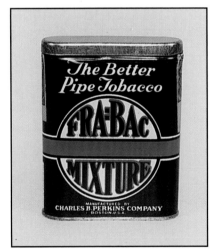

Grade 9: Excellent – near mint condition – nice luster – a few very minor scratches, paint flakes, or rub marks – no fading, dents, or rust.

Grade 8: Fine – starting to show wear from minor scratches, flakes, or chips – possible minute pitting – displays very well – still highly collectible – no serious defects – no fading, dents, or rust.

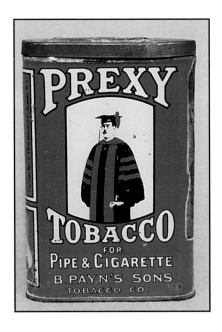

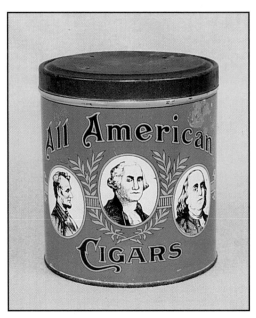

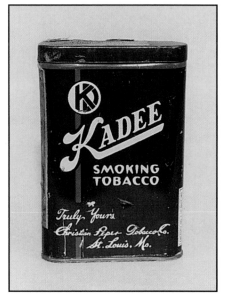

Grade 7: Good – beginning to show major problems – rough edges – several scratches, flakes, or rubs – medium pitting – possible light crazing – minute fading, rust, or dents – still shows with collectible quality.

Grade 6: Poor – rough looking – heavy scratches, flakes, or rubs – heavy pitting or crazing – light fading, dents, or rust – questionable if collectible.

Grade 5: Filler – extensive wear – medium fading, rust, or dents – usually only collectible if scarce or rare.

WHERE TO FIND ANTIQUE TINS

Antique collectibles normally are passed from generation to generation until an heir loses interest and they are sold. Often times items will reappear unexpectedly from an old estate not having seen the light of day for many years. After being rediscovered a large percentage will find their way to a dealer, show, or auction. A subscription to a nationally distributed antique newspaper is very informative on these events. Information concerning these subscriptions may be found at most antique shows or book stores in your area. Below is a very informative weekly antique newspaper for shows, auctions, and articles. For more information write or call:

Antique Week
P.O. Box 90
Knightstown, Indiana 46148
(800) 876-5133

Below are tin clubs, for more information write:

Tins & Signs
P.O. Box 440101
Aurora, Colorado 80044

A.A.A.A.
(Antique Advertising Association of America)
Post Office Box 1121
Morton Grove, Illinois 60053

Ribbon Tin News
28 The Green
Watertown, Connecticut 06795

TIPS FOR CARING, COLLECTING, AND PURCHASING TINS

1. Prepare yourself, know the value of a tin that interests you and the price you are willing to pay before finding it. This will eliminate overpayment and lengthy decision time.

2. If you are at a show or flea market and have not prepared yourself for the price to pay for a tin, you may need a little time to decide whether to purchase it. Pick up the tin, look it over but do not set it down unless you have decided against the purchase. While the tin is in your possession, you will have the option to buy it. Other collectors must await your decision before they will be able to purchase that tin.

3. While attending a highly publicized advertising show, you may find a tin and feel it is a great buy, but again, find yourself in the position of not knowing whether to make the purchase. You should make your decision at that time. Do not make the mistake of shopping around and thinking you may come back to purchase that tin. If it is a good buy, most likely it will be gone in a matter of seconds. Another collector or dealer is right behind you also looking for a great buy.

4. Almost all antique malls, shops, and dealers will offer a small discount. Around 10% is usually the figure and occasionally 20% or more if the dealer has owned the tin for an extended period of time. It never hurts to ask for a discount or to make a reasonable offer, most dealers expect it. Keep in mind, the dealers are doing you a

favor by finding and offering their items for sale. Every collector would like to pay as little as possible, but dealers are trying to make a living and must make profit. The dealers spend time, work, and money enabling you to easily walk up and purchase a tin. If you have an offer in mind that seems extremely low, do not express it. Simply ask the dealer to quote the lowest possible purchase price for that tin. Under no circumatances should you insult the dealer with a counteroffer after the lowest possible price has been quoted. The results of an angry dealer could mean smaller or no discounts in the future. Multiple dealer shops or malls will also accept offers below their customary discounts. Often times, if possible, they will contact the dealer by phone and have an answer before you leave.

5. Beware of auction fever. Participating in a live auction can be very exciting and enjoyable. However, excitement can sometimes spoil the joy. When experiencing a competitive situation, mother nature has instilled within us the desire to win. The overpowering excitement of the auction crowd and competitive bidding can easily motivate a collector into becoming possessed with desire to own a tin. Many collectors refer to this state as the *fever*. This fever can easily be detected by an idle observer or an auctioneer who will sometimes prey upon an unsuspecting victim with luring jesters such as, "don't quit on me now," "I believe I would," "one more time and you'll own it," etc. A fevered bidder will loose concentration and all concept of a tin's condition and value. As a result, the winning purchase price will be two or three times more than the actual value of the tin. When the excitement wears off and the fevered bidder returns to normal, the remorse from the purchase has spoiled the fun.

6. If you purchase a tin by mail or through an auction absentee bid, take the time to research its condition. Make sure the seller or auction host describes every fault of the tin in explicit detail. A few minutes on the telephone may eliminate grief from an unwanted purchase. Make sure you have the option to return the tin if you are not completely satisfied. Most dealers and individuals will offer a return privilege, but some auctions will not.

7. Normally, you will be responsible for payment of a tin prior to shipping. Under these circumstances, if the tin is lost during transport, it will be your loss and not the sellers. Make absolutely sure the seller will purchase adequate insurance for your tin at the time of shipment. One does not like to think of a loss as such, but occasionally it does happen.

8. Do not subject tins to sunlight for even the shortest period of time. The sun's intense ultraviolet radiation will convert the energy in paint pigments to heat or chemical energy, which will decompose or actually burn the coloring medium. The decomposed coloring medium will then reflect light differently presenting a faded look. All tins will fade, but a significant difference will be detected within a matter of minutes if an unstable colorant was used in the paint formula.

9. Fluorescent lighting may save up to 50% of energy and last 10 to 20 times longer than incandescent lighting. The negative aspect is fluorescent lights also produce ultraviolet radiation. Although the intensity is much less than that of the sun, over an extended period of time the results are just as harmful. Do not take this tip lightly, tins in this environment will fade. A corrective filter or ultraviolet protective plastic film should be purchased to block the harmful radiation.

10. A collector's nightmare is to purchase a very expensive tin and discover sometime later, it had numerous defects that were hidden with new paint. Through advanced technology, the colors of old paints are easily duplicated and with the touch of a professional artist, may be difficult to detect under normal lighting. However, to match color and the exact chemical compound of an aged paint is nearly impossible. This unlikely match provides a means of detection with an inexpensive tool known as the ultraviolet or black light. To explain, look around yourself, everything you see is made of molecular structures that are absorbing and

and reflecting light energy. The reflecting energy, measured by wave lengths, is what we refer to as color. Different molecular structures will reflect different sequences of wave lengths which produce different colors. The molecular structures of old and new paints are different, therefore making the reflecting wave lengths different. The paints may appear to be the same color, but by eliminating all lighting and replacing it with a higher energy light source (black light), we can magnify the visual difference of the reflecting wave lengths. A collector of extremely rare tins would be wise to use a black light. It could possibly save hundreds of dollars or help prevent an unwarranted purchase.

11. Displaying tins in an environment with excessive moisture, such as a bathroom, will cause some old paints to degenerate and loose adherence. The final summation will be excessive chalking or flaking.

12. Displaying tins over or near a heat source, such as a furnace register, will cause some old paints to expand, contract, and separate. Crazing or cracking of the paint will be perceived over time.

13. Tins should be lightly dusted on a regular basis, but cleaning is not recommended. If you feel you must clean a tin, use extreme caution. Excess dirt may be removed by gently applying mild soap and water. Do not immerse tins in water or use harsh household cleaning products. Steel wool, brushes, and abrasive wax compounds should never be used. Some collectors will apply a non-abrasive polish to add luster to a tin, but again, use extreme caution. Many thin paints will displace from a tin to a rag with only a few strokes. Never apply polyurethane, varnish, shellac, or sealant to tins at any time.

14. Novice collectors should be selective and refrain from overspending. Although some collectors have tried, it would be foolish to think you could own every tin. Budget overspending is not uncommon at first, but will soon take the fun out of collecting. Some collectors will purchase every tin that appeals to them, while others will limit themselves or specialize in certain types such as store bins, tobacco pockets, key wind coffees, powder samples, etc. I venture to say there is a tin that will correspond with every theme known. Novice collectors are wise to limit themselves to a specific category, type, or theme. They should expand their collections in time after becoming more knowledgeable of the availability and values of tins.

15. All collectors, novice and advanced, should socialize with other collectors. It is impossible for one collector to know everything about tins. Socializing with other collectors will not only keep your interest stirred, it will keep you knowledgeable of current values and quantities. No collector wants to purchase a rare tin and soon find out, it was one of several to surface. Collecting tins is far more enjoyable if you have friends that appreciate your collection as much as you.

TIN MANUFACTURERS

Companies made and distributed their products, however the tin containers in which the products were sold were usually made at another location by a tin can manufacturer. The names of these manufacturers are found on many tins in very small print at various locations. Some collectors use this information when possible to date and locate the production of tins. Tins marked with tin manufacturers are quite appealing to descendants of those who worked at these factories. Many collectors look for tin manufacturer inscriptions to find tins that were produced at a specific location or produced in their local area. To help such collectors, I have listed several tin manufacturers and their locations below.

Acme Can Co. ....Philadelphia, Pennsylvania

American Can Co. (A.C.Co.) .... formed in 1901

American Can Co. 2A ....Waltham, Massachusetts., open until early 1950s

American Can Co. 8A .... New York, New York
American Can Co. 10A .... Brooklyn, New York
American Can Co. 11A .... Brooklyn, New York, open until 1917
American Can Co. 12A .... Brooklyn, New York
American Can Co. 14A .... New York, New York
American Can Co. 17A .... Jersey City, New Jersey
American Can Co. 43A .... Baltimore, Maryland, open until mid 1930s
American Can Co. 48A .... Chatham, Ontario, Canada
American Can Co. 50A .... Richmond, Virginia, open until 1951
American Can Co. 52A .... Cleveland, Ohio
American Can Co. 68A .... Kansas City, Missouri
American Can Co. 69A .... Chicago, Illinois
American Can Co. 73A .... Chicago, Illinois
American Can Co. 004 .... Indianapolis, Indiana
American Can Co. 041 .... Tampa, Florida
American Can Co. 051 .... Atlanta, Georgia
American Can Co. 056 .... Milwaukee, Wisconsin
American Can Co. 068 .... Chicago, Illinois
American Can Co. 082 .... St. Paul, Minnesota
American Can Co. 083 .... St. Louis, Missouri
American Stopper Co. .... Brooklyn, New York
Art Metal Co. .... New York, New York
Aubrey .... Montreal, Canada
Beardsley Mfg. Co. .... Cleveland, Ohio, became A.C. Co. 52A in 1901
Bertels Metalware Co. .... Kingston, Pennsylvania
Buffalo Can Co. .... Buffalo, New York
Calvert Litho Co. .... Detroit, Michigan
Chicago Stamping Co. .... Chicago, Illinois
Columbia Can Co. .... St. Louis, Missouri
Continental Can Co. (C.C.Co.) .... founded in 1904
Diesel Can Co. .... Chicago, Illinois, became A.C. Co. 69A in 1901
Federal Tin Co. .... Baltimore, Maryland, open until early 1930s
Ginna & Co. .... New York, New York, became A.C. Co. 14A in 1901
Hasker & Marcuse Mfg. Co. .... Richmond, Virginia, became A.C. Co. 50A in 1901
Heekin Can Co. .... Cincinnati, Ohio, founded in 1901, circled H trademark
Illinois Can Co. .... Chicago, Illinois
Ilsley S.A. Co. .... New York, New York, became A.C. Co. 8A in 1901
Interprise Stamping Co. .... Pittsburgh, Pennsylvania
Landau & Cormack .... Montreal, Canada
Liberty Can Co. .... Lancaster, Pennsylvania, founded in 1919
Macdonald Mfg. Co. .... Canada, open 1900 – 1930
Mersereau .... Brooklyn, New York
National Can Co. .... Baltimore, Maryland
Norton Bros. .... Chicago, Illinois, became A.C. Co. 73A in 1901
Passaic Metalware .... Passaic, New Jersey
Republic Metalware Co. .... Buffalo, New York
Ritter Can Co. .... Philadelphia, Pennsylvania
Somers Bros. .... Brooklyn, New York, became A.C. Co. 11A in 1901
Southern Can Co. .... Baltimore, Maryland, open 1901 – 1914
Thos. Davidson Mfg. Co. .... Canada
Tindeco (Tin Decorating Co. of Baltimore) .... Baltimore, Maryland, founded in 1900
Towle S.F. Co. .... New York, New York
Vogel Bros. .... Brooklyn New York, became A.C. Co. 12A in 1901
Western Can Co. .... San Francisco, CA.
Wheeling Can Co. .... Wheeling, W. Virginia
Whitall Can Co. .... Montreal, Canada
Wilkes-Barre Can Co. .... Wilkes-Barre, Pennsylvania

1860 by W.T. Hancock, Richmond, Virginia, 4" x 4" x 2¼", $350.00 – 400.00.
Courtesy of Grant Smith

3 Aces flat pocket by R.W. Jenkinson Co., marked A.C. Co., 50A, 1" x 4½" x 2½", $2,500.00 – 3,000.00.
Courtesy of Grant Smith

"Acme" by McGill Tobacco Works, New York, marked Hasker & Marcuse, 1½" x 4½" x 2½", $100.00 – 150.00.
Courtesy of Grant Smith

55 vertical cigar box by W.F. Hinesley Cigar Manufacturing, Lexington, Missouri, 5¼" x 3¼" x 3¼", $50.00 – 75.00.
Courtesy of Ken & Nancy Jones

Admiral cigar canister marked American Can Co. 70A, 6¼" x 5", $250.00 – 300.00.
Courtesy of Grant Smith

After Dinner canister by B. Vander Tak & Co., Rotterdam, Holland, 5¼" x 5", rare, no price available.
Courtesy of Grant Smith

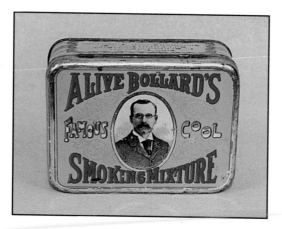

Alive Bollard's by A. Bollard, Toronto, Canada, 2"
x 5" x 3¹/₂", $100.00 – 150.00.
Courtesy of Grant Smith

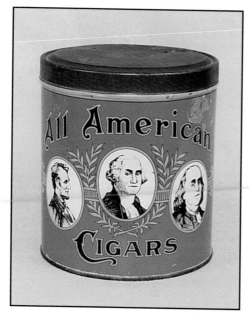

All American cigar canister by C.E. Acton
Co., Belmont, Ohio, marked Heekin Can
Co., 5¹/₂" x 5", $400.00 – 450.00.
Courtesy of Grant Smith

All Nations by J. Wright Co., Richmond, Virginia,
marked Hasker & Marcuse, 1³/₄" x 4¹/₂" x 2¹/₂",
$300.00 – 350.00.
Courtesy of Grant Smith

Alright vertical pocket by Joh Wil Von
Eicken, 4¹/₄" x 3" x 1", $450.00 – 500.00.

Alles & Fisher's cigar box by Alles & Fisher,
Boston, 2¹/₂" x 5¹/₄" x 3¹/₂", $1.00 – 25.00.

Always Cocktail vertical cigarette pocket by United States Cigarette Factories, branches, Pittsburgh, Pennsylvania & Amsterdam, 3" x 3" x 1¼", $500.00 – 600.00.
Courtesy of Bob & Sherri Copeland

Always Cocktail vertical cigarette pocket by United States Cigarette Factories, branches, Pittsburgh, Pennsylvania & Amsterdam, 3" x 3" x 1¼", $500.00 – 600.00.
Courtesy of Roy & Lynne Moseman

American Eagle flat pocket by American Eagle Tobacco Works, Detroit, Michigan, ½" x 3½" x 2¼", small eagle, $1,750.00 – 2,000.00.
Courtesy of Grant Smith

American Eagle flat pocket by American Eagle Tobacco Works, Detroit, Michigan, ½" x 3½" x 2¼", large eagle, $1,250.00 – 1,500.00.
Courtesy of Grant Smith

American Eagle Bird's Eye vertical box by American Eagle Tobacco Co., Detroit, Michigan, marked S.A. Ilsley, 4½" x 3½" x 2", $500.00 – 600.00.
Courtesy of Grant Smith

Americn Eagle concave box by American Eagle Tobacco Co., Detroit, Michigan, 5¼" x 6" x 4½", $150.00 – 200.00.
Courtesy of Grant Smith

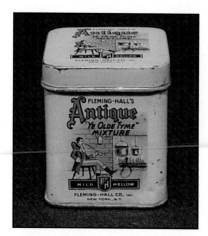

Antique by Fleming-Hall Co. Inc., 2¼" x 2¼" x 2¼", $1.00 – 25.00.

Araks vertical cigarette pocket marked Tchamkerten et Co., 3" x 3¼" x ¾", $150.00 – 200.00.

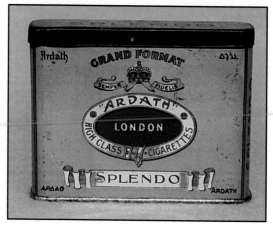

"Ardath" Splendo cigarette vertical pocket by Ardath Tobacco Co. Ltd., London, 3" x 4" x 1", $75.00 – 100.00.

Courtesy of Bob & Sherri Copeland

Auto flat pocket by Continental Tobacco Co., ½" x 3½" x 2¼", $100.00 – 150.00.

Courtesy of Grant Smith

Autobacco vertical pocket by S.S. Pierce Co., Boston, Massachusetts, 4½" x 3" x 1", $2,000.00 – 2,500.00.

B.F. Gravely & Sons vertical pockets by B.F. Gravely of Virginia, left: 4" x 3" x 1"; right: 4½" x 3" x 1", $350.00 – 400.00 each.

Baco-Curo by Eureka Chemical & Manufacturing Co., La Crosse, Wisconsin, 1/2" x 3 1/2" x 2 1/4", $75.00 – 100.00.
Courtesy of Grant Smith

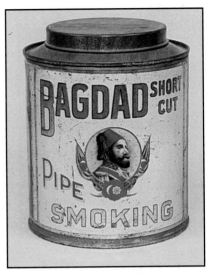

Bagdad small top canister, 6" x 5", $1,250.00 – 1,500.00.
Courtesy of Grant Smith

Bagdad ceramic humador, 6 1/2" x 5", $100.00 – 150.00.

Bank Note vertical cigar box marked Federal Tin Co., 5 1/4" x 3 1/2" x 3 1/2", $25.00 – 50.00.

Banquet vertical box by The American Tobacco Co., Detroit, Michigan, marked S.A. Ilsley, 3 1/2" x 3" x 3", $200.00 – 250.00.
Courtesy of Grant Smith

Bartholdi Mixture by Peter Hauptmann & Co., St. Louis, Missouri, 2 1/4" x 4 1/2" x 3 1/4", $1,000.00 – 1,250.00.
Courtesy of Grant Smith

Battle Royal flat pocket by The United States Tobacco Co., marked Hasker & Marcuse, 1" x 4¹/²" x 2¹/²", $200.00 – 250.00.
Courtesy of Grant Smith

Beech-Nut store bin by P. Lorillard Co., 8³/4" x 10" x 8", $300.00 – 350.00.
Courtesy of Mike & Sharon Hunt

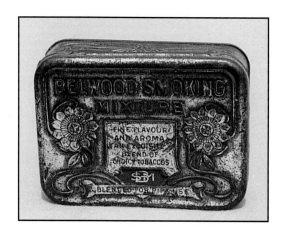

Belwood embossed flat pocket, 1¹/4" x 4¹/²" x 3¹/4", $1.00 – 25.00.

Benson & Hedges cigarette tin, 3¹/4" x 2³/4", $1.00 – 25.00.
Courtesy of Bob & Sherri Copeland

Berriman's cigar canister for Sears Roebuck & Co., 5" x 4", $50.00 – 75.00.
Courtesy of Ken & Nancy Jones

Big Ben (clock) canister by Imperial Tobacco Co. of Canada, Limited Montreal-Granby, 4¹/²" x 5", $25.00 – 50.00.

Black & White by W.L. Gravely & Co., Danville, Virginia, marked Hasker & Marcuse, 1³/₄" x 4¹/₂" x 2¹/₂", $100.00 – 150.00.
Courtesy of Grant Smith

Black and White cigar flat pocket marked 1st Dist. N.Y., ¹/₂" x 3¹/₄" x 1³/₄", $25.00 – 50.00.

Bill William cigar box by H.L. Bowers Cigar Co., Mansfield, Ohio, 1¹/₄" x 3¹/₄" x 5", $25.00 – 50.00.

Black Cat flat 50 cigarette tin, ³/₄" x 5³/₄" x 4¹/₄", $1.00 – 25.00. Note: A yellow version exists.

Blendwell paper label canister, 5¹/₄" x 3³/₄", $25.00 – 50.00.

Blenown vertical pocket by Daniel Frank Co., Boston, marked A.C. Co. 50A, 4" x 3¹/₂" x 1", $500.00 – 600.00.
Courtesy of Grant Smith

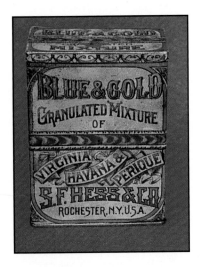

Blue & Gold vertical box by S.F. Hess & Co., Rochester, New York, marked Hasker & Marcuse, 4¹/₂" x 3¹/₂" x 2", $250.00 – 300.00.
Courtesy of Grant Smith

Blue Jay cigar box by Orrison Cigar Co. Inc., Bethesda, Ohio, 5¹/2" x 3¹/2" x 3¹/2", $200.00 – 250.00.
Courtesy of Ken & Nancy Jones

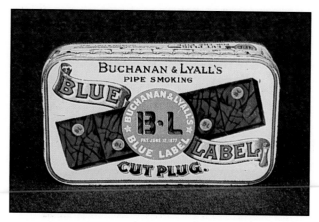

Blue Label flat pocket by Buchanan & Lyall's, marked S.A. Ilsley & Co., Brooklyn, N.Y., 1" x 4¹/2" x 2¹/2", $50.00 – 75.00.
Courtesy of Grant Smith

Bohemian by Surbrug Co., Richmond, Virginia, 1¹/4" x 4¹/2" x 3¹/4", $1.00 – 25.00.

Bohemian by The Surbrug Co., Richmond, Virginia and New York City, 6" x 5" x 5", rare, no price available. Note: A 4¹/2" x 4" x 4" size exists.
Courtesy of Grant Smith

Bon-Air paper label, 5¹/2" x 5", $1.00 – 25.00.
Courtesy of Tom & Lynne Sankiewicz

"*Bond of Union*" by Cope Bros. & Co. Ltd.,
London, 1³/₄" x 5" x 3³/₄", $75.00 – 100.00.

Boot Jack flat pocket by American
Tobacco Co., ¹/₄" x 3¹/₄" x 1³/₄",
$1.00 – 25.00.

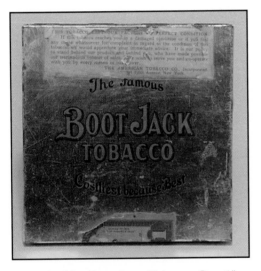

Boot Jack by American Tobacco Co., 1" x
6¹/₄" x 6¹/₄", $1.00 – 25.00.

Boston Slice by F. Abraham & Son, Boston,
Massachusetts, marked S.A. Iksley, 1¹/₄" x
4¹/₂" x 3¹/₄", $75.00 – 100.00.
Courtesy of Grant Smith

Boston Slice by Ehrlich & Kopf, Boston, Massachusetts, 5¹/₂" x 7" x 4¹/₂", $150.00 – 200.00.
Courtesy of Grant Smith

Briggs (complimentary) vertical pocket by P.
Lorillard Co., 4¹/₄" x 3" x 1", $150.00 – 200.00.

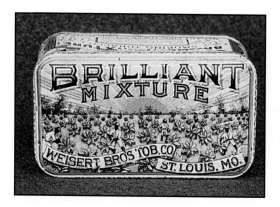

Brilliant Mixture by Weisert Bro's. Tobacco Co., St. Louis, Missouri, marked Hasker & Marcuse, 1³/₄" x 4¹/₂" x 2¹/₂", $100.00 – 150.00.
Courtesy of Grant Smith

Brindley's Mixture paper label vertical pocket by Faber, Coe & Gregg, Inc., 3" x 3¹/₂" x 1", $1.00 – 25.00. Note: A taller version exists with same value.

Brotherhood small top canister by United Brothers, 6¹/₂" x 4³/₄", $250.00 – 300.00.
Courtesy of Grant Smith

Buckingham paper label vertical pocket by John J. Bagley & Co., Detroit, Michigan, 4¹/₂" x 3" x 1", $75.00 – 100.00.
Courtesy of Bob & Sherri Copeland

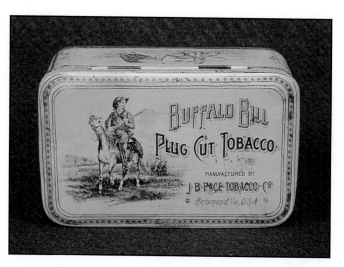

Buffalo Bill by J.B. Pace Tobacco Co., Richmond, Virginia, 2¹/₄" x 6" x 3³/₄", $1,500.00 – 1,750.00.
Courtesy of Grant Smith

Bull Dog by Lovell & Buffington Tobacco Co., Covington, Kentucky, marked A.C. Co. 50A, 5" x 6" x 4", $500.00 – 600.00.
Courtesy of Grant Smith

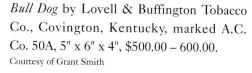

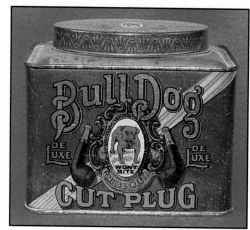

Bull Dog cardboard vertical pocket by Lovell & Buffington Tobacco Co., Covington, Kentucky, 4¼" x 2¼" x 1¼", rare, no price available.

Bull Dog vertical pockets by Lovell & Buffington Tobacco Co., Covington, Kentucky, left to right: #1, #2 & #3 $450.00 – 500.00 each; #4 cardboard, $500.00 – 600.00; #5 oval, $500.00 – 600.00.
Courtesy of Ken & Nancy Jones

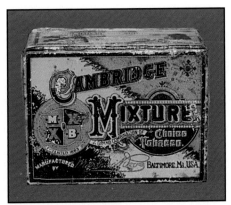

Cambridge Mixture by Marburg Bros., Baltimore, Maryland, 2¼" x 4½" x 3¼", $75.00 – 100.00.
Courtesy of Bob & Sherri Copeland

Camel cigar tin marked Heekin Can Co., Cincinnati, OH., 5½" x 6" x 4¼", $100.00 – 150.00.

Buster Brown cigar canister marked R.F. Outcault, 5" x 5", $3,000.00+.
Courtesy of Grant Smith

Camel vertical pocket cigarette case, 3¾" x 2¼" x 1", $25.00 – 50.00.

Camel cigarette tins by R.J. Reynolds, Winston-Salem, North Carolina, left: 100 count, 3¼" x 3½", $25.00 – 50.00; right: 50 count, 3" x 2¾", $400.00 – 450.00.
Courtesy of Bob & Sherri Copeland

Cameron & Cameron Best by Cameron & Cameron, Richmond, Virginia, marked Hasker & Marcuse, 5$1/2$" x 6" x 4", $300.00 – 350.00.
Courtesy of Grant Smith

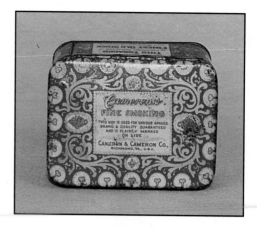

Cameron's by Cameron & Cameron Co., Richmond, Virginia, 2" x 4$1/2$" x 3$1/4$", $25.00 – 50.00.

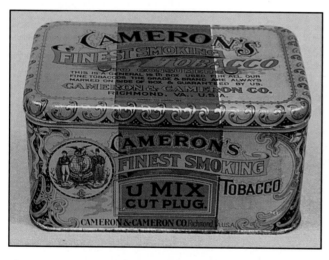

Cameron's by Cameron & Cameron, Richmond, Virginia, 3$1/4$" x 6" x 3$1/4$", $100.00 – 150.00.
Courtesy of Grant Smith

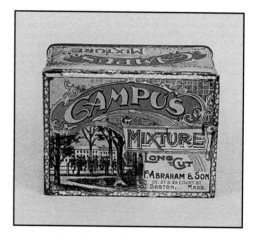

Campus by F. Abraham & Son, Boston, Massachusetts, marked Somers Bros., 2$1/4$" x 4$1/2$" x 3$1/4$", rare, no price available.
Courtesy of Grant Smith

Capstan by W.D. & H.O. Wills, Bristol & London, 2$1/4$" x 2$1/4$" x 2$1/4$", $75.00 – 100.00.

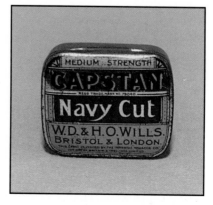

Capstan by W.D. & H.O. Wills, Bristol & London, $3/4$" x 2$1/4$" x 2", $1.00 – 25.00.

Carlton Club, 3" x 2", $25.00 – 50.00.

Carnation Mixture by Cameron & Cameron Manufacturers, Richmond, Virginia, 2¹/₄" x 4¹/₂" x 3¹/₄", $150.00 – 200.00.
Courtesy of Grant Smith

Castle Hall vertical cigar box marked Ritter Manufacturing Co., 5¹/₂" x 3" x 3", $100.00 – 150.00.
Courtesy of Grant Smith

Century flat pockets by P. Lorillard & Co., Jersey City, marked Somers Bros., ¹/₂" x 3¹/₂" x 2¹/₄", left: $500.00 – 600.00; right: $200.00 – 250.00.
Courtesy of Grant Smith

Century flat pocket with working combination lock by P. Lorillard & Co., ¹/₂" x 3¹/₂" x 2¹/₄", $200.00 – 250.00.

Champaign by B. Houde & Co., Quebec, marked Macdonald, 1¹/₄" x 4¹/₂" x 3¹/₄", $50.00 – 75.00.
Courtesy of Grant Smith

Checkerberry Snuff marked Railroad Mills, 2" x 1¹/₂", $25.00 – 50.00.
Courtesy of Bob & Sherri Copeland

Choice by Ogburn, Hill & Co's., 1¹/₂" x 12¹/₂" x 3¹/₄", $75.00 – 100.00.

Courtesy of Bob & Sherri Copeland

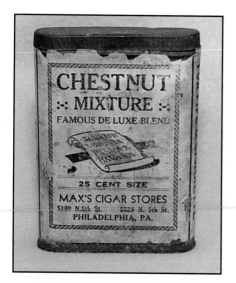

Chestnut paper label vertical pocket by Max's Cigar Stores, Philadelphia, Pennsylvania, 4¹/₂" x 3" x 1", $50.00 – 75.00.

Courtesy of Archie & Carol Ford

Cinco by Otto Eisenlohr & Bros., left: marked A.C. Co., 5¹/₄" x 3" x 3"; right: marked Ritter Can Co., 5" x 5" x 5"; $1.00 – 25.00 each.

Churchman's Wireless Mixture flat pocket by W.A. & A.C. Churchman branch of Imperial Tobacco Co. of Great Britain & Ireland, 1" x 4¹/₂" x 3¹/₄", $25.00 – 50.00.

Climax flat pocket by P. Lorillard Co., ¹/₂" x 3¹/₂" x 2", $1.00 – 25.00.

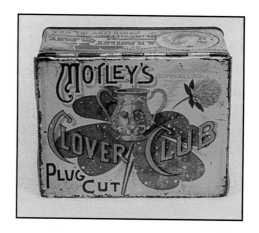

Clover Club by A.H. Motley Co., Reedsville, North Carolina, 2¹/₄" x 4¹/₂" x 3¹/₄", $500.00 – 600.00.

Courtesy of Grant Smith

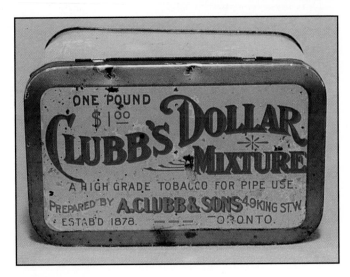

Club by Imperial Tobacco Co. of Canada, Limited, Montreal, Granby, 4¹/₂" x 5", $25.00 – 50.00.

Clubb's Dollar Mixture by A. Clubb & Sons, Toronto, Canada, 4¹/₄" x 6¹/₂" x 4", $1.00 – 25.00.

Coarse French Rappee flat pocket by P. Lorillard & Co., Jersey City, New Jersey, marked Somers Bros., ¹/₂" x 2³/₄" x 1¹/₂", $450.00 – 500.00.

Columbia for Sears, Roebuck & Co., 6¹/₂" x 5", $150.00 – 200.00.
Courtesy of Grant Smith

Commander (Hunt Bros.) by Fergus Falls Cigar Factory, Fergus Falls, Minnesota, 5" x 3³/₄", $75.00 – 100.00.
Courtesy of Mike & Sharon Hunt

Commodore vertical pocket by Weideman Co., Cleveland, Ohio, marked American Can Co. 11A, 3¹/₂" x 3¹/₂" x 1¹/₄", rare, no price available. Note: Two variations exist with and without statue of Commodore Perry on reverse side.

Courtesy of Roy & Lynne Moseman

Continental Cubes 5" x 5" x 5", rare, $3,000.00+.

Courtesy of Grant Smith

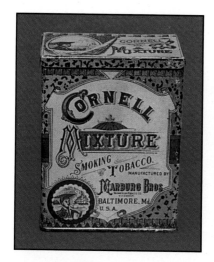 

Cosmos by Fauth & Ogden, Philadelphia, 2¹/₄" x 4¹/₂" x 3¹/₄", $250.00 – 300.00.

Courtesy of Grant Smith

Coronation flat 100 cigarette tin by S.S. Pierce Co., Boston, Massachusetts, 1¹/₂" x 5¹/₂" x 4¹/₄", $25.00 – 50.00.

Cornell vertical box by Marburg Bros., Baltimore, Maryland, American Tobacco Co. Successor, marked Somers Bros., 4¹/₂" x 3¹/₂" x 2", $100.00 – 150.00.

Courtesy of Grant Smith

Counsellor vertical box marked
Cressman's & Rothschilds, 5¹/₄"
x 3¹/₄" x 3¹/₄", $100.00 – 150.00.

Country Club cigar vertical box by
W.H. Snyder & Sons, marked Liberty
Can Co., Lancaster, PA., 5¹/₂" x 3¹/₂" x
3¹/₂", $250.00 – 300.00.
Courtesy of Ken & Nancy Jones

Court Royal by San Telmo
Cigar Manufacturing Co.,
Detroit, Michigan, marked
Passaic Metalware Co., 5¹/₄" x
3" x 3", $75.00 – 100.00.

Crane's Private Mixture paper
label vertical pocket marked
Indianapolis, 4¹/₄" x 3¹/₄" x
1¹/₄", $75.00 – 100.00.
Courtesy of Bill & June Mason

Craven "A" flat 50 cigarette tin by Carreras
Limited, Acadia Works, London, England,
³/₄" x 5³/₄" x 4¹/₄", $1.00 – 25.00.

Crescent Club, 2" x 4¹/₂" x 3¹/₄", $150.00 –
200.00.
Courtesy of Grant Smith

Crest large flat pocket by Allen H. Wright, Hicksville, Ohio, 1¹/₄" x 5¹/₄" x 3¹/₂", $1.00 – 25.00.

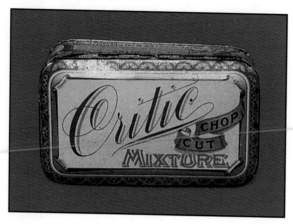

Critic by Daniel Scotten & Co., Detroit, Michigan, marked Ginna & Co., N.Y., 1³/₄" x 4¹/₂" x 2¹/₂", $75.00 – 100.00.
Courtesy of Grant Smith

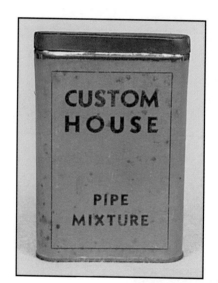

Custom House paper label vertical pocket by Aufder Heider & Son, Philadelphia, Pennsylvania, 4¹/₂" x 3" x 1", $25.00 – 50.00.
Courtesy of Tom & Mary Lou Slike

Cutty Pipe store bin by Weyman & Bros., 12" x 8" x 7", $400.00 – 450.00.
Courtesy of Tom & Mary Lou Slike

Daily Habit cigar canister marked Liberty Can Co., Lancaster, PA., 5¹/₄" x 5¹/₂", $150.00 – 200.00. Note: A smaller size exists with same value.

Diadem flat pocket by J.G. Flint Jr., Milwaukee, marked Chicago Stamping Co., 1/2" x 3 1/2" x 2 1/4", $250.00 – 300.00.

De Voe's concaved vertical pockets by The United States Tobacco Co., Richmond, Virginia, left: 4 1/2" x 3" x 1", right: 4 1/4" x 3" x 1", $300.00 – 350.00 each. Note: another exists that is not concaved.
Courtesy of Grant Smith.

Della Rocca paper label vertical box by Alexander Gordon, Detroit, Michigan, 5 1/4" x 3 1/2" x 3 1/2", $75.00 – 100.00. Note: a canister also exists.
Courtesy of Bob & Sherri Copeland

Dill's Best vertical pockets by J.G. Dill Co., Richmond, Virginia, left to right: #1 & #2, $200.00 – 250.00 each; #3, $75.00 – 100.00; #4 & #5, $25.00 – 50.00 each.

Dill's Best short canister by J.G. Dill Co., Richmond, Virginia, 2 3/4" x 5", $25.00 – 50.00.

Dill's Best by J.G. Dill Co., Richmond, Virginia, 3/4" x 3 1/2" x 2 1/4", left: $25.00 – 50.00; center and right: $1.00 – 25.00 each.

Dill's Best vertical pockets by J.G. Dill Co., Richmond, Virginia, 4¹/₂" x 3" x 1", from left to right: #1, $1.00 – 25.00; #2, $100.00 – 150.00; #3, $200.00 – 250.00; #4 & #5, $50.00 – 75.00 each.

Dill's Best vertical pockets by J.G. Dill & Co., Richmond, Virginia, left: 2³/₄" x 3¹/₄" x 1", $25.00 – 50.00; others: $150.00 – 200.00 each. Note: The four tall tins read CUBE CUT PLUG, the common variation reads RUBBED CUBE CUT.

Dixie Maid paper label marked Factory No. 57, 11th Dist. OH., 5¹/₂" x 3¹/₂" x 1¹/₄", $50.00 – 75.00.

Courtesy of Archie & Carol Ford

Don Porto oval cigar tin marked Liberty Can Co., 5¹/₂" x 6¹/₂" x 4¹/₄", $75.00 – 100.00.

Courtesy of Richard & Ann Lehmann

Doublets flat cigarette pocket by Axton-Fisher Tobacco Co., Louisville, Kentucky, ¹/₄" x 3¹/₂" x 3", $1.00 – 25.00.

Courtesy of Bob & Sherri Copeland

Dubonnet De Luxe marked Factory No. 132 3rd Dist. of New York, 1" x 5" x 3½", $1.00 – 25.00.

Courtesy of Bob & Sherri Copeland

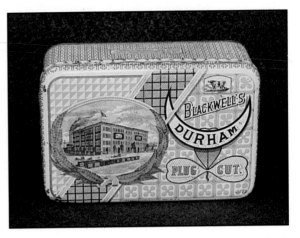

Durham by W.T. Blackwell & Co., Durham, North Carolina, 2¼" x 6" x 4", $800.00 – 900.00.

Courtesy of Grant Smith

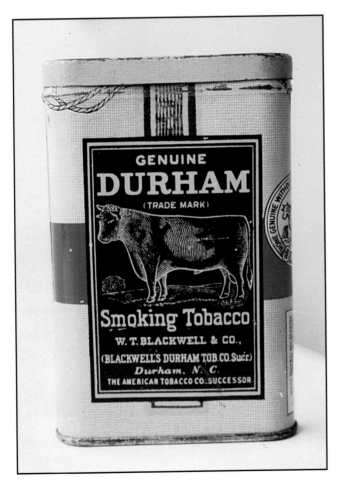

Durham vertical pocket by W.T. Blackwell & Co., Durham, North Carolina, 4½" x 3" x 1", $3,000.00+.

Eagle Brand Snuff by C.W. Patterson & Son, Chicago, Illinois, 1½" x 2¼" x 1¼", $25.00 – 50.00.

Courtesy of Richard & Ann Lehmann

Egret by G.A. Strobeck, Red Lion, Pennsylvania, 5¹/2" x 4³/4" x 4³/4", $250.00 – 300.00.
Courtesy of Ken & Nancy Jones

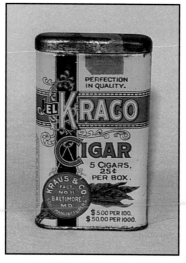

El Kraco cigar vertical pocket by Kraus & Co., Baltimore, Maryland, marked A.C. Co., 50A., 5" x 3" x 1", $500.00 – 600.00.

El Parmela cigar tin marked Factory No. 57, 11th Dist. of OH., 5¹/2" x 6¹/4" x 4¹/4", $100.00 – 150.00.

El Teano cigar tin marked Factory #666 1st Dist. of PA., 5¹/2" x 6¹/4" x 4¹/4", $100.00 – 150.00.
Courtesy of Bob & Sherri Copeland

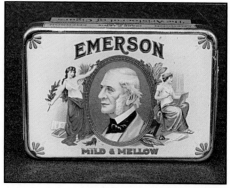

Emerson large flat pocket by Frank P. Lewis Cigar Co., 1¹/4" x 5" x 3¹/2", $50.00 – 75.00.
Courtesy of Bob & Sherri Copeland

Emilia Garcia cigar tin marked Factory No. 620, 14th Dist. of N.Y., 5" x 5¹/2", $50.00 – 75.00.

English Bird's Eye vertical box by The American Tobacco Co. Successor to Wm. S. Kimball & Co., Rochester, New York, marked Hasker & Marcuse, 4¹/2" x 3¹/2" x 2", $200.00 – 250.00.
Courtesy of Grant Smith

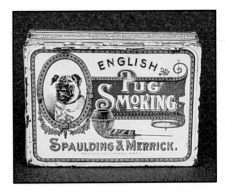

English Pug by Spaulding & Merrick, 1¼" x 4½" x 3¼", $300.00 – 350.00.
Courtesy of Grant Smith

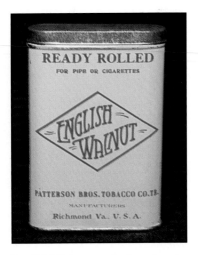

English Walnut vertical pocket by Patterson Bros. Tobacco Co., Richmond, Virginia, 4½" x 3" x 1", $800.00 – 900.00.
Courtesy of Allen & Judy Kimmel

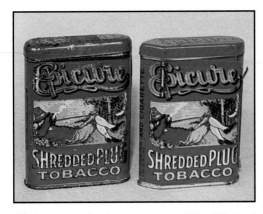

Epicure vertical pockets by The United States Tobacco Co., 4" x 3" x 1", left: without v-corner, $350.00 – 400.00; right: v-corner, $150.00 – 200.00.

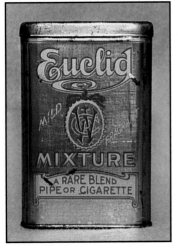

Eutopia by Cameron Tobacco Co., Richmond, Virginia, left: 4½" x 7" x 4½", $350.00 – 400.00; right: vertical pocket 4½" x 3½" x 1", $1,000.00 – 1,250.00.
Courtesy of Grant Smith

Essex vertical pocket by Montreal Tobacco Co., Boston, Massachusetts, 4½" x 3" x 1", rare, $3,000.00+.

Euclid vertical pocket by The Weideman Co., Cleveland, Ohio, 4½" x 3" x 1", $1,250.00 – 1,500.00.
Courtesy of Allen & Judy Kimmel

Even Steven vertical cigar box by C.E. Bair & Sons, Harrisonburg, Pennsylvania, marked P.J. Ritter Co., Philadelphia, 5½" x 3" x 3", $300.00 – 350.00.
Courtesy of Grant Smith

Exquisite by Larus & Bros., Richmond, Virginia, marked Hasker & Marcus, 1½" x 4½" x 2½", $2,500.00 – 3,000.00.
Courtesy of Grant Smith

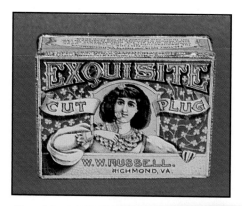

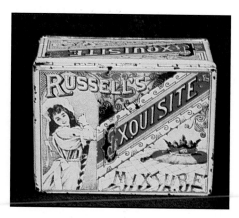

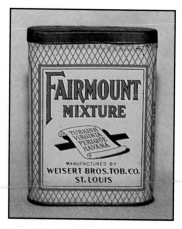

Exquisite by W.W. Russell, Richmond, Virginia, marked Hasker & Marcuse, 1¹/₂" x 4¹/₂" x 3¹/₄", rare, $3,000.00+.
Courtesy of Grant Smith

Exquisite by W.W. Russell, Richmond, Virginia, marked Hasker & Marcuse, 2¹/₄" x 4¹/₂" x 3¹/₄", rare, $3,000.00+.
Courtesy of Grant Smith

Fairmount Mixture (without 10 cents) vertical pocket by Weisert Bros. Tobacco Co., St. Louis, Missouri, 4¹/₄" x 3¹/₄" x 1", $300.00 – 350.00.

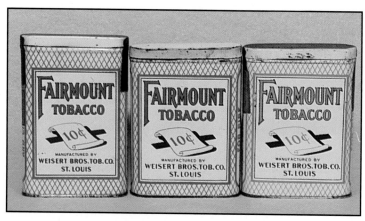

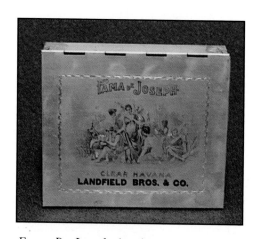

Fairmount Tobacco (10 cents) vertical pockets by Weisert Bros. Tobacco Co., St. Louis, left: 4¹/₂" x 3" x 1"; center & right: 4¹/₄" x 3" x 1", $200.00 – 250.00 each. Note: The orange color tin is consistent under the lid and tax stamp, not faded.

Fama De Joseph aluminum cigar box by Landfield Bros. & Co., 1¹/₄" x 5" x 4", $1.00 – 25.00.

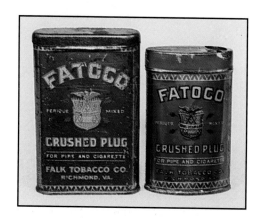

Fatima by Cameron & Cameron, Richmond, Virginia, 3¹/₄" x 2³/₄", $25.00 – 50.00.
Courtesy of Bob & Sherri Copeland

Fatima flat 50 cigarette tin by Cameron & Cameron, Richmond, Virginia, ³/₄" x 5³/₄" x 4¹/₂", $25.00 – 50.00.
Courtesy of Archie & Carol Ford

Fatoco vertical pockets by Falk Tobacco Co., Richmond, Virginia, left: 4¹/₂" x 3" x 1", rare, no price available; right: 4" x 2¹/₄" x 1¹/₄", $200.00 – 250.00.

Fatoco paper label vertical pocket by Falk Tobacco Co., Richmond, Virginia, 4" x 2¹/₂" x 4¹/₄", $100.00 – 150.00.

Courtesy of Bob & Sherri Copeland

Finest Grade by Cameron & Cameron, Richmond, Virginia, 5¹/₂" x 7" x 4¹/₂", $100.00 – 150.00.

Courtesy of Grant Smith

Finest Grade by Cameron & Cameron, Richmond, Virginia, 5¹/₂" x 7" x 4¹/₂", $100.00 – 150.00.

Courtesy of Grant Smith

Finest Grade by Cameron & Cameron, 5¹/₂" x 7" x 4¹/₂", $100.00 – 150.00.

Courtesy of Grant Smith

Flor De Franklin vertical box by Hull Grummond & Co. Inc., Binghampton, New York, 5¹/₄" x 3" x 3", $200.00 – 250.00.
Courtesy of Grant Smith

Flor De Haynie cigar canister, 5¹/₄" x 5³/₄", $100.00 – 150.00.
Courtesy of Grant Smith

Flor De Leon cigar canister marked Factory No. 118, 16th Dist. of MO., 5¹/₂" x 4¹/₄", $150.00 – 200.00.
Courtesy of Ken & Nancy Jones

Forest and Stream (canoe) 4¹/₂" x 4", $450.00 – 500.00.

Forest and Stream screw top canister by Imperial Tobacco Co., Canada, 4" x 4¹/₂", $50.00 – 75.00.

Forest Giant cardboard with tin top and bottom by Scotten, Dillon Co., Detroit, Michigan, 4" x 4", $500.00 – 600.00.

Four Roses vertical pockets by Nall & Williams Tobacco Co., left: 4¹/₂" x 3" x 1", $350.00 – 400.00; center: 4" x 3¹/₂" x 1¹/₄", $100.00 – 150.00; right: 3¹/₂" x 3¹/₂" x 1¹/₄", $150.00 – 200.00. Note: another silver variation with stripes exists.

Courtesy of Bob & Sherri Copeland

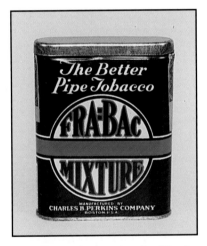

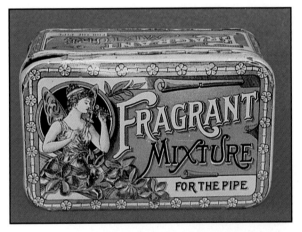

Fra-Bac vertical pocket by Charles B. Perkins Co., Boston, marked A.C. Co., 4¹/₂" x 3¹/₂" x 1", $1,000.00 – 1,250.00.

Courtesy of Grant Smith

Fragrant Mixture marked Hasker & Mascuse, Richmond, VA., 2³/₄" x 6" x 4", $200.00 – 250.00.

Courtesy of Grant Smith

Full Dress for Sears, Roebuck & Co., Chicago, Dallas, Seattle, left: sample vertical pocket, 3" x 2¹/₄" x ³/₄", $900.00 – 1,000.00; center: canister, 6" x 5", $200.00 – 250.00; right: vertical pocket, 4¹/₂" x 3" x 1", $700.00 – 800.00.

Courtesy of Grant Smith

Gallaher's Honeydew by Gallahers Ltd., London, 1½" x 6¼" x 3¾", $50.00 – 75.00.

Garcia cigar tin marked Factory #417 1st Dist. of PA., 5½" x 6¼" x 4¼", $25.00 – 50.00.

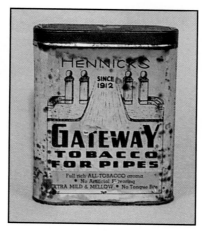

Gazi flat pocket marked Monopole Des Tabacs De Turquie, ¾" x 3" x 1¾", $1.00 – 25.00.

Gateway paper label vertical pocket by Hennick's Pipe Shop, Columbus, Ohio, 4" x 3¼" x 1¼", $100.00 – 150.00.

Garcia y Vega cigar tin marked Factory No. 17 Dist. of FLA., made in Tampa, 5½" x 5½", $25.00 – 50.00.

Globe sample flat pocket by Globe Tobacco Co., Detroit, Michigan, marked Ginna & Co., ½" x 2½" x 1½", $300.00 – 350.00.

Goal marked Heekin Can Co., Factory No. 463, 9th Dist. of Pa., 5¼" x 2½" x 2", $100.00 – 150.00.
Courtesy of Ken & Nancy Jones

Gloriana Mixture by Surbrug Co., New York City, New York, Patent 1888, marked Somers Bros., 1¾" x 6½" x 3", $25.00 – 50.00.

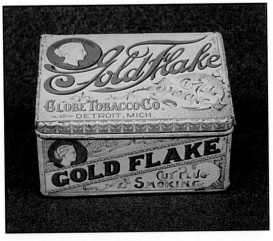

Gold Flake by Globe Tobacco Co., Detroit, Michigan & Windsor, Ontario, 2½" x 6" x 4", $200.00 – 250.00.
Courtesy of Grant Smith

Gold Flake by Globe Tobacco Co., Detroit, Michigan, marked Hasker & Marcuse, 2¼" x 4½" x 3¼", $200.00 – 250.00.
Courtesy of Grant Smith

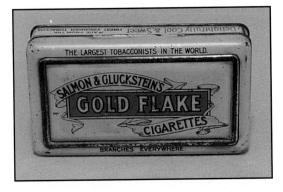

Gold Medal flat pocket by Cameron & Cameron, Richmond, Virginia, marked Melbourne & Sydney, ¾" x 4½" x 2½", $150.00 – 200.00.
Courtesy of Grant Smith

Gold Flake by Salmon & Gluckstein, 1½" x 5½" x 3", $1.00 – 25.00.

Gold Flake paper label by W.D. & H.O. Wills, Bristol & London, 3" x 2½", $1.00 – 25.00.
Courtesy of Bob & Sherri Copeland

Gold Medal flat pocket by Cameron & Cameron, Richmond, Virginia, marked S.A. Ilsley, ³/₄" x 4¹/₂" x 2¹/₂", $150.00 – 200.00.
Courtesy of Grant Smith

Golden Arrow by Micheliose Ltd., Perth, Australia, 1" x 4¹/₄" x 3", $100.00 – 150.00.
Courtesy of Ken & Nancy Jones

Golden Leaf by B. Houde Co., Quebec, 3" x 5" x 3³/₄", $75.00 – 100.00.

Golden Lustre by S.M. Johnson & Bros., New York, marked S.A. Ilsley, 2¹/₄" x 4¹/₂" x 3¹/₄", $250.00 – 300.00.
Courtesy of Grant Smith

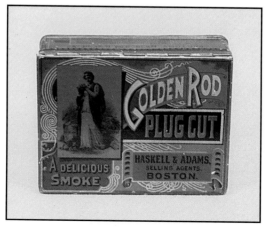

Golden Rod by Haskell & Adams, Boston, 1¹/₄" x 4¹/₂" x 3¹/₄", $150.00 – 200.00.
Courtesy of Grant Smith

Golden Wedding by Daniel Scotten & Co., marked Ginna & Co., 1¹/₂" x 4¹/₂" x 3¹/₄", $100.00 – 150.00.
Courtesy of Grant Smith

Green Seal flat pocket by The Surbrug Co.,
New York, marked A.C. Co. 50A, $^3/4$" x $4^1/2$" x
$2^3/4$", $75.00 – 100.00.
Courtesy of Grant Smith

Granulated 54 vertical pockets by John Weisert Tobacco Co.,
St. Louis, Missouri, left: $4^1/2$" x 3" x 1", $75.00 – 100.00; cen-
ter: sample, 3" x $2^1/4$" x $^3/4$", $150.00 – 200.00; right: sample,
2" x 2" x 1", $200.00 – 250.00.
Courtesy of Roy & Lynne Moseman

H-O small top canister by R.A.
Patterson Tobacco Co., Richmond,
Virginia, 6" x 5", $100.00 – 150.00.
Courtesy of Grant Smith

Hand Made small top canister by
Globe Tobacco Co., Detroit, Michi-
gan, marked S.A. Ilsley, $6^1/2$" x 5",
$300.00 – 350.00.
Courtesy of Grant Smith

Handsome Dan paper label by Philip
Morris & Co. Ltd. Inc., $4^1/2$" x $5^1/2$",
$25.00 – 50.00.
Courtesy of Bob & Sherri Copeland

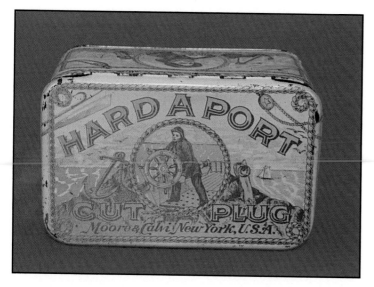

Hard A Port by Moore & Calvi, New York, 3¹/₄" x 6" x 3¹/₄", $250.00 – 300.00.

Courtesy of Grant Smith

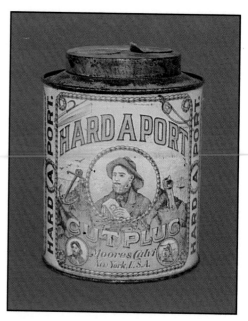

Hard A Port small top canister by Moore & Calvi, New York, 6¹/₄" x 5", $2,000.00 – 2,500.00.

Courtesy of Grant Smith

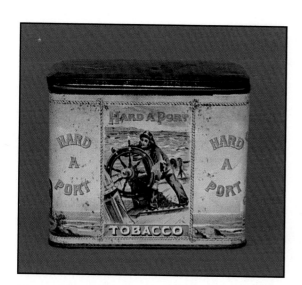

Hard A Port paper label by Thompson Moore & Co., New York, 5" x 6" x 3³/₄", $200.00 – 250.00.

Courtesy of Grant Smith

Havana Cadet cigar canister marked Liberty Can Co., Lancaster, PA., 5" x 5¹/₂", $75.00 – 100.00.

Havana Sparks cigar canister marked Bethesda, OH., 6" x 4¹/₄", $25.00 – 50.00.

Courtesy of Tom & Mary Lou Slike

*Havanette*s by Cameron & Cameron Co., Richmond, Virginia, 1³/₄" x 5¹/₄" x 4³/₄", $1.00 – 25.00.

Herald flat box, 1" x 6¹/₄" x 4³/₄", $25.00 – 50.00.

Heine's Blend by Sutliff Tobacco Co., San Francisco, California, 5" x 4¹/₄", $1.00 – 25.00.

Hi-Plane vertical pockets by Larus & Bros. Co., Richmond, Virginia, 4¹/₂" x 3" x 1", left to right: #1, $75.00 – 100.00; #2, $100.00 – 150.00; #3, 200.00 – 250.00; #4, $500.00 – 600.00.

Courtesy of Allen & Judy Kimmel

Hi-Plane by Larus & Bro. Co., Richmond, Virginia, marked A.C. Co. 70A, 6¹/₂" x 5", $100.00 – 150.00.

Courtesy of Grant Smith

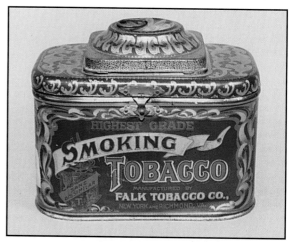

Hickey & Nicholson by Hickey & Nicholson Tobacco Co., 2" x 5" x 3³/₄", $1.00 – 25.00 each.

Highest Grade by Falk Tobacco Co., New York & Richmond, Virginia, 5¹/₂" x 7" x 4¹/₂", $100.00 –150.00.

Courtesy of Grant Smith

Highest Grade by Falk Tobacco Co., 2" x 4¹/₂" x 3¹/₄", $25.00 – 50.00.

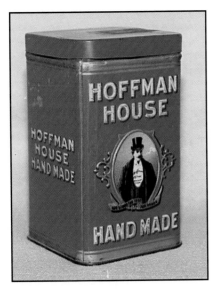

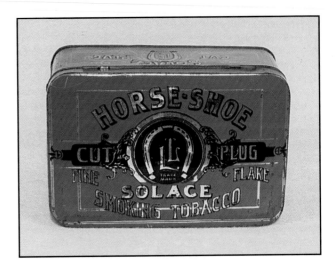

Hoffman House embossed cigar box marked Factory No. 143, 1st Dist. of OH., 5³/4" x 3¹/2" x 3¹/2", $150.00 – 200.00.
Courtesy of Ken & Nancy Jones

Horse-Shoe by B. Houde Co., 2¹/2" x 6" x 4", $25.00 – 50.00.
Courtesy of Grant Smith

Hot Spur marked Factory No. 26 2nd Dist. of Virginia, 2¹/4" x 4¹/2" x 3¹/4", $150.00 – 200.00.
Courtesy of Grant Smith

Hunt Club vertical pocket by The United States Tobacco Co., Richmond, Virginia, marked A.C. Co. 50A, 4¹/4" x 3" x 1", rare, $3,000.00+.

Hunter paper label marked Factory No. 8, 11th Dist. of OH., 5¹/4" x 6" x 4¹/4", $75.00 – 100.00.

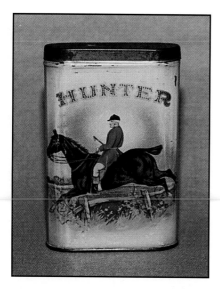

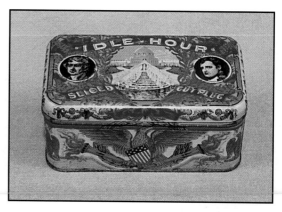

Idle Hour by The United States Tobacco Co., Richmond, Virginia, 2¹/₂" x 5¹/₂" x 3", $350.00 – 400.00.
Courtesy of Grant Smith

Hunter vertical cigar tin marked 11th Dist. State of Ohio, 5¹/₄" x 3¹/₂" x 1¹/₂", $200.00 – 250.00.

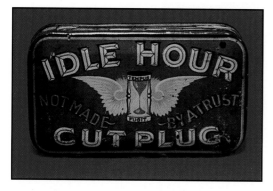

Idle Hour flat pocket by The United States Tobacco Co., Richmond, Virginia, marked A.C. Co. 50A, 1" x 4¹/₂" x 2³/₄", $75.00 – 100.00.

Imported and Domestic paper label vertical pocket by Rusine's, Lorain, Ohio, 3" x 3¹/₂" x 1", $1.00 – 25.00.
Courtesy of Bob & Sherri Copeland

Imperial Cube Cut paper label by Allen & Ginter, 2" x 2¹/₂", $1.00 – 25.00.

Indian Brand flat box with glass insert in lid by Toledo Tobacco Works, Toledo, Ohio, marked Norton Bros., Chicago, 3" x 10" x 6¹/₄", rare, $2,500.00 – 3,000.00.
Courtesy of Grant Smith

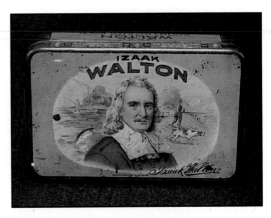

Italia, vertical pocket, 4¼" x 3" x 1", rare, no price available.

Ivy Leaf paper label by Daniel Scotten & Co., Detroit, Michigan, 1¾" x 4½" x 3¼", $75.00 – 100.00.
Courtesy of Grant Smith

Izaak Walton by W.W. Davis Cigar Co., Coffyville, Kansas, marked Heekin Can Co., 1¼" x 5½" x 3½", $50.00 – 75.00.

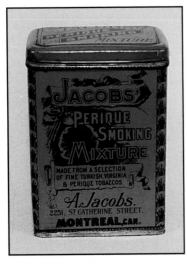

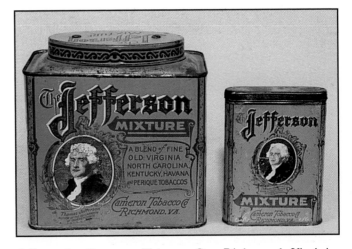

Jacobs vertical box by A. Jacobs, Montreal, Canada, 5" x 3½" x 2½", $150.00 – 200.00.
Courtesy of Grant Smith

Jefferson by Cameron Tobacco Co., Richmond, Virginia, left: 6" x 6" x 4", $1,750.00 – 2,000.00; right: vertical pocket, 4½" x 3½" x 1", $3,000.00+.
Courtesy of Grant Smith

Jewel of Virginia by Cameron & Cameron, Richmond, Virginia, marked Hasker & Marcuse, 1¾" x 4½" x 2½", $25.00 – 500.00.
Courtesy of Grant Smith

John Storm marked Heekin Can Co., 5½" x 6¼" x 4", $200.00 – 250.00.
Courtesy of Grant Smith

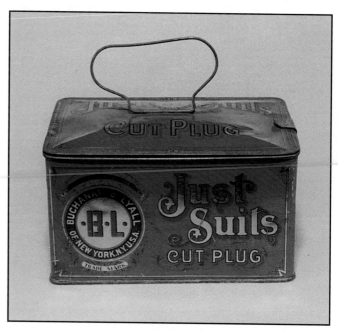

Just Suits by Buchanan & Lyall, New York, New York, American Tobacco Co. successor, 6¹/₄" x 4³/₄", $100.00 – 150.00.

Just Suits lunch box by Buchanan & Lyall, New York, New York, 4¹/₂" x 7³/₄" x 5", $50.00 – 75.00.

Kanona by John Blakely, New York City, marked A.C. Co. 50A, 2¹/₄" x 4¹/₂" x 3¹/₄", $500.00 – 600.00.

Courtesy of Grant Smith

Karel 1 Elegant cigarette tin by H.J. Van Abbe, ¹/₂" x 5¹/₄" x 4³/₄", $25.00 – 50.00.

Courtesy of Bob & Sherri Copeland

Kennebec cigar tin marked Factor No. 89 1st Dist. of OH., 2¼" x 8½" x 4¾", $200.00 – 250.00.
Courtesy of Bob & Sherri Copeland

Kensitas flat 50 cigarette tin by J. Wix & Sons Ltd., London, ¾" x 5¼" x 4¼", $25.00 – 50.00.

Khaki by B. Houde & Co., Montreal & Quebec, marked Macdonald Manufacturing Co. Toronto, 2" x 5" x 3¾", $200.00 – 250.00.
Courtesy of Grant Smith

King George's Navy by Rock City Tobacco Co. Limited, Quebec, marked Whittall Can Co., 4¾" x 4½" x 3½", $25.00 – 50.00.
Courtesy of Bob & Sherri Copeland

King of All paper label box by A.H. Motley & Co., 1¾" x 3¼" x 4½", $150.00 – 200.00.
Courtesy of Grant Smith

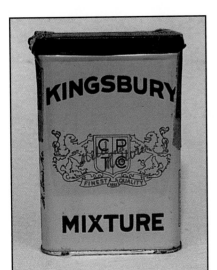

Kingsbury vertical pocket by Christian Peper Tobacco Co., St. Louis, Missouri, 4½" x 3" x 1", $500.00 – 600.00.
Courtesy of Bob & Sherri Copeland

Kipling flat pocket by Harry Weissinger, Louisville, Kentucky, marked Hasker & Marcuse, 1" x 4¹/₂" x 2¹/₂", $100.00 – 150.00.
Courtesy of Grant Smith

Knapsack marked Hasker & Marcuse, 1¹/₂" x 4¹/₂" x 3¹/₄", $100.00 – 150.00.
Courtesy of Grant Smith

Kolb's vertical box marked Liberty Can Co., 5¹/₄" x 3¹/₂" x 3¹/₂", $50.00 – 75.00.
Courtesy of Richard & Ann Lehmann

L.A.W. flat pocket marked Hasker & Marcuse, Richmond, VA., ³/₄" x 4¹/₂" x 2¹/₂", $400.00 – 450.00.
Courtesy of Grant Smith

La Azora cigar canister marked Liberty Can Co., Lancaster, PA., 5¹/₂" x 5¹/₂", $200.00 – 250.00.
Courtesy of Grant Smith

La Costa cigar box by Joseph J. Schaefer Manufacturer, Dayton, Ohio, 5¹/₂" x 3¹/₂" x 3¹/₂", $100.00 – 150.00.
Courtesy of Ken & Nancy Jones

La Belle Creole by S. Hernsheim Bros. & Co., New Orleans, Louisiana, 1" x 4¹/₂" x 2¹/₂", $450.00 – 500.00. Note: a yellow variation exists.
Courtesy of Grant Smith

Lady Churchill flat cigar box, 1¼" x 5¼" x 3½", $1.00 – 25.00.

La Palina by General Cigar Co. Ltd., 5½" x 5½", $50.00 – 75.00.

Courtesy of Richard & Ann Lehmann

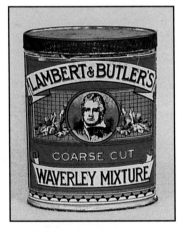

Lambert & Butler's flat pocket by Lambert & Butler, London, England, 1" x 4¼" x 3¼", $25.00 – 50.00.

Lambert & Butler's paper label vertical pocket by Imperial Tobacco Co. of Great Britain & Ireland, 4" x 3" x 1¼", $250.00 – 300.00. Note: a more valuable litho version exists.

Courtesy of Grant Smith

Latakia paper label vertical pocket by Falk Tobacco Co. Inc., 4" x 3¼" x 1", $25.00 – 50.00.

Courtesy of Bob & Sherri Copeland

Lenox vertical pockets by L. Warnick Brown & Co., Utica, New York, 4" x 3½" x 1", left: rare, 3,000.00+; right: $2,000.00 – 2,500.00.

Courtesy of Grant Smith

Lewis' Beauty vertical box by W.B. Lewis & Co., Milton, North Carolina, marked S.A. Ilsley, 4" x 3¹/₂" x 2", $1,000.00 – 1,250.00.
Courtesy of Grant Smith

Lipschutz's 44 vertical cigar box, 5¹/₂" x 3¹/₄" x 3¹/₄", $25.00 – 50.00.
Courtesy of Ken & Nancy Jones

Log Cabin by Lambert & Butler, England, 1¹/₄" x 4³/₄" x 3¹/₄", $50.00 – 75.00.
Courtesy of Grant Smith

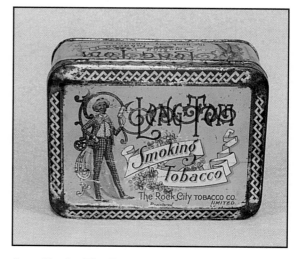

Log Cabin flat pocket by Lambert & Butler, England, 1" x 5¹/₂" x 3¹/₄", $50.00 – 75.00.

Long Tom by The Rock City Tobacco Co. Limited, 2" x 5" x 3¹/₂", $150.00 – 200.00.
Courtesy of Grant Smith

Lookout by J.G. Dill's, Richmond, Virginia, left: vertical pocket, 4" x 3" x 1", $1,000.00 – 1,250.00; center: 5" x 6" x 4", $1,000.00 – 1,250.00; right: flat pocket, 1" x 4¹/₂" x 2¹/₂", $200.00 – 250.00.
Courtesy of Grant Smith

Louisiana Perique by Cameron & Cameron, Richmond, Virginia, 1½" x 4" x 3", $100.00 – 150.00.

Louisiana Perique paper label vertical pocket by Falk Tobacco Co., 4¼" x 3" x 1", $25.00 – 50.00.

Lucky Strike by The American Tobacco Co., 3¼" x 4", $25.00 – 50.00.

Maccoboy Snuff by P. Lorillard & Co's., marked Ginna & Co., New York, 6½" x 7½" x 4¾", $350.00 – 400.00.

Courtesy of Grant Smith

Maccoboy Snuff by P. Lorillard & Co., Jersey City, N.J., $25.00 – 50.00.

Macdonald's flat 50 cigarette tin by MacDonald Inc., Montreal, Canada, ½" x 5¾" x 4¼", $1.00 – 25.00.

Macdonald's by W.C. MacDonald Inc., Montreal, Canada, 1½" x 5¾" x 4¼", $25.00 – 50.00.

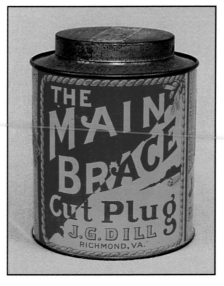

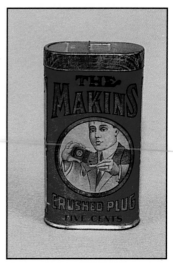

Magnet by Myers-Cox Co., Dubuque, Iowa, marked Heekin Can Co., 6¼" x 5¼", no price available.

Courtesy of Grant Smith

Main Brace small top canister by J.G. Dill, Richmond, Virginia, 6" x 5", $200.00 – 250.00.

Courtesy of Grant Smith

Makins cardboard vertical pocket with tin top and bottom by Globe Tobacco Co., Detroit, Michigan, 4" x 2¼" x 1", $500.00 – 600.00.

Courtesy of Grant Smith

Manco vertical pocket by Joseph P. Manning Co., 4½" x 3" x 1", $1,000.00 – 1,250.00.

Courtesy of Allen & Judy Kimmel

Mapacuba by Bayuk Cigars Inc., marked Tindeco, 5" x 4¾" x 4¾", $50.00 – 75.00.

Courtesy of Richard & Ann Lehmann

Marlboro cigarette tin by Philip Morris Inc., Richmond, Virginia, 3½" x 2¾", $50.00 – 75.00.

Marlboro flat 100 cigarette tin by Philip Morris &
Co., 1¹/₄" x 5³/₄" x 4¹/₄", $25.00 – 50.00.

Master Guard cigar pail marked Heekin
Can Co., Cincinnati, OH., 6¹/₄" x 6",
$600.00 –700.00.
Courtesy of Grant Smith

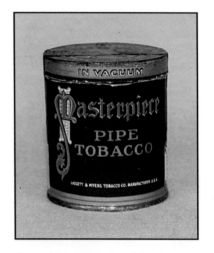

Masterpiece paper label by Liggett
& Myers Tobacco Co., 3¹/₄" x
2³/₄", $1.00 – 25.00.

Mastiff by J.B. Pace Tobacco Co., Richmond, Virginia, marked Hasker & Marcuse, 5¹/₄" x 6" x 4",
rare, $3,000.00+.
Courtesy of Grant Smith

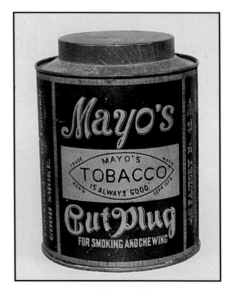

Mayo's small top canister,
6¹/₄" x 5", $100.00 – 150.00.
Courtesy of Grant Smith

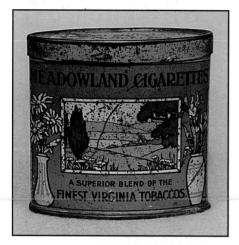

Meadowland vertical pocket by Co-Operative Wholesale Society Ltd., Manchester-London-New Castle, 3" x 3" x 1¼", $50.00 – 75.00.

Mercantile Cigars glass container with tin top, 6" x 4½", $25.00 – 50.00.
Courtesy of Bob & Sherri Copeland

Mid-Channel vertical pocket by Standard Tobacco Co., Fayetteville, New York, 2¾" x 3½" x 1", $500.00 – 600.00.

Model vertical pockets by The United States Tobacco Co., Richmond, Virginia, from left to right: #1, #3, #4, $25.00 – 50.00 each; #2, $400.00 – 450.00; #5 sample & #6 complimentary, $100.00 – 150.00 each.

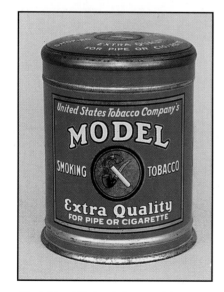

Model by United States Tobacco Co., Richmond, Virginia, 6¼" x 5", $75.00 – 100.00.

Courtesy of Bob & Sherri Copeland

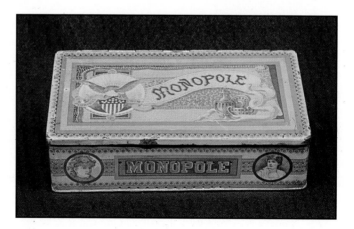

Monopole box marked Colorado Maduro, 2¼" x 8½" x 4¼", $150.00 – 200.00.
Courtesy of Grant Smith

Moonstone vertical pocket by Frishmuth Bro. & Co. Inc., Philadelphia, Pennsylvania, marked F.S. Towle Co., New York & Germany, 3³/₄" x 3³/₄" x 1", rare, $3,000.00+.

Monte Cristo flat box by Wm. S. Kimball & Co., 1" x 8¹/₂" x 2", $50.00 – 75.00.

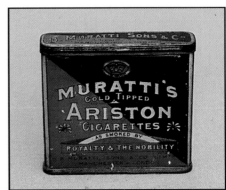

Muratti's vertical pocket by B. Muratti Sons & Co. Ltd., Manchester-London, 3" x 3¹/₄" x ³/₄", $50.00 – 75.00.

Murad by S. Anargyros owned by P. Lorillard Co., top left: vertical pocket, 3" x 3" x 1", $75.00 – 100.00; bottom left: 1¹/₂" x 5¹/₂" x 3", $25.00 – 50.00; right: ³/₄" x 5¹/₂" x 4¹/₂", $25.00 – 50.00.

My Own by Wright Tobacco Stores, marked Barclay & Fry, London, 8¹/₂" x 6" x 3", $50.00 – 75.00.

Myrtle T & B by The Tuckett Tobacco Co., Hamilton, Canada, 3³/₄" x 4¹/₄", $25.00 – 50.00.
Courtesy of Bob & Sherri Copeland

N.C.S. vertical box, 5¹/₂" x 3¹/₂" x 3¹/₂", no price available.
Courtesy of Grant Smith

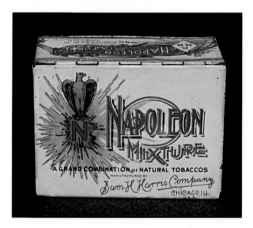

Napoleon by Sam H. Harris Co., Chicago, Illinois, 2¹/₂" x 4¹/₂" x 3¹/₄", $500.00 – 600.00.
Courtesy of Grant Smith

Napoleon by W. C. Macdonald Inc., Montreal, Canada, 4" x 5", $25.00 – 50.00.
Courtesy of Bob & Sherri Copeland

Natural Leaf by the J.G. Dill Co., Richmond, Virginia, 1¹/₂" x 4¹/₂" x 3¹/₄", $150.00 – 200.00.
Courtesy of Grant Smith

Natural Leaf paper label vertical pocket by Falk Tobacco Co., 4" x 3¹/₄" x 1", $25.00 – 50.00.
Courtesy of Bob & Sherri Copeland

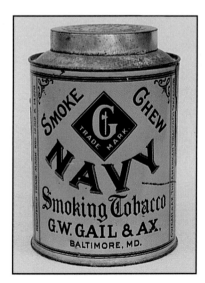

Navy small top canister by G.W. Gail & Ax, Baltimore, Maryland, marked Hasker & Marcuse, 7" x 5", $250.00 – 300.00.
Courtesy of Grant Smith

Navy Snuff paper label by
Goe W. Helm, New Jersey,
1³/₄" x 1¹/₂", $1.00 – 25.00.
Courtesy of Bob & Sherri Copeland

No-To-Bac by The Sterling Remedy Co.,
Chicago, ¹/₂" x 3¹/₂" x 2¹/₄", $50.00 – 75.00.
Courtesy of Grant Smith

No. H.H. Aromatic Blender paper
label vertical pocket by Crimson
Coach Inc., Toledo, Ohio, 3" x
3¹/₂" x 1", $1.00 – 25.00.
Courtesy of Bob & Sherri Copeland

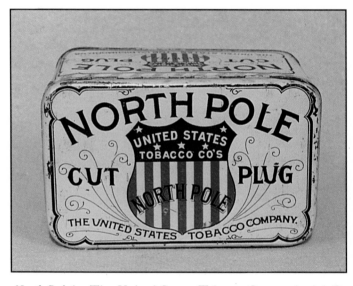

None-Such vertical pocket by McNeil &
Higgins Co., Chicago, 3³/₄" x 3¹/₂" x 1",
rare, no price available.

North Pole by The United States Tobacco Co., marked A.C.
Co., 3¹/₄" x 6" x 3³/₄", $100.00 – 150.00.
Courtesy of Grant Smith

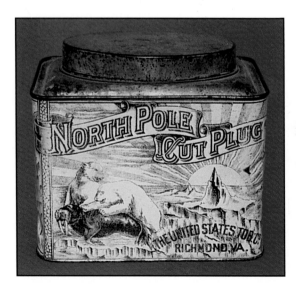

North Pole by The United States Tobacco Co., Richmond,
Virginia, marked Hasker & Marcuse, 5¹/₄" x 6" x 4",
$300.00 – 350.00.
Courtesy of Grant Smith

Nutt's cigarette tin by A. Baker & Co., London, 1¼" x 6" x 3", $50.00 – 75.00.
Courtesy of Ken & Nancy Jones

O.S.U. paper label by Levy Mendel & Co., Columbus, Ohio, 1¼" x 4½" x 4¼", $1.00 – 25.00.

Oceanic by Scotten Dillon Co., Detroit, Michigan, 3¼" x 6" x 4", $100.00 – 150.00. Note: a reproduction exists from Cheinco that measures 4½" x 6" x 5".

Ojibwa store bin canister by Scotten Dillon Co., Detroit, Michigan, 11½" x 8¼", $450.00 – 500.00.
Courtesy of Grant Smith

Ojibwa by Scotten-Dillon Co., Detroit, Michigan, 6¼" x 5½", $150.00 – 200.00.

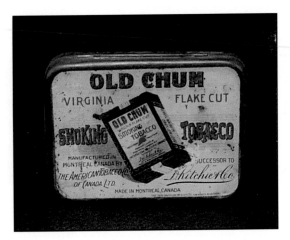

Old Chum by The American Tobacco Co., of Canada Successor to D. Ritchie & Co., 1" x 5½" x 3½", $50.00 – 75.00.

Old Chum vertical box by D. Ritchie & Co., Montreal, Canada, $25.00 – 50.00. Note: a white variation exists.

Old Glory flat pocket by Spaulding & Merrick, Chicago, marked Ginna & Co., ½" x 3½" x 2½", $150.00 – 200.00.
Courtesy of Grant Smith

Old Glory cigar canister marked A.C. Co. 43A, 5" x 5", $300.00 – 350.00.
Courtesy of Grant Smith

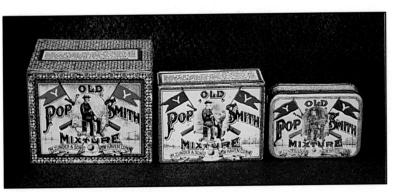

Old Pop Smith by M. Zunder & Sons, New Haven, Connecticut, left: 4" x 5" x 4", $1,000.00 – 1,250.00; center: 1¾" x 4½" x 3¼", $2,500.00 – 3,000.00; right: 1" x 4" x 2¾", $700.00 – 800.00.
Courtesy of Grant Smith

Old Rip vertical box by Allen & Ginter, Richmond, Virginia, American Tobacco Co., Successor, 4³/₄" x 3¹/₄" x 2", $400.00 – 450.00. Note: a larger size exists with less value.
Courtesy of Grant Smith

Old Seneca cigar canister, 5³/₄" x 3¹/₄", $300.00 – 350.00.
Courtesy of Ken & Nancy Jones

Old Virginia vertical pocket by Sparrow & Gravely Tobacco Co., Martinsville, Virginia, marked A.C. Co. 50A, 4¹/₂" x 3" x 1", $700.00 – 800.00.

Omar by the Shenkberg Co., Sioux City, Iowa, 2¹/₄" x 8¹/₂", $500.00 – 600.00.
Courtesy of Grant Smith

Option by Joseph Scwartz, Cleveland, Ohio, 6" x 4¹/₄", $25.00 – 50.00.

Orange Flower cigar canister by Henry B. Grauley Manufacturing, Quakertown, Pennsylvania, marked Liberty Can Co., 5¹/₂" x 6", $250.00 – 300.00.
Courtesy of Grant Smith

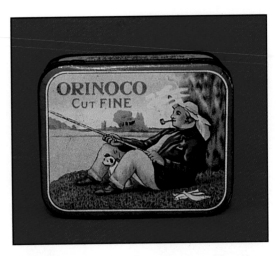

Orinoco by Tuckett Tobacco Co., Hamilton, Canada, 1½" x 3½" x 2¾", $75.00 – 100.00.
Courtesy of Tom & Mary Lou Slike

Orange Flower by Henry B. Grauley, Quakertown, Pennsylvania, marked Liberty Can Co., Lancaster, PA., 5¼" x 4¼", $250.00 – 300.00.

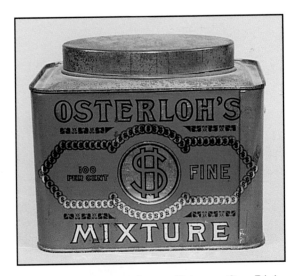

Osterloh's by United States Tobacco Co., Richmond, Virginia, 5¼" x 6" x 4", $150.00 – 200.00.
Courtesy of Grant Smith

Ostro vertical cigar box by Rothenberg & Schloss Co., Kansas City, Missouri, marked National Can Co., 5½" x 3½" x 3½", $150.00 – 200.00.
Courtesy of Grant Smith

Our Hobby flat pocket by O.C. Taylor & Co., Burlington, Vermont, marked A.C. Co. 50A, 1" x 4½" x 2½", rare, no price available.
Courtesy of Grant Smith

P. Lorillard's Fine Cuts marked Ginna & Co., 1" x 4½" x 3¼", $150.00 – 200.00.
Courtesy of Grant Smith

Pall-Mall vertical pocket cigarette tin, 3" x 3¼" x ¾", $100.00 – 150.00.

Pastora vertical cigar tin by Elwood Myers Co., Springfield, Ohio, 5½" x 3½" x 1½", $450.00 – 500.00.

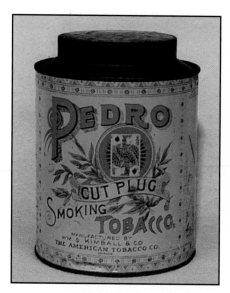

Perfection flat pocket by Oudgon & Arnell Ltd., Melbourne, Australia, ¾" x 3¼" x 2", $75.00 – 100.00.
Courtesy of Grant Smith

Philadelphia Hand Made cigar box by Bayuk Cigars Inc., 3½" x 5½" x 3¾", $1.00 – 25.00.

Pedro by Wm. S. Kimball & Co., American Tobacco Co. Successor, 6½" x 4¾", $500.00 – 600.00.

Philadelphia Phillies cigar tin by Bayuk Cigar Co. Inc., 3" x 7¼" x 5¼", $1.00 – 25.00.

Philip Morris by Philip Morris & Co. Ltd., London, 1" x 6" x 3", $1.00 – 25.00.

Picobac (quality mark) vertical pocket by Imperial Tobacco Co. of Canada, 4¹/₂" x 3" x 1", $100.00 – 150.00.
Courtesy of Bill & June Mason

Pig-Skin football-shaped tin by J. Wright Co., Richmond, Virginia, 2" x 4" x 2³/₄", rare, no price available.
Courtesy of Grant Smith

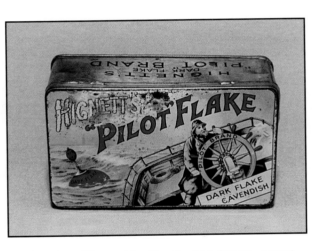

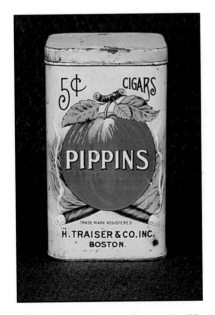

Pilot Flake by Hignett Co., 2" x 6" x 3¹/₂", $75.00 – 100.00.

Pippins vertical cigar box by H. Traiser & Co. Inc., Boston, 5¹/₂" x 3" x 3", $100.00 – 150.00.
Courtesy of Grant Smith

Player's by Player & Sons, left: gold leaf, 1" x 3¹/₄" x 2", $1.00 – 25.00; center: 2³/₄" x 4", $1.00 – 25.00; right: airman, 1" x 3¹/₄" x 2", $25.00 – 50.00.

Player's Navy Cut cigarette tin by Player
& Sons, 1¹/₂" x 4" x 3¹/₄", $25.00 – 50.00.

Player's Navy Cut flat 50 cigarette tin, ¹/₂" x 5³/₄" x 4¹/₄",
$50.00 – 75.00.
Courtesy of Bob & Sherri Copeland

Poet's Dream, 1³/₄" x 4¹/₂" x 2¹/₂", $75.00 – 100.00.
Courtesy of Grant Smith

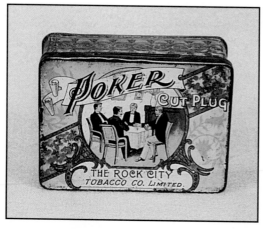

Poker by The Rock City Tobacco Co., marked
Macdonald Manufacturing Co., Toronto, 1³/₄" x
4¹/₂" x 3", $200.00 – 250.00.
Courtesy of Grant Smith

Polar Bear store bin by Luhrman & Wilbern
Tobacco Co., 13" x 20" x 15", $600.00 – 700.00.
Courtesy of Tom & Mary Lou Slike

Popper's Ace store bin by E. Popper & Co. Inc., New York, 8" x 5¼" x 6", $500.00 – 600.00.

Courtesy of Allen & Judy Kimmel

Portuondo cigar canister by Juan F. Portuondo, Philadelphia, Pennsylvania, 5" x 5", $200.00 – 250.00.

Courtesy of Ken & Nancy Jones

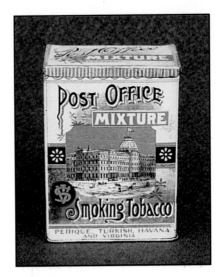

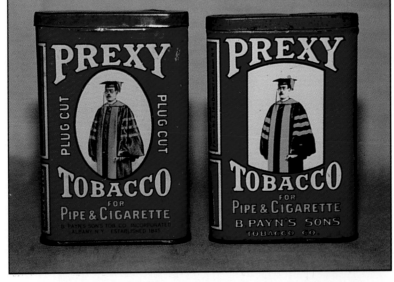

Post Office vertical box by E.G. Teane & Co., marked Hasker & Marcuse, 4¾" x 3½" x 2", $1,250.00 – 1,500.00.

Courtesy of Grant Smith

Prexy vertical pockets by B. Payn's Sons, Albany, New York, left: plug cut, 4½" x 3" x 1", right: 4½" x 3" x 1", $1,250.00 – 1,500.00 each.

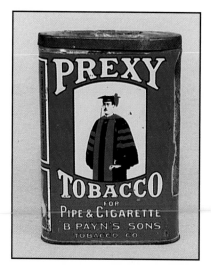

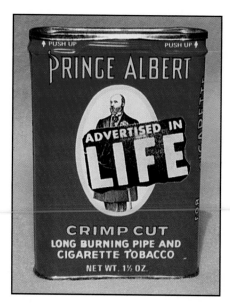

Prexy (red robe) vertical pocket by B. Payn's Sons Tobacco Co., Albany, New York, 4¹/₂" x 3" x 1", $1,250.00 – 1,500.00.

Prince Albert (life ad) vertical pocket by R.J. Reynolds Tobacco Co., Winston-Salem, North Carolina, 4¹/₂" x 3" x 1", $25.00 – 50.00.

Courtesy of Archie & Carol Ford

Princess Royal vertical box by Wm. S. Kimball & Co., Rochester, New York, marked Somers Bros., 4¹/₂" x 3¹/₂" x 2", $100.00 – 150.00.

Courtesy of Grant Smith

Private Stock paper label vertical pocket by Straus Bros. & Co., Cincinnati, Ohio, 4" x 3¹/₂" x 1", $25.00 – 50.00.

Courtesy of Bob & Sherri Copeland

Prune Nugget by Harry Weissinger Tobacco Co., Louisville, Kentucky, 1¹/₂" x 6¹/₄" x 3", $150.00 – 200.00.

Courtesy of Grant Smith

Pure Gold by L.P. Langlois & Co., 2¹/₂" x 6" x 4", $75.00 – 100.00.

Courtesy of Grant Smith

The Puritan by D. Ritchie & Co., American Tobacco Co. of Canada successor, 2¹/₅" x 6" x 4¹/₄", $75.00 – 100.00. Note: A smaller size exists.

Puritan paper label vertical pocket by Estabrook & Eaton, Boston, 4¹/₄" x 3¹/₄" x 1", $100.00 – 150.00.
Courtesy of Bill & June Mason

Quaker Doctor cigar canister marked Factory No. 43, 11th Dist. State of OH., 6" x 4¹/₄", $250.00 – 300.00.
Courtesy of Ken & Nancy Jones

Queen City by Wm. Goldstein & Co., Toronto, Canada, 3" x 5" x 3³/₄", $100.00 – 150.00.

Queen of Virginia by W.W. Russell, Richmond, Virginia, marked Hasker & Marcuse, 2³/₄" x 4¹/₂" x 3¹/₄", $400.00 – 450.00.
Courtesy of Grant Smith

R•B flat box, 1¹/₂" x 4¹/₂" x 4¹/₂", $1.00 – 25.00.

Raleigh cigarette bank by Brown & Williamson Tobacco Corp., Louisville, Kentucky, 2³/₄" x 2¹/₄" x 1¹/₄", $75.00 – 100.00. Note: reverse side is Kool.
Courtesy of Bob & Sherri Copeland

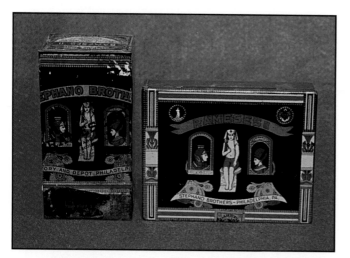

Rameses II cigarette tins by Stephano Brothers, Philadelphia, Pennsylvania, left: paper label, 2¹/₄" x 5¹/₂" x 2³/₄"; right: 1¹/₂" x 5¹/₂" x 4¹/₄", $25.00 – 50.00 each.

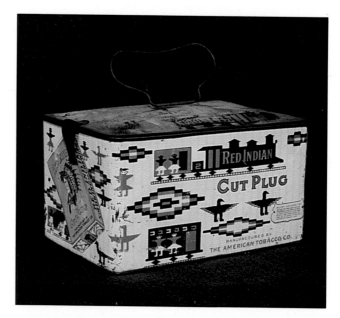

Red Indian lunch box by The American Tobacco Co., 4³/₄" x 7³/₄" x 5", $1,250.00 1,500.00.
Courtesy of Grant Smith

Red Indian small top canister by The American Tobacco Co., 6³/₄" x 5", $450.00 – 500.00.
Courtesy of Grant Smith

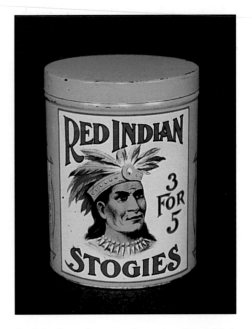

Red Indian cigar canister by David M. Zolla, Chicago, Illinois, marked Heekin Can Co., Cin. O., 5¹/₂" x 4¹/₂", rare, no price available.
Courtesy of Bob & Sherri Copeland

Red Label flat pocket by Buchanan & Lyall, marked S.A. Ilsley & Co., 1" x 4¹/₂" x 2¹/₂", $75.00 – 100.00.
Courtesy of Grant Smith

Reio marked Factory No. 304, 1st Dist. of OH., 1¹/₄" x 4³/₄" x 3¹/₂", $25.00 – 50.00.
Courtesy of Tom & Lynne Sankiewicz

Revelation vertical pockets, tall: 4" x 3¹/₂" x 1", short: 3" x 3¹/₂" x 1", far right: sample, 2" x 3", 1", $25.00 – 50.00; all others, $1.00 – 25.00 each.

Resolute paper label vertical box by F.A. Goetze & Bros., 4¹/₂" x 3" x 2", $200.00 – 250.00.
Courtesy of Grant Smith

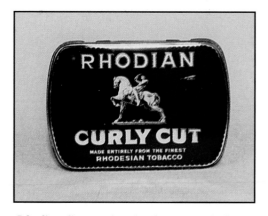

Revelation paper label vertical pockets by Continental Tobacco Co., New York & Richmond, left: 4" x 3¹/₂" x 1", $50.00 – 75.00; right: 3" x 3¹/₂" x 1", $1.00 – 25.00.
Courtesy of Bob & Sherri Copeland

Rhodian flat pocket by Lambert & Butler, London, England, 1" x 4¹/₂" x 3", $1.00 – 25.00.

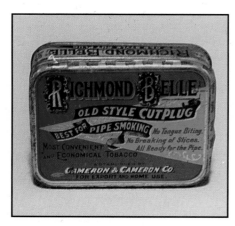

Richmond Belle by Cameron & Cameron, Richmond, Virginia, 2¹/₄" x 4¹/₂" x 3¹/₄", $1,000.00 – 1,250.00.
Courtesy of Grant Smith

Richmond Belle by Cameron & Cameron Co., Richmond, Virginia, 1¹/₄" x 4¹/₂" x 3¹/₄", $1.00 – 25.00.

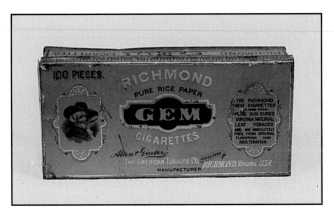

Richmond Gem cigarette box by Allen & Ginter, The American Tobacco Co. Successor, 1³/₄" x 6³/₄" x 3", $75.00 – 100.00.

Courtesy of Grant Smith

Richmond Gem by Allen & Ginter, Richmond, Virginia, 2¹/₂" x 4¹/₂" x 3¹/₄", $75.00 – 100.00.

Courtesy of Bob & Sherri Copeland

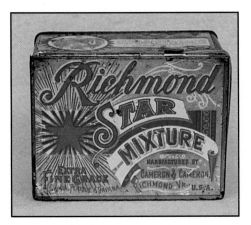

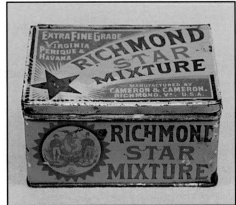

Richmond Star Mixture (pink) by Cameron & Cameron, Richmond, Virginia, 2¹/₄" x 4¹/₂" x 3¹/₄", $300.00 – 350.00.

Courtesy of Grant Smith

Richmond Star Mixture (green) by Cameron & Cameron, Richmond, Virginia, 2¹/₄" x 4¹/₂" x 3¹/₄", $300.00 – 350.00.

Courtesy of Grant Smith

Rigby's paper label, 18th Dist. State of Ohio, 5¹/₂" x 3¹/₂" x 3¹/₂", $25.00 – 50.00.

Robert Emmet by Spietz Cigar Co., Detroit, Michigan, left: 4" x 5" x 1¹/₄", $25.00 50.00; right: 1³/₄" x 5³/₄" x 5¹/₄", $25.00 – 50.00.

Roosevelt cigar box by H. Simon & Sons Ltd., Montreal, Canada, 1³/₄" x 5" x 3³/₄", $100.00 – 150.00.

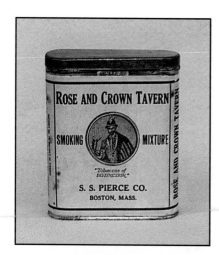

Rose and Crown Tavern paper label vertical pocket by S.S. Pierce Co., Boston, Massachusetts, 4" x 3¹/₂" x 1", $200.00 – 250.00.
Courtesy of Grant Smith

Rose Quesnel by Rock City Tobacco Co. Ltd., Quebec, 2¹/₄" x 6¹/₂" x 4", $25.00 – 50.00.
Courtesy of Tom & Lynne Sankiewicz

Rose's Makings vertical pocket with rolling paper stored in its lid, by The Makings Co., Fort Worth, Texas, 4¹/₂" x 3" x 1", rare, no price available.

Rothenberg and Schloss (old style) marked Factory No. 39, 1st Dist. of Mich., 5³/₄" x 3¹/₂" x 3¹/₂", $25.00 – 50.00.
Courtesy of Ken & Nancy Jones

Rover Canadian tin, 4" x 4", $500.00 – 600.00.

Royal Cannon vertical pocket made in England, 3¹/₂" x 2¹/₄" x 1", $1.00 – 25.00. Note: Questionable if tobacco.

Royal Navy vertical box by Imperial Tobacco Co. of Canada, 5" x 3³/₄" x 2¹/₂", $100.00 – 150.00.
Courtesy of Ken & Nancy Jones

Royal Standard by Surbrug Co., New York, 2¹/₄" x 4¹/₂" x 3¹/₄", $350.00 – 400.00.

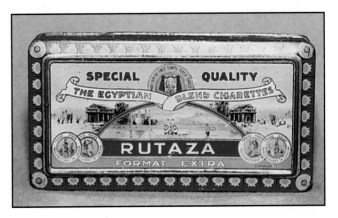

Rutaza by Major Drapkin & Co., London, 1¹/₄" x 5³/₄" x 3", $25.00 – 50.00.
Courtesy of Richard & Ann Lehmann

Safety First paper label by Kohlberg Bros., El Paso, Texas, 6" x 3¹/₂" x 3¹/₂", $1.00 – 25.00.

Sailor's Pride flat pocket by Huntoon & Gorham, Providence, Rhode Island, 1" x 4¹/2" x 2¹/2", $500.00 – 600.00.
Courtesy of Grant Smith

Sailor's Pride by Bland Tobacco Co., American Tobacco Co. Successor, 6¹/2" x 5", $400.00 – 450.00.
Courtesy of Grant Smith

Schermerhorn's paper label vertical pockets by Schermerhorn Cigar Stores Inc., Chicago, Illinois, 4" x 3" x 1", $25.00 – 50.00 each.
Courtesy of Bob & Sherri Copeland

Schermerhorn's paper label by Schermerhorn Cigar Stores Inc., Chicago, Illinois, 4¹/4" x 4", $1.00 – 25.00.

Schinasi Bros. Natural flat 100 cigarette box by Schinasi Bros., 1¹/2" x 5¹/2" x 4¹/4", $25.00 – 50.00.

Scotty flat pocket by Barry Cigar Factory, Quebec, Canada, 1/4" x 3¹/4" x 3", $50.00 – 75.00.

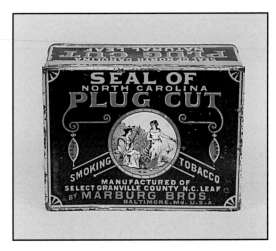

Seal of North Carolina by Marburg Bros., Baltimore, Maryland, marked S.A. Ilsley & Co., 2" x 4¹/2" x 3¹/4", $500.00 – 600.00.
Courtesy of Grant Smith

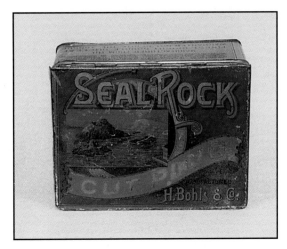

Seal Rock by H. Bohls & Co., marked S.A. Ilsley, 2" x 4¹/2" x 3¹/4", $100.00 – 150.00.
Courtesy of Grant Smith

Seven Up pail marked A.C. Co., American Can Co., 6" x 6", $450.00 – 500.00.
Courtesy of Grant Smith

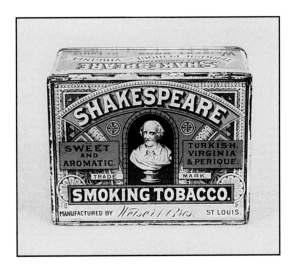

Shakespeare by Weisert Bros., St. Louis, 2¹/4" x 4¹/2" x 3¹/4", $400.00 – 450.00.
Courtesy of Grant Smith

Shandigaf flat pocket by L. Miller & Sons, New York, marked Hasker & Marcuse, ³/₄" x 4¹/₂" x 2¹/₂", rare, no price available.
Courtesy of Grant Smith

Sir Walter Raleigh cardboard (1943) war canister by Brown & Williamson, Louisville, Kentucky, 5¹/₄" x 5¹/₄", $25.00 – 50.00.

Signum by B. Houde & Co., Quebec & Montreal, 2" x 5" x 3³/₄", $100.00 – 150.00.
Courtesy of Grant Smith

Sir Walter Raleigh cardboard vertical pocket by Brown & Williamson Tobacco Co., Louisville, Kentucky, 5" x 3" x 1", $200.00 – 250.00.
Courtesy of Ben Labudde

Sir Walter Raleigh paper label Christmas canister, 5" x 5", $25.00 – 50.00.
Courtesy of Bob & Sherri Copeland

"*Skipper*" by Richard Lloyd & Sons, London, 1¹/₂" x 6¹/₂" x 4", $25.00 – 50.00.

Courtesy of Ken & Nancy Jones

Smith's Glasgow paper label vertical pocket marked F. & J. Smith Tobacco Manufacturers, issued by Imperial Tobacco Co. of Great Britain & Ireland, 3³/₄" x 3" x 1¹/₄", $100.00 – 150.00.

Courtesy of Ken & Nancy Jones

Snake Charmer by Salmon & Gluckstein Ltd., London, 1¹/₂" x 3" x 4¹/₂", $50.00 – 75.00.

Spanish Lassie embossed vertical pocket marked Factory No. 6, 23rd Dist. of PA., 5" x 3" x 1", $450.00 – 500.00.

Spanish Puffs by H. Mandelbaum, New York, marked Hasker & Marcuse, 2¹/₄" x 4¹/₂" x 3¹/₄", $200.00 – 250.00.

Courtesy of Grant Smith

Sphinx by The United States Tobacco Co., marked Hasker & Marcuse, 1³/₄" x 4¹/₂" x 2¹/₂", $100.00 – 150.00.

Courtesy of Grant Smith

St. Leger by Butler-Butler Inc., New York, New York, ¹/₄" x 3¹/₄" x 3", $25.00 – 50.00.

Courtesy of Bob & Sherri Copeland

St. James Parish Perique by Wm. S. Kimball & Co., Rochester, New York, 2" x 3¹/₂" x 2¹/₄", $25.00 – 50.00.

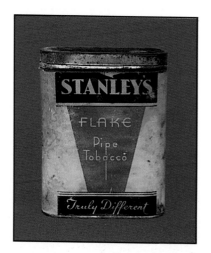

Stanley's paper label vertical pocket by L & I Rubovits, Chicago, Illinois, 4" x 3¹/₂" x 1", $50.00 – 75.00.

Courtesy of Bob & Sherri Copeland

Stanwix vertical pockets by Falk Tobacco Co., New York & Richmond, 4¹/₂" x 3" x 1", left: blue, $600.00 – 700.00; right: black, $450.00 – 500.00.

Staple Grain vertical pocket by M.A. Gunst & Co., 3¹/₂" x 3" x 1", $1,250.00 – 1,500.00.

State Express 555 by Ardath Tobacco Co. Ltd., Piccadilly, London, 3/4" x 3½" x 3", $1.00 – 25.00.

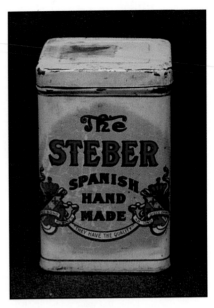

Star and Crescent cigar canister by A.J. Dimmig & Co., East Greenville, Pennsylvania, marked Liberty Can Co., 5" x 5½", $250.00 – 300.00.
Courtesy of Grant Smith

Steber marked Heekin Can Co., Cincinnati, Ohio, 5" x 3" x 3", $25.00 – 50.00.

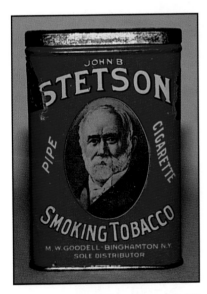

Sultan's by J. Wright Co., Richmond, Virginia, 5½" x 6" x 4", $800.00 – 900.00.
Courtesy of Grant Smith

Stetson vertical pocket by M. W. Goodell, Binghamton, New York, 4½" x 3" x 1", rare, $3,000.00+.

Success Stogies by Duquesne Cigar Co., Pittsburgh, Pennsylvania, marked Lockwood Mfg. Co., Cinn. O., 6" x 4¼", $75.00 – 100.00.
Courtesy of Ken & Nancy Jones

Sultan's by J. Wright & Co., Richmond, Virginia, marked Hasker & Marcuse, 1³/4" x 4¹/2" x 2³/4", $100.00 – 150.00.

Courtesy of Grant Smith

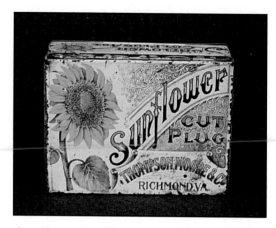

Sunflower by Thompson Moore & Co., Richmond, Virginia, 1¹/4" x 4¹/2" x 3¹/4", $1,750.00 – 2,000.00.

Courtesy of Grant Smith

Sunset Trail vertical box by Roby Cigar Co., Barnesville, Ohio, 5¹/2" x 3¹/2" x 3¹/2", $1,000.00 – 1,250.00.

Courtesy of Ken & Nancy Jones

Surbrug's High Grade by The Surbrug Co., New York & Richmond, Virginia, 6" x 7" x 4¹/2", $250.00 – 300.00.

Courtesy of Grant Smith

Sweet Caporal flat 50 cigarette tin by Kinney Bros., 1/2"
x 5³/4" x 4¹/4", $50.00 – 75.00.
Courtesy of Bob & Sherri Copeland

Sweet Clover store bin by Lovell-Buffington
Tobacco Co., Covington, Kentucky, 11"
x 7" x 7", $600.00 – 700.00.
Courtesy of Alex & Marilyn Znaiden

Sweetser's Snuff by
Sweetser Bros., Boston,
2" x 1¹/2", $1.00 – 25.00.
Courtesy of Bob & Sherri Copeland

T. & B. Renowned by Geo. Tuckett & Son Co.
Ltd., Hamilton, Ontario, 3" x 5" x 3¹/2",
$100.00 – 150.00.
Courtesy of Grant Smith

Sweet Mist cardboard store bin with tin
top and bottom by Scotten Dillion Co.,
Detroit, Michigan, 11" x 8" x 6¹/4",
$200.00 – 250.00.

Tally Ho! flat pocket by F.F. Adams & Co.,
Milwaukee, marked Chicago Stamping
Co., 1/2" x 3³/4" x 2¹/2", $700.00 – 800.00.
Courtesy of Grant Smith

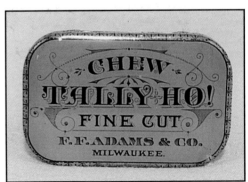

"Tam O' Shanter" by Stephen Mitchell & Son, 1¹/₄" x 6¹/₄" x 4³/₄", $25.00 – 50.00.

Tee-To-Green paper label vertical pocket by J.B. Back & Co., Brooklyn, New York, 4" x 3" x 1", $200.00 – 250.00.
Courtesy of Bob & Sherri Copeland

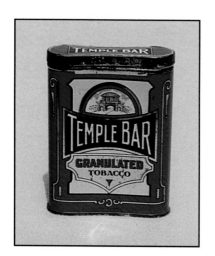

Temple Bar double concaved vertical pocket by The British-Australasian Tobacco Co., Melbourne, Australia, 4" x 3" x 1", rare, $1,250.00 – 1,500.00.

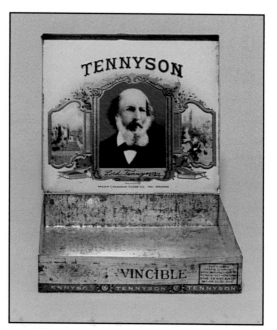

Tennyson cigar tin by Mazer Cressman Cigar Co. Inc., ³/₄" x 6¹/₄" x 5¹/₂", $25.00 – 50.00.

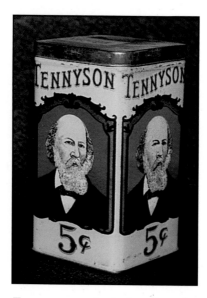

Tennyson vertical cigar box by Mazer Cressman Cigar Co., Detroit, Michigan, 5¹/₂" x 3" x 3", $75.00 – 100.00.
Courtesy of Ken & Nancy Jones

Tiger flat pocket by The American Tobacco Co., ½" x 3½" x 2½", $75.00 – 100.00.

Times Square paper label by United Cigar Stores, 4½" x 4", $25.00 – 50.00. Note: a more valuable litho version exists.

Tiger store bin canister by P. Lorillard Co., Jersey City, New Jersey, 11¼" x 8¼", $150.00 – 200.00. Note: a more valuable blue variation exists.

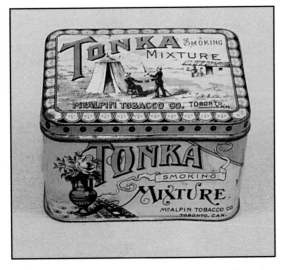

"Travellers Companion" by Elliot, Ottenheimer & Elliot, Baltimore, 2" x 4½" x 2¾", $1.00 – 25.00.

Tonka by McAlpin Tobacco Co., Toronto, Canada, $300.00 – 350.00.

Courtesy of Grant Smith

Tuckett's by Tuckett's Tobacco Co., Canada, 1¼" x 4¼" x 3", $1.00 – 25.00.

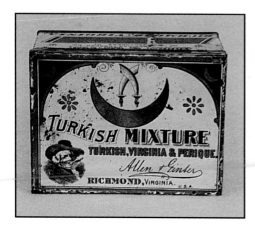

Turkish Mixture by Allen & Ginter, Richmond, Virginia, 2¼" x 4½" x 3¼", $150.00 – 200.00.

Courtesy of Grant Smith

Turkish Patrol cardboard vertical pocket with tin top and bottom by John Bagley & Co., 4¼" x 2¼" x 1", $250.00 – 300.00.

Courtesy of Bob & Sherri Copeland

Turmac flat 50 cigarette tin by Turkish-Macedonia Tobacco Co., 1" x 6" x 4¾", $50.00 – 75.00.

Turret flat 50 cigarette tin by Imperial Tobacco Co. of Canada, ½" x 5¾ 2 4¼", $25.00 – 50.00.

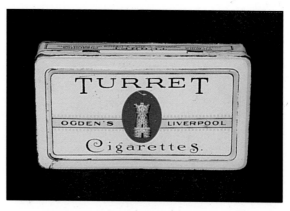

Turret cigarette tin by Imperial Tobacco Co. of Canada, 1" x 5½" x 3", $1.00 – 25.00.

Tuxedo (gold) vertical pocket by R.A. Patterson Tobacco Co., American Tobacco Co. Successor, 4¹/4" x 3" x 1". Reflecting a slight universal cast of green and showing green under its tax stamp, this tin appears to have been originally green. Its (gold) authenticity is highly controversial among collectors. Some believe it to be an anniversary promotional item and consider it rare. No price available.

Tuxedo vertical pockets by R.A. Patterson Tobacco Co., left: 4¹/4" x 3" x 1", $1.00 – 25.00; right: 4" x 3" x 1", $25.00 – 50.00. Note: the tin on the right has four items on the table and the man's hands are separate.

U.C. Mixture (University of California), 1¹/2" x 5" x 3¹/2", $100.00 – 150.00.
Courtesy of Grant Smith

Two Orphans cigar canister marked factory No. 17, 2nd Dist. of VA., 5" x 5", $250.00 – 300.00.
Courtesy of Ken & Nancy Jones

U.S. Marine vertical pockets by American Tobacco Co., left: 4¹/2" x 3" x 1"; right: 4¹/4" x 3" x 1", $300.00 – 350.00 each.

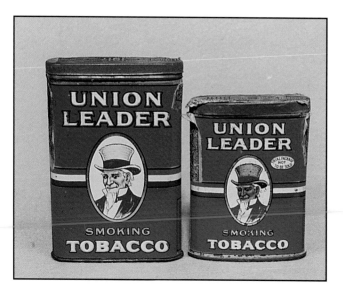

Union Slice flat pocket, ³/₄" x 4¹/₂" x 2¹/₂", rare, no price available.
Courtesy of Grant Smith

Union Leader (no pipe) by P. Lorillard Co., left: 4¹/₂" x 3" x 1", $100.00 – 150.00; right: trial, 3¹/₂" x 2³/₄" x 1", rare, $450.00 – 500.00. Note: another trial variation of Uncle Sam with a pipe exists.

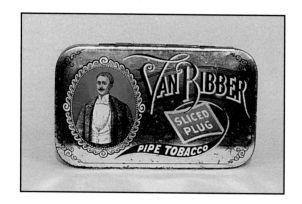

Van Bibber flat pocket, ³/₄" x 4¹/₂" x 2¹/₂", $50.00 – 75.00.
Courtesy of Grant Smith

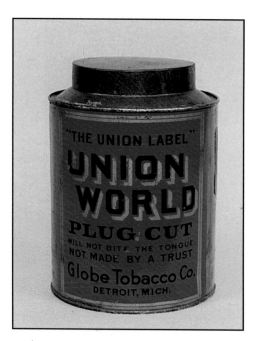

Union World small top canister by Globe Tobacco Co., Detroit, Michigan, marked A.C. Co. 11A, 6¹/₂" x 5", $400.00 – 450.00.
Courtesy of Grant Smith

Van-Loo by Van-Loo Cigar Co. Ltd., 5¹/₄" x 5¹/₂", $150.00 – 200.00.
Courtesy of Richard & Ann Lehmann

Vaporia paper label by Falk Tobacco Co., Richmond, Virginia, 2³/4" x 2³/4", $1.00 – 25.00.

Victor by Moonelis Cigarette Co., New York, marked S.A. Ilsley, Brooklyn, New York, ¹/4" x 3¹/2" x 3¹/4", $75.00 – 100.00.

Victor flat pocket by Charles W. Allen, Chicago, ¹/2" x 3¹/2" x 2¹/4", $300.00 – 350.00. Note: Reverse side is Darey and Joan Plug.
Courtesy of Grant Smith

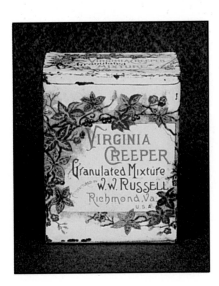

Virginia Creeper vertical box by W.W. Russell, Richmond, Virginia, marked Hasker & Marcuse, 4¹/2" x 3¹/2" x 2", $350.00 – 400.00.
Courtesy of Grant Smith

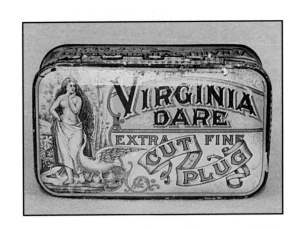

Virginia Dare marked Hasker & Marcuse, 1³/4" x 4¹/2" x 2¹/2", $250.00 – 300.00.
Courtesy of Grant Smith

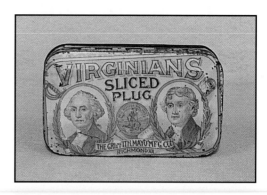

Virginia Dare flat pocket marked Hasker & Marcuse, Richmond, VA., 1" x 4¹/₂" x 2¹/₂", $400.00 – 450.00.
Courtesy of Grant Smith

Virginians flat pocket by The Griffith, Mayo Manufacturing Co., Richmond, Virginia, marked Hasker & Marcuse, 1" x 4¹/₂" x 2³/₄", $1,000.00 – 1,250.00.

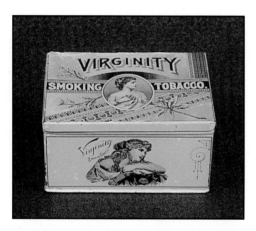

Virginity by G.W. Gail & Ax, branch of The American Tobacco Co., Baltimore, Maryland, 2¹/₂" x 4¹/₂" x 3¹/₄", $500.00 – 600.00.
Courtesy of Grant Smith

War Eagle (green) cigar canister, 5¹/₂" x 5", $200.00 – 250.00.
Courtesy of Grant Smith

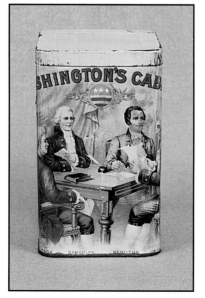

Washington's Cabinet paper label vertical box by Sam Telmo Cigar Manufacturing Co., Detroit, Michigan, 5" x 3" x 3", $150.00 – 200.00.
Courtesy of Grant Smith

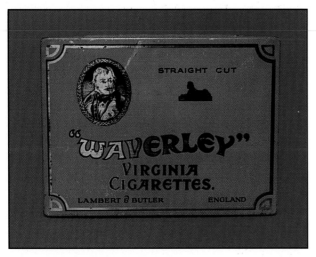

"Waverley" flat 50 cigarette tin by Lambert & Butler, England, ³/₄" x 5¹/₄" x 4¹/₂", $25.00 – 50.00.

Waverley Navy Cut by Hodge Tobacco Co., Henderson, Kentucky, 1³/₄" x 4¹/₂" x 3¹/₄", $800.00 – 900.00.
Courtesy of Grant Smith

Week End Special paper label canister by Stone & Ordean Wells Co., 5³/₄" x 4¹/₂", rare, no price available.
Courtesy of Grant Smith

Weldon vertical pockets by S.S. Pierce Co., Boston, Massachusetts, left: 4¹/₂" x 3" x 1", $400.00 – 450.00; right: 3¹/₂" x 3¹/₄" x 1", $350.00 – 400.00.

Weldon flat pocket by S.S. Pierce Co., Boston, 1" x 4¹/₂" x 3¹/₄", $25.00 – 50.00.
Courtesy of Bob & Sherri Copeland

Wheeling Maids cigar canister by Allan H. Wright, Hicksville, Ohio, marked Heekin Can Co., 5¹/₂" x 5¹/₄", $350.00 – 400.00.
Courtesy of Grant Smith

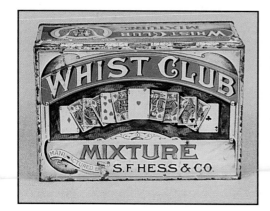

Whist Club by S.F. Hess & Co., marked
Hasker & Marcuse, Richmond, VA., 2" x
4¹/2" x 3", $1,000.00 – 1,250.00.
Courtesy of Grant Smith

White Fowl by H.W. Lewis Cigar Co.,
Belmont, Ohio, marked Heekin Can
Co., 6" x 4¹/2", $200.00 – 250.00.
Courtesy of Alex & Marilyn Znaiden

White Lion cigar box marked Liberty Can Co., 5¹/2" x 3¹/2" x 3¹/2",
$100.00 – 150.00.
Courtesy of Ken & Nancy Jones

White Seal pail by Lovell & Buffington
Tobacco Co's., 6¹/2" x 5¹/4", $250.00 – 300.00.
Courtesy of Grant Smith

Willoughby Taylor by Penn Tobacco
Co., Wilkes-Barre, Pennsylvania,
4¹/4" x 5" x 3¹/4", $1.00 – 25.00.

Willoughby Taylor by Bloch Bros.
Tobacco Co., Wheeling, West
Virginia, 4" x 4¹/4", $25.00 – 50.00.
Courtesy of Bob & Sherri Copeland

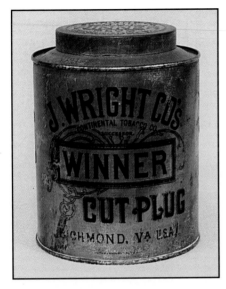

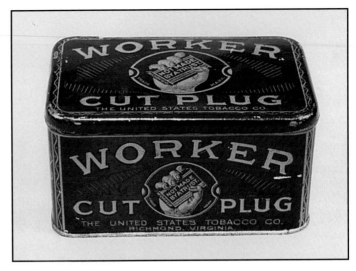

Worker by The United States Tobacco Co., Richmond, Virginia, 3¼" x 6" x 4", $200.00 – 250.00.
Courtesy of Grant Smith

Winner by J. Wright Co., Richmond, Virginia, Continental Tobacco Co. Successor, marked Hasker & Marcuse, 6" x 5", $100.00 – 150.00.
Courtesy of Grant Smith

Yacht flat pocket by United States Tobacco Co., marked Hasker & Marcuse, 1" x 4½" x 2½", $250.00 – 300.00.
Courtesy of Grant Smith

Worker lunch box marked Factory No. 15, 2nd Dist. of VA., 5½" x 7½" x 4½", $100.00 – 150.00. Note: a brown variation exists with the same value.

Yale flat pocket by Marburg Bros., Baltimore, Maryland, American Tobacco Co. Successor, ¾" x 4½" x 2½", $300.00 – 350.00.
Courtesy of Grant Smith

Yankee Clipper vertical pocket by Brown & Williamson Tobacco Corp., Louisville, Kentucky, marked Brown & Williamson (export) Ltd., 4¹/₄" x 3" x 1", rare, $3,000.00+.
Courtesy of Ben Labudde

Yoc-O-May by John J. Bagley & Co., Detroit, Michigan, 1¹/₂" x 4¹/₂" x 2¹/₂", $75.00 – 100.00.
Courtesy of Grant Smith

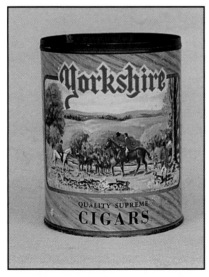

Yorkshire paper label by Sears, Roebuck & Co., 5" x 4", $25.00 – 50.00.
Courtesy of Bob & Sherri Copeland

Yum Yum by Aug. Beck & Co., American Tobacco Co. Successor, 6¹/₂" x 5¹/₂", $300.00 – 350.00.
Courtesy of Grant Smith

TOBACCO TINS NOT SHOWN:

A. Zaphiro & Co., 1¹/₂" x 5¹/₂" x 4¹/₄", $50.00 – 75.00
Achiever (man) paper label, 5" x 5¹/₂", $75.00 – 100.00
All Dutch Panetelas (children), 6" x 4¹/₄", $300.00 – 350.00
Alverez Lopez, 5³/₄" x 5¹/₄", $75.00 – 100.00
American Mixture, 4¹/₂" x 4", $25.00 – 50.00
American Sweets, 5¹/₄" x 4¹/₄" x 4¹/₄", $50.00 – 75.00
Americus (man), 4" x 3" x 3", $150.00 – 200.00
Amicus (woman) paper label, 5¹/₂" x 4¹/₂", $200.00 – 250.00
Aquilas Habana, 2" x 6" x 4", $75.00 – 100.00
Archer, 4" x 4¹/₄", $50.00 – 75.00
Argood Cigar (white), 5" x 5¹/₄", $25.00 – 50.00
As You Like It, paper label, 5¹/₂" x 6", $75.00 – 100.00
At–A–Boy (yellow), 5¹/₄" x 3" x 3", $1.00 – 25.00
Azora, 5¹/₂" x 4¹/₂", $75.00 – 100.00
B.D.V., ¹/₄" x 3¹/₄" x 2³/₄", $25.00 – 50.00
Badminton (Hill's), 4¹/₂" x 3", $100.00 – 150.00
Bamboo, ¹/₄" x 3¹/₂" x 3¹/₄", $25.00 – 50.00
Bando (yellow), 5¹/₂" x 3" x 3", $1.00 – 25.00
Banker Hand Made, 5¹/₄" x 3¹/₂" x 3¹/₂", $25.00 – 50.00
Barrett Stables, 5¹/₂" x 6" x 4", $100.00 – 150.00
Bella Mundo (girl), 5" x 3¹/₂" x 3¹/₂", $250.00 – 300.00
Besco Cigar paper label, 5¹/₂" x 6", $1.00 – 25.00
Big Value (Stickney), 5¹/₂" x 3¹/₂" x 3¹/₂", $25.00 – 50.00
Bilt Rite (pyramid) paper label, 6" x 6" x 4", $100.00 – 150.00
Bit and Spur Mixture, 2³/₄" x 7" x 2³/₄", $75.00 – 100.00
Black Friar Lake (yellow), 1¹/₄" x 5" x 4", $25.00 – 50.00
Bluebird, 1¹/₂" x 5" x 3¹/₂", $25.00 – 50.00
Boar's Head, 5" x 8" x 5", $75.00 – 100.00
Bon Voyage, paper label, 4¹/₂" x 3¹/₂" x 1¹/₂", $50.00 – 75.00
Boston Bankers (green), 5¹/₂" x 3" x 3", $25.00 – 50.00
Brown Bear Blend paper label, 2" x 3" x 1", $75.00 – 100.00
Buckeye (stag), 5¹/₂" x 3" x 2", $100.00 – 150.00
Canada Straight, 4" x 4¹/₄", $25.00 – 50.00
Canadian Club, 5¹/₂" x 5¹/₂", $75.00 – 100.00
Careme Topangos, 4¹/₂" x 4", $25.00 – 50.00
Carmelo paper label, 5" x 4", $75.00 – 100.00
Charles Denby, 5¹/₂" x 3¹/₂" x 3¹/₂", $75.00 – 100.00
Checkers cardboard, 2" x 2¹/₄" x 1", $350.00 – 400.00
Class (peacock), 5¹/₄" x 3¹/₂" x 3¹/₂", $25.00 – 50.00
Clifton Park Special (fountain), 5" x 5¹/₄", $400.00 – 450.00
Coiner (eagle), 5¹/₄" x 3¹/₂" x 3¹/₂", $150.00 – 200.00
Colombo's Egyptian, 1¹/₂" x 5¹/₂" x 3", $50.00 – 75.00
Colonial Warlock, ¹/₄" x 3¹/₄" x 3", $1.00 – 25.00
Combination Stogies, 6" x 4", $150.00 – 200.00
Commercial, 5¹/₂" x 6", $75.00 – 100.00
Cornelius Cigars (yellow), 5" x 3¹/₄", $150.00 – 200.00
Cortez (man), 6¹/₂" x 5¹/₂", $100.00 – 150.00
Cremo, 14" x 6" x 6", $50.00 – 75.00
Cremo, 5¹/₂" x 6¹/₂" x 3¹/₄", $50.00 – 75.00
Crosse & Blackwell, ³/₄" x 5" x 3³/₄", $25.00 – 50.00
Cyana, 1" x 5" x 3", $25.00 – 50.00
Cyco (woman), 1¹/₄" x 5¹/₄" x 3¹/₂", $50.00 – 75.00
Cyrus The Great paper label, 5¹/₂" x 5¹/₂", 25.00 – 50.00
Dinty Moore cardboard, 5" x 3¹/₂" x 1¹/₄", $1.00 – 25.00
Diplomat Mixture, 3" x 2³/₄" x 1¹/₄", $150.00 – 200.00
Dominion Line (boat), ¹/₂" x 4¹/₄" x 3", $200.00 – 250.00
Earl Marshal (horse/rider), 5¹/₄" x 3" x 3", $150.00 – 200.00
Egyptian Belle (Monopol), ¹/₄" x 3¹/₄" x 3", $25.00 – 50.00
Ekctpa, 3³/₄" x 3¹/₄" x 1¹/₄", $350.00 – 400.00
El Corsicano (rider) paper label, 6" x 4¹/₂", $200.00 – 250.00

El Dallo, 6" x 3¹/₄" x 3¹/₂", $50.00 – 75.00
El Retina (man w/hat), 1¹/₄" x 5¹/₄" x 3¹/₂", $50.00 – 75.00
El Verdaro (woman), 5" x 3¹/₄" x 3¹/₄", $100.00 – 150.00
Ember, 5¹/₂" x 3¹/₂" x 3¹/₂", $1.00 – 25.00
Estabrook & Eaton's, 1³/₄" x 4¹/₂" x 3¹/₄", $50.00 – 75.00
Federal Judge, 5¹/₂" x 3¹/₂" x 3¹/₂", $100.00 – 150.00
Fiona, 5¹/₂" x 6", $250.00 – 300.00
First Cabin cardboard, 5¹/₂" x 4¹/₂" x 4¹/₂", $400.00 – 450.00
Flag Heads (yellow), 6" x 4" x 4", $50.00 – 75.00
Fort Garry, 4³/₄" x 4" x 2¹/₂", $100.00 – 150.00
Garcia Mystery, 5" x 5¹/₄", $1.00 – 25.00
Gen. Good paper label, 5" x 3¹/₄" x 3¹/₄", $75.00 – 100.00
Golden Eagle, ¹/₄" x 3¹/₄" x 3", $100.00 – 150.00
Good Cheer (stein shape), 5" x 3³/₄", $100.00 – 150.00
Gott Mituns 1870 (bird), ¹/₄" x 3¹/₄" x 3", $75.00 – 100.00
Grand Central Mixture, 1³/₄" x 4¹/₂" x 3¹/₄", rare, no price available
Great Auk, 1¹/₂" x 5¹/₂" x 3", $350.00 – 400.00
Great International paper label, 2" x 4" x 3", $50.00 – 75.00
Great International Mixture, 2" x 4" x 3", $300.00 – 350.00
Grizzly paper label, 6¹/₂" x 4³/₄", $250.00 – 300.00
Grouse-Moore (dogs), 1" x 4¹/₂" x 3¹/₄", $25.00 – 50.00
Hake's New York Hand Made, 5¹/₂" x 4", $25.00 – 50.00
Half Spanish, 5³/₄" x 5", $100.00 – 150.00
Hav–A–Tampa paper label, 5¹/₄" x 5¹/₂", $25.00 – 50.00
Havana Consul paper label, 5" x 3¹/₂", $75.00 – 100.00
Henry George paper label, 5¹/₄" x 3" x 3", $75.00 – 100.00
Hensel's No. 78 (blue), 5" x 6", $50.00 – 75.00
Hignett's Golden Butterfly, 2" x 7³/₄" x 4", $75.00 – 100.00
Hipp, 2¹/₄" x 6¹/₂" x 5³/₄", $25.00 – 50.00
His Master's Voice (dog) paper label, 5" x 4", $200.00 – 250.00
Holt Pipe Shop paper label, 4¹/₂" x 3" x 1", $100.00 – 150.00
Houston Club Mixture, 1" x 6¹/₂" x 2³/₄", $150.00 – 200.00
Hudson's Bay, 5" x 3" x 3", $25.00 – 50.00
Hugh Cambells Shag, 4" x 6" x 4", $150.00 – 200.00
Hyman's Sun Cured, 4¹/₂" x 3¹/₄" x 1¹/₂", $50.00 – 75.00
Ibex Flake (gazelle), 1¹/₄" x 6¹/₂" x 4³/₄", $25.00 – 50.00
Illustrator paper label, 5¹/₂" x 5¹/₂", $75.00 – 100.00
Intermission, ¹/₂" x 3¹/₄" x 3", $25.00 – 50.00
J–A–Z, 5¹/₄" x 4¹/₂" x 4¹/₂", $25.00 – 50.00
James G. Blaine, 5" x 3" x 3", $150.00 – 200.00
Jefferson Chums, ¹/₂" x 3¹/₄" x 3", $25.00 – 50.00
Joan of Arc paper label, 5¹/₄" x 4", $100.00 – 150.00
Keg, 6" x 4³/₄", $1.00 – 25.00
Kenway, 5¹/₂" x 5", $25.00 – 50.00
Key Mark (red), 5¹/₂" x 4¹/₂" x 4¹/₂", $25.00 – 50.00
La Mavita, 5" x 4³/₄" x 4³/₄", $25.00 – 50.00
La Nora (woman), 5¹/₂" x 3¹/₂" x 3¹/₂", $200.00 – 250.00
La Primadora, 5³/₄" x 5¹/₂" x 4³/₄", $100.00 – 150.00
La Tisona (woman), 5¹/₄" x 3" x 3", $100.00 – 150.00
La Vendor paper label, 1¹/₄" x 5¹/₄" x 3¹/₂", $1.00 – 25.00
Limit, 4" x 2¹/₂" x 1³/₄", $100.00 – 150.00
Lincoln Highway (U.S.), 5¹/₄" x 3" x 3", $100.00 – 150.00
Little Barrett, 4¹/₂" x 3" x 3", $75.00 – 100.00
Little Bobbie, 4¹/₂" x 3" x 3", $50.00 – 75.00
Lord Lister paper label, 5¹/₄" x 5¹/₄", $50.00 – 75.00
Lord Salisbury, ¹/₂" x 5³/₄" x 4¹/₂", $50.00 – 75.00
Lord Tennyson Puritanos, 5¹/₄" x 5", $100.00 – 150.00
Los Tres (3-men), 4¹/₄" x 5¹/₂", $50.00 – 75.00
Lotus (standing woman), ¹/₄" x 3¹/₄" x 3¹/₄", $100.00 – 150.00
Louisville Perfectos, 5³/₄" x 3¹/₄" x 3¹/₄", $25.00 – 50.00

Lucky Hit, 3/4" x 41/4" x 31/4", $25.00 – 50.00

Marksman paper label, 51/2" x 5", $500.00 – 600.00

Maude Hale (woman) paper label, 51/2" x 3" x 3", $75.00 – 100.00

Medalist, 1/2" x 31/4" x 3", $25.00 – 50.00

Meerchaum, 5" x 33/4" x 31/2", $75.00 – 100.00

Melrose (woman), 51/4" x 31/4" x 31/4", $150.00 – 200.00

Mexican Commerce (eagle), 5" x 31/2" x 31/2", $200.00 – 250.00

Mexican Tiger Stogies, 61/2" x 51/4", $300.00 – 350.00

Mi Wauki, 11/4" x 5" x 31/2", $25.00 – 50.00

Millbank, 1" x 5" x 3", $1.00 – 25.00

Mitchell's Cut Golden Bar, 1" x 6" x 4", $1.00 – 25.00

Mitchell's Navy Cut (ship), 11/4" x 6" x 43/4", $25.00 – 50.00

Mohar, 1/4" x 31/4" x 23/4", $50.00 – 75.00

Moneymaker (Clark's), 11/4" x 6" x 43/4", $50.00 – 75.00

Na-Bocklish (trees), 5" x 51/2", $100.00 – 150.00

National Trade Mark, 51/2" x 6" x 4", $100.00 – 150.00

Nebraska Blossom paper label, 51/2" x 41/2", $400.00 – 450.00

New Capitol, 53/4" x 31/4" x 31/4", $150.00 – 200.00

Niles & Mose's, 53/4" x 31/2" x 31/2", $1.00 – 25.00

Nonpareil paper label, 5" x 31/4" x 31/4", $25.00 – 50.00

Normandie, 4" x 41/4", $25.00 – 50.00

Ohio State, 51/4" x 5", $75.00 – 100.00

Old Caelic, 1/4" x 31/4" x 3", $25.00 – 50.00

Old Tar, 4" x 6" x 4", $75.00 – 100.00

Ology, 5" x 3" x 3", $1.00 – 25.00

Omega knob top, 5" x 3", $100.00 – 150.00

Oriental Mixture, 13/4" x 61/2" x 3", $25.00 – 50.00

Osceola embossed, 43/4" x 31/2" x 31/2", $200.00 – 250.00

Osmundo, 11/4" x 43/4" x 31/2", $1.00 – 25.00

Our Straight Fives, 51/2" x 31/2" x 31/2", $25.00 – 50.00

Parker-Gordon, 51/4" x 31/4" x 31/4", $25.00 – 50.00

Paul Mayo Habana, 5" x 3" x 3", $100.00 – 150.00

Philadelphia Leader paper label, 51/2" x 6", $1.00 – 25.00

Philip Morris cardboard, 4" x 31/2" x 1", $350.00 – 400.00

Pictou Twist, 61/2" x 5", $50.00 – 75.00

Pinzon (man), 5" x 51/2", $100.00 – 150.00

Plantista paper label, 53/4" x 41/4", $50.00 – 75.00

Pontiac, 4" x 41/4", $25.00 – 50.00

Press Agent, 5" x 51/4", $1.00 – 25.00

Pridemark, 51/4" x 31/2" x 3", $25.00 – 50.00

Prime Puff, 1/2" x 31/4" x 3", $25.00 – 50.00

Prince Cuban (knight), 51/4" x 41/4", $100.00 – 150.00

Prince Hamlet, 5" x 51/4", $50.00 – 75.00

Puffit, 31/2" x 31/2" x 11/4", rare, no price available

Punch, 51/2" x 51/4", $25.00 – 50.00

Pure Stock, 51/2" x 51/2", $25.00 – 50.00

Queen Cigar (building), 51/2" x 3" x 3", $150.00 – 200.00

R.G. Dunn, 11/4" x 5" x 3", $25.00 – 50.00

Raptco Wafers, 3/4" x 31/4" x 2", $1.00 – 25.00

Real Thing cut plug, 3" x 6" x 31/4", $100.00 – 150.00

Recollection (brown), 11/4" x 51/4" x 3", $1.00 – 25.00

Red Crest cardboard, 81/4" x 5" x 5", $200.00 – 250.00

Riverhead Gold, 6" x 41/4", $100.00 – 150.00

Royal Gold, 51/4" x 31/2" x 31/2", $100.00 – 150.00

Royal Kid Cigar (red), 5" x 51/4", $50.00 – 75.00

Royal Moore paper label, 51/2" x 5", $75.00 – 100.00

Security (knight) paper label, 51/2" x 3" x 3", $100.00 – 150.00

Serenade, 1/4" x 31/4" x 3", $25.00 – 50.00

Seven Stars paper label, 1" x 41/2" x 31/4", $25.00 – 50.00

Sir Haig, 51/2" x 6", $100.00 – 150.00

Smart (seated woman), 1/4" x 31/4" x 3", $75.00 – 100.00

Soldier Boy, 3/4" x 31/4" x 23/4", $75.00 – 100.00

Sportsman, 1/4" x 31/4" x 23/4", $100.00 – 150.00

Square American (blue), 51/4" x 31/4" x 31/4", $1.00 – 25.00

Star Five, 41/2" x 51/4", $100.00 – 150.00

Star Green, 5" x 3" x 3", $75.00 – 100.00

Strause's, 4" x 21/2" x 13/4", $200.00 – 250.00

Sunstar (2 women), 51/2" x 3" x 3", $200.00 – 250.00

Sweet Alberta (peach) cardboard, 5" x 5", $75.00 – 100.00

Sweet Bouquet, 1" x 5" x 31/2", $600.00 – 700.00

Tango Stogies, 6" x 5", $50.00 – 75.00

Temple Bar, 1/2" x 31/4" x 23/4", $50.00 – 75.00

Terrier Brown Flake (dog), 1" x 6" x 41/2", $200.00 – 250.00

Three Kings, 4" x 3" x 3", $25.00 – 50.00

Three States (oval), 3/4" x 41/2" x 21/2", $150.00 – 200.00

Thunder Clouds, 11/2" x 5" x 4", $25.00 – 50.00

Tiz (man w/hat), 51/2" x 51/2", $100.00 – 150.00

Train Master, 51/2" x 43/4" x 43/4", $75.00 – 100.00

Trolly, 10" x 71/4" x 7", $1,250.00 1,500.00

True Blue paper label, 5" x 5", $25.00 – 50.00

Two Belles, 11/4" x 43/4" x 31/2", $100.00 – 150.00

Tyon paper label, 5" x 41/2", $50.00 – 75.00

Uncle Green, 51/2" x 51/2", $100.00 – 150.00

Union Blend, 41/2" x 73/4" x 5", $150.00 – 200.00

Varsity Blend, 2" x 5" x 31/2", $25.00 – 50.00

Vintage Blend paper label, 21/2" x 21/4", $1.00 – 25.00

Wake Up (rooster) paper label, 6" x 41/4", $700.00 – 800.00

Wave Line, 3" x 6" x 4", $25.00 – 50.00

White Ash (cigar), 11/4" x 51/4" x 31/4", $25.00 – 50.00

White Horse, 1/4" x 31/4" x 3", $50.00 – 75.00

Winsome (woman), 1/4" x 31/4" x 3", $75.00 – 100.00

Wonder Cigar (yellow), 5" x 51/4", $25.00 – 50.00

Zeybec Queens, 1/4" x 3" x 23/4", $100.00 – 150.00

20-more by H.H. Hixon & Co. Inc., Chicago, Illinois, 3½" x 5", $25.00 – 50.00.

Courtesy of Tom & Lynne Sankiewicz

5th Avenue by The DeWitt-Nash Co., Cleveland, Ohio, marked Buffalo Can Co., 6" x 4¼", $75.00 – 100.00.

Courtesy of Tom & Mary Lou Slike

Abbey Garden by Mission Garden Co. Inc., New York, 6¼" x 4", $600.00 – 700.00.

Courtesy of Alex & Marilyn Znaiden

Acorn paper label by The Harnit & Hewitt Co., Toledo, Ohio, 5½" x 4¼", $100.00 – 150.00.

Courtesy of Ken & Nancy Jones

Aero by Thompson, Elliott, Limited, Vancouver, British Columbia, marked A.C. Co., 5¾" x 4¼", $350.00 – 400.00.

Courtesy of Grant Smith

Aladdin by M.J.B. Co's., marked Western Can Co., San Francisco, California, 5" x 4¼", $150.00 – 200.00.

Courtesy of Bob & Sherri Copeland

Alice Foote MacDougall marked Continental Can Co., 4" x 5", $50.00 – 75.00.
Courtesy of Bob & Sherri Copeland

All Pure by Ocean Coffee Co., Shreveport, Louisiana, 11½" x 5¼", $600.00 – 700.00.
Courtesy of Alex & Marilyn Znaiden

Allen Square by Allen, Quinlan Co., St. Paul, Minnesota, 9" x 7½", $2,000.00 – 2,500.00.
Courtesy of Alex & Marilyn Znaiden

Arabian Banquet by Blogett, Beckley Co., Toledo, Ohio, left: 9½" x 5½", $300.00 – 350.00; right: 6" x 4¼", $200.00 – 250.00.
Courtesy of Alex & Marilyn Znaiden

Aragon by Aragon Coffee Co., Richmond, Virginia, 5½" x 4¼", $500.00 – 600.00.
Courtesy of Alex & Marilyn Znaiden

Arcadia manufacturer unknown, marked A.C. Co. 68A, 4" x 5¼", $150.00 – 200.00.
Courtesy of Alex & Marilyn Znaiden

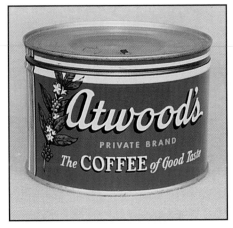

Atwood's by Atwood Coffee Co., Minneapolis, Minnesota, marked A.C. Co. 50A, 3½" x 5", $25.00 – 50.00.
Courtesy of Bob & Sherri Copeland

Autocrat by Brownell & Field Co., Providence, Rhode Island, 8¼" x 6¼", $50.00 – 75.00.
Courtesy of Tom & Mary Lou Slike

B.B. Java by Bennett, Sloan & Co., New York & New Haven, marked Ginna & Co., 9" x 5" x 5", $300.00 – 350.00.
Courtesy of Alex & Marilyn Znaiden

Barrington Hall by Baker Importing Co. Inc., Division of Hygrade Products Corp., New York, New York, 3½" x 5", $25.00 – 50.00.
Courtesy of Tom & Lynne Sankiewicz

Bartley's Honor by The R.A. Bartley Co., Toledo, Ohio, 3¾" x 5", $150.00 – 200.00.
Courtesy of Tom & Lynne Sankiewicz

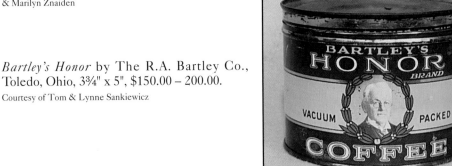

Beech-Nut sample by Beech-Nut Packing Co., Canajoharie, New York, marked A.C. Co. 10A, 2¼" x 2¾", $100.00 – 150.00.
Courtesy of Bob and Sherri Copeland

Better Cup by N.C.D. Inc., Pittsburgh, Pennsylvania, 3½" x 5", $1.00 – 25.00.
Courtesy of Bob & Sherri Copeland

Beacon by The Floom-Fleck Co., Tiffin, Ohio, 4" x 5", $100.00 – 150.00.
Courtesy of Tom & Lynne Sankiewicz

Big Hit by Euclid Coffee Co., Cleveland, Ohio, marked A.C. Co. 68A, 4" x 5", $25.00 – 50.00.
Courtesy of Bob & Sherri Copeland

Big Horn by The Inter-State Coffee & Spice Co., Joplin, Missouri, 6" x 4¼", $350.00 – 400.00.
Courtesy of Grant Smith

Blackstone by Blackhawk Coffee & Spice Co., Waterloo, Iowa, 5¾" x 4¼", $300.00 – 350.00.
Courtesy of Alex & Marilyn Znaiden

Blanke's by C. F. Blanke Tea & Coffee Co., St. Louis, 4" x 8" x 4", $100.00 – 150.00.
Courtesy of Bob & Correna Anderson

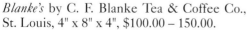

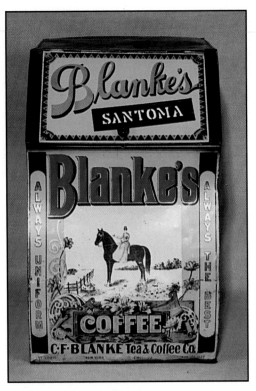

Blue and Whtie by Red & White Corp., Buffalo, New York, 3½" x 5", $50.00 – 75.00.
Courtesy of Tom & Lynne Sankiewicz

Blanke's store bin by C.F. Blanke Tea & Coffee Co., St. Louis, Missouri, 25" x 15¾" x 19½", $1,000.00 – 1,250.00.
Courtesy of Alex & Marilyn Znaiden

Bo-Kā by Reid, Murdoch & Co., 4" x 5", $25.00 – 50.00.
Courtesy of Bob & Sherri Copeland

Blue Parrot by C.W. Griffin & Co., New York, New York, marked A.C. Co. 10A, 6" x 4¼", $3,000.00+.
Courtesy of Alex & Marilyn Znaiden

Boscul by Wm. S. Scull, Camden, New Jersey, 4¼" x 5", $1.00 – 25.00.
Courtesy of Tom & Lynne Sankiewicz

Boscul by William S. Scull, Camden, New Jersey, 3½" x 5", $1.00 – 25.00 each.

Courtesy of Tom & Lynne Sankiewicz

Breakfast Cheer by The Campbell & Woods Co., Pittsburgh, Pennsylvania, 6" x 4¼", $1,250.00 – 1,500.00.

Courtesy of Alex & Marilyn Znaiden

Brundage by The Brundage Bros. Inc., Toledo, Ohio, 4" x 5", $50.00 – 75.00.

Courtesy of Tom & Lynne Sankiewicz

Brundage Urn by The Brundage Bros. Inc., Toledo, Ohio, 4" x 5", $100.00 – 150.00.

Courtesy of Tom & Lynne Sankiewicz

Bubbling Over by Fletcher-Wilson Coffee Co.,
Nashville, Tennessee, 4" x 5", $250.00 – 300.00.
Courtesy of Alex & Marilyn Znaiden

Bunker Hill by Delano Potter & Co., Boston,
Massachusetts, 3¾" x 5", $200.00 – 250.00.
Courtesy of Alex & Marilyn Znaiden

Butter-Nut by Paxton & Gallagher Co., Omaha, Nebraska, top
right: half pound, 3" x 4", $25.00 – 50.00; others: 3½" x 5",
$1.00 – 25.00 each.
Courtesy of Tom & Lynne Sankiewicz

Byerly's by J.A. Byerly Co. Inc., Owosso, Michigan, 3½"
x 5", $25.00 – 50.00.
Courtesy of Tom & Lynne Sankiewicz

Caffé Pastene by Pastene & Co., New York, New York & Boston, Massachusetts, marked A.C. Co. 17A, 4½" x 5", $25.00 – 50.00.

Courtesy of Bob & Sherri Copeland

Capitol by Andrus-Scofield, Columbus, Ohio, marked Wheeling Can Co., left: 5½" x 4¼", $200.00 – 250.00; right: 4" x 5", $100.00 – 150.00.

Courtesy of Bob & Sherri Copeland

Camp Fire by Blue Ribbon Products Co. Inc., San Francisco, California, marked A.C. Co. 94A, 8" x 5¼", $450.00 – 500.00.

Courtesy of Alex & Marilyn Znaiden

Casino by Wepper-Wile Co., Cleveland Ohio, 4" x 5", $25.00 – 50.00.

Courtesy of Bob & Sherri Copeland

Caswell's (Yellow and Blue Brand) by Geo. W. Caswell Co., San Francisco, California, 8¾" x 5¼", $25.00 – 50.00.

Courtesy of Tom & Mary Lou Slike

Caswell's by Geo. W. Caswell Co., San Francisco, California, 8¾" x 5¼", $150.00 – 200.00.
Courtesy of Alex & Marilyn Znaiden

Clipper by Merchants Coffee Co. Inc., New Orleans, 7½" x 6", $2,000.00 – 2,500.00.
Courtesy of Alex & Marilyn Znaiden

Clover Farm by Grain Babcock Co., Cleveland, Ohio, 5¾" x 4¼". $100.00 – 150.00.
Courtesy of Tom & Mary Lou Slike

Commodore pail by W.F. McLauhein & Co., marked Illinois Can Co., Chicago, Ill., 8" x 5½", $450.00 – 500.00.
Courtesy of Grant Smith

Community Brand by Community Coffee Mills, Baton Rouge, Louisiana, 8" x 6½", $200.00 – 250.00.
Courtesy of Mike & Sharon Hunt

Condor by E.D. Marceau Wholesale, Montreal, 6¾" x 4", rare, no price available.
Courtesy of Grant Smith

Country Club by Kroger Grocery & Baking Co., Cincinnati, Ohio, 3½" x 5", $1.00 – 25.00 each.
Courtesy of Tom & Lynne Sankiewicz

Coronet by Euclid Coffee Co., Cleveland, Ohio, 3½" x 5", $25.00 – 50.00.

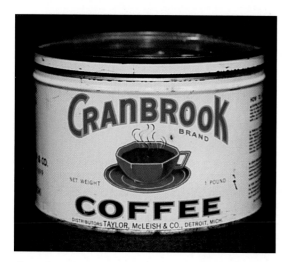

Cranbrook by Taylor, McLeish & Co., Detroit, Michigan, marked Canco, 3½" x 5", $50.00 – 75.00.
Courtesy of Tom & Lynne Sankiewicz

Dairy Brand by Foley Bros. Grocery Co., St. Paul, Minnesota, 8¾" x 7½", $800.00 – 900.00.
Courtesy of Alex & Marilyn Znaiden

Daisee by The Herman Co, Paterson, New Jersey, 6" x 4", $50.00 – 75.00.
Courtesy of Ken & Nancy Jones

Dale Bros. by Dale Bros., Fresno, California, marked Western Can. Co., San Francisco, CA., 3½" x 5", $50.00 – 75.00.

Del Haven by Federated Foods Inc., San Francisco
& Chicago, 4" x 5", $25.00 – 50.00.
Courtesy of Tom & Lynne Sankiewicz

Devotion by Page Coffee Co., St. Joseph, Missouri,
4" x 5", $200.00 – 250.00.
Courtesy of Alex & Marilyn Znaiden

Dining Car by Norwine Coffee Co., St. Louis, Missouri,
left: 8" x 5"; right: 4" x 5", $400.00 – 450.00 each.
Courtesy of Alex & Marilyn Znaiden

Dot by The Janszen Co., Cincinnati, Ohio, left: 5¾" x 4¼",
$75.00 – 100.00; right: 3½" x 5", $25.00 – 50.00.
Courtesy of Bob & Sherri Copeland

Drummer by S.E. Lux Jr. Merchantile Co., Topeko
& Frankfort, Kansas, 4" x 5", $350.00 – 400.00.
Courtesy of Alex & Marilyn Znaiden

Drinkmor by Drinkmor Coffee Co.,
Toronto, Canada, 5¾" x 4¼",
$700.00 – 800.00.
Courtesy of Alex & Marilyn Znaiden

Drummer by S.E. Lux Jr. Mercantile Co., Topeko & Frankfort, Kansas,
4" x 9¾", $250.00 – 300.00.
Courtesy of Mike & Sharon Hunt

E.C.H. Special by E.C. Harley
Co., Dayton, Ohio, 5½" x 4¼",
$300.00 – 350.00.
Courtesy of Bob & Sherri Copeland

El Perco by Caravan Coffee Co., Toledo, Ohio, 4" x 5¼", $25.00 – 50.00.
Courtesy of Tom & Lynne Sankiewicz

Eagle by The Eagle Grocery Co., Jersey City, New Jersey, 6¼" x 4", $100.00 – 150.00.
Courtesy of Bob & Correna Anderson

Elkay by The Lasalle & Koch Co., Toledo, Ohio, 6" x 4", $25.00 – 50.00.
Courtesy of Tom & Lynne Sankiewicz

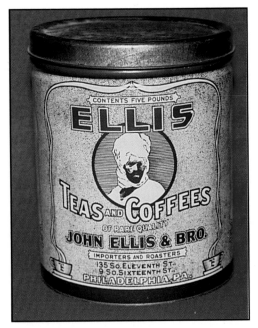

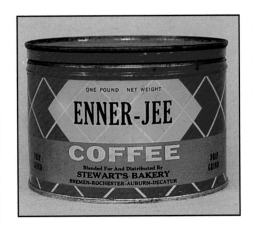

Enner-Jee paper label by Stewart's Bakery, 3½" x 5", $1.00 – 25.00.
Courtesy of Tom & Lynne Sankiewicz

Empire by T. Eaton Co., Toronto, Canada, marked A.C. Co. 31A, 6" x 4¼", $250.00 – 300.00.
Courtesy of Grant Smith

Ellis by John Ellis & Bro., Philadelphia, Pennsylvania, 8" x 8", $200.00 – 250.00.
Courtesy of Bob & Correna Anderson

Fairway by Twin City Wholesale Grocers Co., St. Paul & Minneapolis, Minnesota, marked A.C. Co. 68A, 4" x 5", $75.00 – 100.00.

Courtesy of Bob & Sherri Copeland

Epicure by America Mills, New York, marked S.A. Ilsley, Brooklyn, N.Y., 11½" x 3", $400.00 – 450.00.

Courtesy of Bob & Sherri Copeland

Epicure by John S. Sills & Son Inc., New York, marked Passaic Metalware Co., 6" x 4", $250.00 – 300.00.

Courtesy of Alex & Marilyn Znaiden

Fairway by Twin City Wholesale Grocers Co., marked A.C. Co. 66A, 4" x 5", $100.00 – 150.00.

Farmers Pride sample by Hulman & Co., Terre Haute, Indiana, left: paper label, 2½" x 1¾", $150.00 – 200.00; right: cardboard, 2" x 1¾", $300.00 – 350.00.

Courtesy of Mike & Sharon Hunt

Fall-leaf by Henry Soodsma & Co., Peterson, New Jersey, 6¼" x 4", $250.00 – 300.00.

Courtesy of Alex & Marilyn Znaiden

Faultless by E.D. Keyes & Co., Rutland, Virginia, 6¼" x 3½" x 3½", $100.00 – 150.00.
Courtesy of Alex & Marilyn Znaiden

Ferndell by Sprague, Warner & Co., Chicago, Illinois, 6" x 4¼", $25.00 – 50.00.
Courtesy of Bob & Sherri Copeland

Festal Hall by Goddard Grocer Co., St. Louis, Missouri, 10" x 5½", $300.00 – 350.00.
Courtesy of Alex & Marilyn Znaiden

First Call by Woolson Spice Co., Toledo, Ohio, marked Canco, 3½" x 5", $25.00 – 50.00.
Courtesy of Bob & Sherri Copeland

First Pick by Carroll, Brough & Robinson Co., Oklahoma City, Oklahoma, left: 8" x 5"; right: 4" x 5"; $400.00 – 450.00 each.
Courtesy of Alex & Marilyn Znaiden

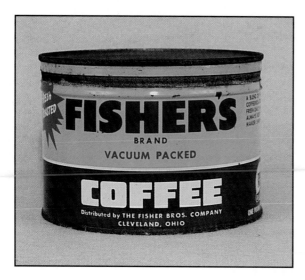

Fisher's by Fisher Bros. Co., Cleveland, Ohio, 3½"
x 5", $1.00 – 25.00.
Courtesy of Tom & Lynne Sankiewicz

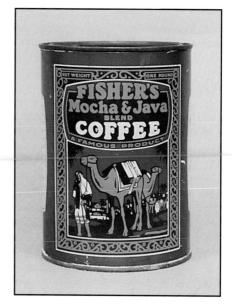

Fisher's by The Fisher Brothers Co.,
Cleveland, Ohio, 5¾" x 4¼",
$150.00 – 200.00.
Courtesy of Alex & Marilyn Znaiden

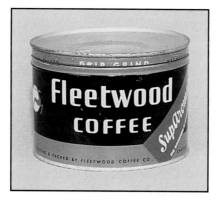

Flavorite by George W. Howe Co. Inc.,
Grove City, Pennsylvania, marked
Canco, 3½" x 5", $25.00 – 50.00.
Courtesy of Bob & Sherri Copeland

Fleetwood by Fleetwood Coffee
Co., Chattanooga, Tennessee, 3½"
x 5", $1.00 – 25.00.
Courtesy of Bob & Sherri Copeland

Folger's Golden Gate by A.J. Folger Co.,
Kansas City & San Francisco, 9¼" x 7",
$250.00 – 300.00.
Courtesy of Alex & Marilyn Znaiden

Food King by Central Retailer Owned Grocers Inc., marked C.C. Co., 3½" x 5", $1.00 – 25.00.
Courtesy of Bob & Sherri Copeland

Forbes by Jas. H. Forbes Tea & Coffee Co., Saint Louis, 3¾" x 9¾", top to bottom: #1, $25.00 – 50.00; #2, $75.00 – 100.00; #3, $50.00 – 75.00; #4, $75.00 – 100.00.
Courtesy of Mike & Sharon Hunt

Forbes by Woolson Spice Co., Toledo, Ohio & New York, New York, marked Canco, 3½" x 5", $50.00 – 75.00.

Fort Western by Holmes-Swift Co., Augusta & Waterville, Maine, 5¾" x 4¼", $250.00 – 300.00.
Courtesy of Grant Smith

Franklin Blend store bin by Bennett, Sloan & Co., New York & Cleveland, 20½" x 14" x 15", $450.00 – 500.00.
Courtesy of Alex & Marilyn Znaiden

French Brand by Wesco Foods Co., Cincinnati, Ohio, 6" x 4½", $25.00 – 50.00.

G.C. French's Special by Pritz & French Co.,
Springfield, Ohio, 3¾" x 5¼", $350.00 – 400.00.
Courtesy of Alex & Marilyn Znaiden

Frontier by Western Grocer Mills, Marshalltown, Iowa,
marked A.C. Co. 70A, 4" x 5¼", $300.00 – 350.00.

Gillies store bin, marked New York,
19½" x 13" x 15½", $350.00 – 400.00.
Courtesy of Alex & Marilyn Znaiden

Gillies' Good Health paper label by
Edwin J. Gillies & Co., New York,
5½" x 4¼", $200.00 – 250.00.
Courtesy of Alex & Marilyn Znaiden

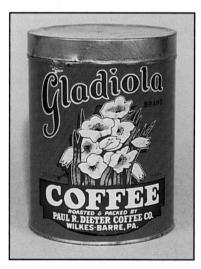

Gladiola by Paul R. Dieter Coffee
Co., Wilkes-Barre, Pennsylvania,
marked Wilkes-Barre Can Co.,
5½" x 4¼", $350.00 – 400.00.
Courtesy of Alex & Marilyn Znaiden

Gold Coast by Swanson Bros., Chicago, Illinois, 6" x 4", $150.00 – 200.00.

Courtesy of Alex & Marilyn Znaiden

Gold Medal by B.H. Voskamp's Sons, Pittsburgh, Pennsylvania, marked Enterprise Stamping Co., Pittsburgh, PA., 5¾" x 4¼", $350.00 – 400.00.

Courtesy of Grant Smith

Gold Medal by Sanitary Coffee & Butter Stores, Chicago, Illinois, 6" x 4¼", $100.00 – 150.00.

Courtesy of Grant Smith

Gold Standard by Eppens Smith Co., Secaucus, New Jersey, 3½" x 5", $25.00 – 50.00.

Courtesy of Bob & Sherri Copeland

Golden Light by Junior Coffee Co., Amarillo, Texas, 6" x 4¼", $450.00 – 500.00.

Courtesy of Alex & Marilyn Znaiden

Golden Robin by Ottawa Wholesale Grocery Co., Ottawa, Kansas, 4" x 5¼", $600.00 – 700.00.

Courtesy of Alex & Marilyn Znaiden

Great West by Western Grocers Limited, marked American Can Co., 3¾" x 5", $150.00 – 200.00.

Green Mill cardboard with tin top & bottom by John A. Tolman & Co., Chicago, 6½" x 4¾" x 3½", $200.00 – 250.00.

Courtesy of Alex & Marilyn Znaiden

Griffin's by Griffin Coffee Co., Muskogee, Oklahoma, 3½" x 5", $1.00 – 25.00.

Gypsy Boy by The Dolan Merchantile Co., 9" x 6", $1,000.00 – 1,250.00.

Courtesy of Alex & Marilyn Znaiden

H & H by Harnit & Hewitt Co., Toledo, Ohio, 3½" x 5", $1.00 – 25.00.

Courtesy of Tom & Lynne Sankiewicz

H & H paper label by Harnit & Hewitt Co., Toledo, Ohio, 5¼" x 4¼", $25.00 – 50.00.

Courtesy of Tom & Lynne Sankiewicz

H & K cardboard with tin top & bottom by Hanley & Kinsella Coffee & Spice Co., 9½" x 6¼" x 4¼", $50.00 – 75.00.

Courtesy of Tom & Mary Lou Slike

Harvest Queen by Red Owl Stores, Minneapolis, Minnesota, 3½" x 5", $25.00 – 50.00.

Courtesy of Bob & Sherri Copeland

Haserot's by The Haserot Co., Cleveland, Ohio, marked Canco, 3½" x 5", $25.00 – 50.00.

Courtesy of Bob & Sherri Copeland

Hatchet by The Twitchell-Champlin Co., Portland, Maine & Boston, Massachusetts, 6" x 4¼", $75.00 – 100.00.

Courtesy of Bob & Correna Anderson

Hercules by Winslow, Rand & Watson Coffee Co., 7¼" x 3½" x 3½", $250.00 – 300.00.

Courtesy of Alex & Marilyn Znaiden

Hi-Lander by H. Runyan & Sons, Louisville, Kentucky, marked A.C. Co., 3¾" x 5", $100.00 – 150.00.
Courtesy of Alex & Marilyn Znaiden

Hi-Test (*Tinsmans*) cardboard with tin top and bottom by Findlay Coffee, Tea & Spice Co., Findlay, Ohio, 3¾" x 5¼", $150.00 – 200.00.
Courtesy of Bob & Sherri Copeland

High Park by Loblaw Grocery Co., Toronto, Canada, 4" x 5", $25.00 – 50.00.
Courtesy of Bob & Sherri Copeland

Holland House, left: by Holland House Coffee & Tea Corp., 4" x 5", $50.00 – 75.00; right: by Eppens, Smith Co., 3½" x 5", $25.00 – 50.00.

Holland Brand by Winston, Harper, Fisher Co., Minneapolis, Minnesota, 10" x 5½", $350.00 – 400.00.
Courtesy of Alex & Marilyn Znaiden

Homestead by Standard Brands Limited, Chase & Sanborn Products, Montreal, 7¾" x 8½", $100.00 – 150.00.

121

Hoosier Poet by M. O'Conner & Co.,
Indianapolis, Indiana, marked A.C.
Co. 68A, 3½" x 5", $350.00 – 400.00.
Courtesy of Bob & Sherri Copeland

Huggins Young by Huggins-Young Co. Inc.,
Vernon, California, 3½" x 5", $1.00 – 25.00.
Courtesy of Bob & Sherri Copeland

Hoosier Club by The Hoosier
Coffee Co., Indianapolis, 6" x
4¼", $350.00 – 400.00.
Courtesy of Grant Smith

Hurrah by W.H. Hood Co., Portland,
Indiana, 4" x 5", $25.00 – 50.00.
Courtesy of Bob & Sherri Copeland

Hunt paper label by Hunt Tea & Coffee
Co., Birmingham, Michigan, 9" x 7½",
$25.00 – 50.00.
Courtesy of Mike & Sharon Hunt

Inca Maiden by McAtee Newell Coffee
Co., Bloomington, Illinois, 7½" x 7½",
$400.00 – 450.00.
Courtesy of Alex & Marilyn Znaiden

Isbest by Associated Food Dist., Coldwater, Michigan, 3¾" x 5¼", $25.00 – 50.00 each.
Courtesy of Tom & Lynne Sankiewicz

Isbrandtsen by Isbrandtsen Co., New York, New York, marked Canco, 3¾" x 5", $75.00 – 100.00.

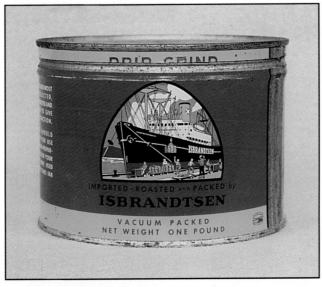

Jack Sprat by Jack Sprat Foods Inc., Marshalltown, Iowa, marked Continental Can Co., 4" x 5", $300.00 – 350.00.

Isbrandtsen by Isbrandtsen Co., New York, N.Y., 3½" x 5", $50.00 – 75.00.
Courtesy of Tom & Lynne Sankiewicz

Java by Joseph Stiner & Co., New York, 4" x 7½" x 6", $200.00 – 250.00.
Courtesy of Alex & Marilyn Znaiden

Jewel by Jewel T. Co. Inc., Barrington, Illinois, 4" x 3¼", $50.00 – 75.00.

Courtesy of Mike & Sharon Hunt

Kamargo by Peck Calen & Co., Watertown, New Jersey marked Passaic Metalware Co., Passaic, N.J., 6" x 4", $800.00 – 900.00.

Courtesy of Grant Smith

Kar-A-Van by Gasser Coffee Co., Toledo, Ohio, 5¼" x 4¼", $75.00 – 100.00.

Kept-fresh by W.F. McLaughlin & Co., Chicago, marked A.C. Co., 4" x 5", $25.00 – 50.00.

King Appetite by Odelsa Manufacturing Co., Oklahoma City, Oklahoma, 10" x 5½", $3,000.00+.

Courtesy of Alex & Marilyn Znaiden

King Cole by G.E. Barbour Co. Ltd., marked A.C. Co. 31A, 3¾" x 5", $50.00 – 75.00.

Courtesy of Bob & Sherri Copeland

Knighthood by Reeves Parvin & Co., marked A.C. Co. 10A, 3½" x 5", $100.00 – 150.00.
Courtesy of Bob & Sherri Copeland

Knighthood by Reeves-Parvin & Co., Philadelphia, Pennsylvania, 4" x 5", $200.00 – 250.00.
Courtesy of Alex & Marilyn Znaiden

Kleeko by P.H. Butler Co., Pittsburgh, Pennsylvania, marked A.C. Co. 53A, 6" x 4¼", $50.00 – 75.00. Note: a red and white variation exists with the same value.
Courtesy of Tom & Lynne Sankiewicz

Lafer Brothers by Lafer Bros., Detroit, Michigan, 3½" x 5", $25.00 – 50.00 each.
Courtesy of Bob & Sherri Copeland

Ladyette by United Buyers Corp. Dist., Chicago & San Francisco, 3½" x 5", $25.00 – 50.00.
Courtesy of Tom & Lynne Sankiewicz

Latona by J.A. Folger & Co., Kansas City & San Francisco, 3½" x 5", $200.00 – 250.00.
Courtesy of Alex & Marilyn Znaiden

Life by James E. Hart, Cincinnati, Ohio, marked Continental Can Co., 4" x 5", $50.00 – 75.00.
Courtesy of Bob & Sherri Copeland

Lidco by John Liddle Co. Inc., Glens Falls, New York, 6" x 4¼", $100.00 – 150.00.
Courtesy of Alex & Marilyn Znaiden

Light House paper label by National Grocer Co. Mills, Detroit, Michigan, marked Calvert Litho Co., Detroit, Mich., 6" x 4¼", $200.00 – 250.00.
Courtesy of Grant Smith

Lion by The Woolson Spice Co., New York, New York & Toledo, Ohio, 3½" x 5", $25.00 – 50.00.

Lipton's by Thomas J. Lipton Inc., Hoboken, New Jersey, marked A.C. Co., 4" x 5", $100.00 – 150.00.

Little Boy Blue by Lansing Wholesale Grocer Co., Lansing, Michigan, 3½" x 5", $200.00 – 250.00.
Courtesy of Bob & Sherri Copeland

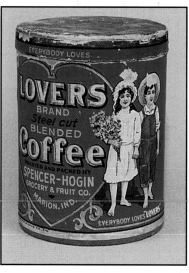

Louis by William-Hassel-Frasier Co., Oklahoma City, Oklahoma, 4" x 5½", $350.00 – 400.00.

Courtesy of Alex & Marilyn Znaiden

Love Nest by Love Nest Products Co. Inc., New York, New York, marked Canco, 3½" x 5", $300.00 – 350.00.

Courtesy of Bob & Sherri Copeland

Lovers Brand cardboard by Spencer-Hogin Grocery & Fruit Co., Marion, Indiana, 5½" x 4¼", rare, no price available.

Courtesy of Mike & Sharon Hunt

Luzianne sample by Wm. B. Reily & Co. Inc., New Orleans, 3" x 2½", left: $200.00 – 250.00; right: $150.00 – 200.00.

Courtesy of Mike & Sharon Hunt

Luzianne by Wm. B. Reily & Co. Inc., New Orleans, 7½" x 6¼", $350.00 – 400.00.

Courtesy of Alex & Marilyn Znaiden

M-K Deluxe by M-K Stores, Barnesville, Ohio, 3½" x 5", $1.00 – 25.00.

Courtesy of Bob & Sherri Copeland

Manning's by Manning's Coffee Co., San Francisco, California, marked Canco, 3½" x 5", $1.00 – 25.00.

Courtesy of Bob & Sherri Copeland

Manor House paper label by W.F. McLaughlin & Co., Chicago, 6" x 4", $75.00 – 100.00.

Courtesy of Ken & Nancy Jones

Mansion Inn by Economy Grocery Stores, Boston, Massachusetts, 3½" x 5", $75.00 – 100.00.

Courtesy of Bob & Sherri Copeland

Mauna cardboard with tin top and bottom by Acker, Merrall & Condit Co., 6" x 4½" x 3", $100.00 – 150.00.

Courtesy of Bob & Sherri Copeland

Max-i-mum by Max-i-mum Coffee Co., Oakland, California, 3½" x 5", $200.00 – 250.00.

Courtesy of Bob & Sherri Copeland

May-Flower store bin by Beckham, McKnight & Co., Kansas City, Missouri, 14" x 19" x 13½", $2,000.00 – 2,500.00.

Courtesy of Alex & Marilyn Znaiden

Mayflower by Joannes Bros. Co., Green Bay, Wisconsin, 6½" x 4¾" x 3½", $2,000.00 – 2,500.00.

Courtesy of Alex & Marilyn Znaiden

McLaughlin's by W.F. McLaughlin & Co., Chicago, 3¾" x 5¼", $1.00 – 25.00.

Courtesy of Bob & Sherri Copeland

Medaglia D' oro by S.A. Schonbrunn & Co., left: 4" x 5", $50.00 – 75.00; right: 3½" x 5", $25.00 – 50.00.

Courtesy of Bob & Sherri Copeland

Mello Glo by Browning & Baines Inc., Washington, D.C., 4" x 5", $25.00 – 50.00.

Courtesy of Tom & Lynne Sankiewicz

Mi-Lady by Michigan Coffee & Spice Co., Menominee, Michigan, 6" x 4¼", $500.00 – 600.00.

Courtesy of Alex & Marilyn Znaiden

Military by Nave-McCord Merchantile Co., St. Joseph, Missouri, and Denver, Colorado, 4" x 5", $400.00 – 450.00.

Courtesy of Alex & Marilyn Znaiden

Millar's Nut-Brown by E.B. Millar & Co., Denver & Chicago, 4" x 5", $25.00 – 50.00.

Courtesy of Tom & Lynne Sankiewicz

Minuet by Sanitary Food Manufacturing Co., St. Paul, Minnesota, 4" x 5", $50.00 – 75.00.

Mocha & Java by Woolson Spice
Co., Toledo, Ohio, marked Norton
Bros., Chicago, 6¾" x 6" x 3¾",
$100.00 – 150.00.
Courtesy of Bob & Sherri Copeland

Monarch by Consolidated Foods Corp., Chicago, Illinois, 3½" x 5",
$25.00 – 50.00 each.
Courtesy of Tom & Lynne Sankiewicz

Montco by Family Products Co., Philadelphia,
Pennsylvania, 3½" x 5", $1.00 – 25.00.
Courtesy of Tom & Lynne Sankiewicz

Monterey by The Woolson Spice
Co., Toledo, Ohio, marked Canco,
3½" x 5", $1.00 – 25.00.
Courtesy of Bob & Sherri Copeland

Monumental No. 1 store bin by
Merchants Coffee Co., Baltimore, Maryland, 25" x 13¼" x
13¼", $450.00 – 500.00.
Courtesy of Alex & Marilyn Znaiden

Morning Cup paper label by Thomson & Taylor Co., Chicago, 4" x 5¼", $25.00 – 50.00.
Courtesy of Bob & Sherri Copeland

Morning Sip by Alex Sheppard & Sons Inc., Philadelphia, 5¾" x 4½", $50.00 – 75.00.
Courtesy of Bob & Correna Anderson

Mother Parker's by Mother Parker Tea Co., Toronto, Canada, 3¾" x 5", left: $50.00 – 75.00; right: $25.00 – 50.00.

Mrs. Lane's by Foodland Inc., Cleveland, Ohio, 3½" x 5", $25.00 – 50.00.
Courtesy of Tom & Lynne Sankiewicz

Nescafé by Nestlé's Milk Products Inc., New York, 3¼" x 2½", $1.00 – 25.00. Note: a smaller version exists with more value.

Niagara by Buffalo Coffee Co. Inc., Buffalo, New York, 6" x 4¼", $500.00 – 600.00.

Courtesy of Alex & Marilyn Znaiden

Noon-Day by Tri-City Grocery Co., Granite City, Illinois, marked Columbia Can Co., St. Louis, 6" x 4¼", $600.00 – 700.00.

Courtesy of Alex & Marilyn Znaiden

North Woods by North Woods Coffee Co., Chicago, Illinois, marked Continental Can Co., 3½" x 5", $25.00 – 50.00.

Courtesy of Bob & Sherri Copeland

Northland by Northland Associate Grocers Inc., marked Canco, 3½" x 5", $25.00 – 50.00.

Courtesy of Bob & Sherri Copeland

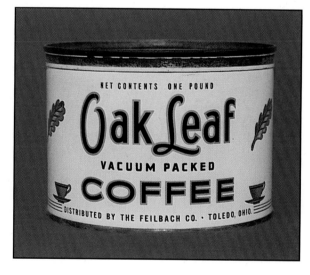

Oak Leaf by The Feilbach Co., Toledo, Ohio, 3½" x 5", $25.00 – 50.00.

Courtesy of Tom & Lynne Sankiewicz

O'Connor's by James J. O'Connor Coffee Co., St. Louis, Missouri, marked Continental Can Co., 3½" x 5", $50.00 – 75.00.

Old Dutch by Old Dutch Coffee Co. Inc., New York, New York, marked Canco, 3½" x 5", $25.00 – 50.00.

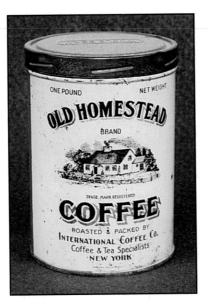

Old Homestead by International Coffee Co., New York, marked Passaic Metalware Co., Passaic, N.J., 6" x 4¼", $100.00 – 150.00.
Courtesy of Grant Smith

Old N'Orleans by Love Nest Products Co. Inc., New York, New York, marked Canco, 3½" x 5", $25.00 – 50.00.
Courtesy of Bob & Sherri Copeland

Old Tavern by Lee & Cady, Detroit, Michigan, marked Canco, 3½" x 5", left: $50.00 – 75.00; right: $25.00 – 50.00.
Courtesy of Tom & Lynne Sankiewicz

Old Time by Roundy's Inc., Milwaukee, Wisconsin, 3½" x 5", $25.00 – 50.00.
Courtesy of Tom & Lynne Sankiewicz

Orchard Park by Orchard Park Foods Inc., Buffalo, New York, 3½" x 5", $25.00 – 50.00.
Courtesy of Bob & Sherri Copeland

Orienta by Browning & Baines Inc., Washington, D.C., 6½" x 4", $50.00 – 75.00.

Courtesy of Richard & Ann Lehmann

Overland store bin by Shaw, Hammond & Carney, Portland, Maine, 17¾" x 18" x 14¼", $500.00 – 600.00.

Courtesy of Alex & Marilyn Znaiden

Paul De Lima by Paul De Lima Co. Inc., Syracuse, New York, 3½" x 5", $1.00 – 25.00.

Courtesy of Bob & Sherri Copeland

Perfect's P Brand by A.H. Perfect & Co., 4" x 5", $25.00 – 50.00.

Courtesy of Bob & Sherri Copeland

Pal-O-Mine by McAtee Newell Coffee Co., Bloomington, Illinois, 6¼" x 4", $400.00 – 450.00.

Courtesy of Alex & Marilyn Znaiden

Petring's Kake Kan by H.P. Coffee Co., St. Louis, Missouri, marked Columbia Can Co., St. Louis, 3¾" x 9¾", $150.00 – 200.00.

Courtesy of Mike & Sharon Hunt

Pheasant by Young & Griffin Coffee Co. Inc., New York City, 7½" x 7½", $350.00 – 400.00.

Courtesy of Alex & Marilyn Znaiden

Pickwick, left: by Kansas City Wholesale Grocery Co., 4" x 5", $50.00 – 75.00; right: by Holsum Products, Kansas City, Missouri, 3½" x 5", $25.00 – 50.00.

Pilot-Knob by Bowers Brothers Inc., Richmond, Virginia, 3½" x 5", $150.00 – 200.00.

Pilot-Knob by Bowers Brothers Inc., Richmond, Virginia, 8¼" x 5¾", $300.00 – 350.00.

Plee-zing by Dannemiller Coffee Co., Brooklyn, New York, 3¾" x 5", $25.00 – 50.00.

Courtesy of Bob & Sherri Copeland

Plee-zing by George W. Simmons Corp., 4" x 5", $75.00 – 100.00.

Courtesy of Bob & Sherri Copeland

Planters House by Hanley & Kinsella Coffee & Spice Co., St. Louis, 6" x 4¼", $400.00 – 450.00.

Courtesy of Ken & Nancy Jones

Pot o' Gold by Fisher Foods, Cleveland, Ohio, marked Canco, 3½" x 5", $1.00 – 25.00.

Courtesy of Bob & Sherri Copeland

Premier by Francis H. Leggett & Co., New York, New York, 3½" x 5", $25.00 – 50.00.

Courtesy of Bob & Sherri Copeland

Pride of Arabia by Loblaw Groceterias Ltd., Toronto, Canada, marked A.C. Co. 31A, 6" x 4¼", $300.00 – 350.00.

Courtesy of Grant Smith

Pride of Arabia ½ pounder by Loblaw Groceterias, Toronto, Canada, 2½" x 4¼", $100.00 – 150.00.

Courtesy of Bob & Sherri Copeland

Purity by The Stokes Coffee Co., Baltimore, Maryland, marked Southern Can Co., Baltimore, MD., 6¼" x 4¾" x 3½", $1,500.00 – 1,750.00.

Courtesy of Alex & Marilyn Znaiden

Quail by Ridenour Baker Merchantile Co., 9" x 5¼", $500.00 – 600.00.

Courtesy of Alex & Marilyn Znaiden

Queen B by A.L. Ross & Son Distributing, Muncie, Indiana, 3½" x 5", $50.00 – 75.00.

Courtesy of Tom & Lynne Sankiewicz

Quinn's by Quinn Coffee Co., Springfield, Ohio, 3½" x 5", $25.00 – 50.00.

Courtesy of Tom & Lynne Sankiewicz

Real Java Coffee by The Manhattan Rubber Manufacturing Division, Passaic, New Jersey, 6" x 4", $50.00 – 75.00.

Courtesy of Bob & Sherri Copeland

Red Label by S.S. Pierce Co., Boston, Massachusetts, 3½" x 5", $25.00 – 50.00.

Red Rose (½" pound) by Brooke Bond Canada Limited, 2½" x 4", $50.00 – 75.00.

Courtesy of Bob & Sherri Copeland

Red Star by Meyer's Bros. Coffee & Spice Co., St. Louis, Missouri, 4" x 10", $150.00 – 200.00.
Courtesy of Mike & Sharon Hunt

Red Wolf by Ridenour-Baker Grocery Co., Kansas City, Missouri, 9½" x 8½", $250.00 – 300.00.
Courtesy of Ken & Nancy Jones

Regent by The U & J Lenson Corp., Brooklyn, New York, marked Canco, 3½" x 5", $50.00 – 75.00.

Rex sample paper label by Hulman & Co., Terre Haute, Indiana, 3½" x 2¼", $75.00 – 100.00.
Courtesy of Mike & Sharon Hunt

Rideau Hall by Gorman Eckert & Co. Limited, London & Toronto, 6" x 4¼", $300.00 – 350.00.
Courtesy of Grant Smith

Rideau Hall ½ pound by Gorman, Eckert & Co. Ltd., London & Winnipeg, 2¼" x 4½", $100.00 – 150.00.
Courtesy of Tom Sankiewicz

Rose of Kansas by Ennis-Hanley-Blackburn Coffee Co., Kansas City, Missouri, 3¾" x 5¼", $500.00 – 600.00.
Courtesy of Alex & Marilyn Znaiden

Roseco by Roach & Seeber Co., 4" x 5¼", $100.00 – 150.00.
Courtesy of Alex & Marilyn Znaiden

Roundy's by Roundy's Inc., Milwaukee, Wisconsin, 3½" x 5", $25.00 – 50.00.
Courtesy of Tom & Lynne Sankiewicz

Royal Star by McMahan & Leib Co., Anderson & Marion, Indiana, 4" x 5", $50.00 – 75.00.

Courtesy of Bob & Sherri Copeland

Royal Ceylon Java by Royal Ceylon Coffee Co., Chicago, marked Norton Bros., 8" x 4¼", $450.00 – 500.00.

Courtesy of Alex & Marilyn Znaiden

Royal Corona by Commercial Importing Co., Seattle, Washington, 12" x 10", $150.00 – 200.00.

Courtesy of Alex & Marilyn Znaiden

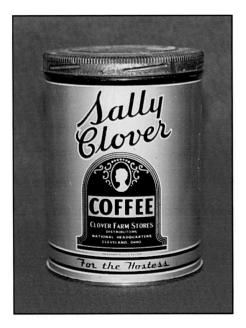

Santa Fe by Jones Thierbach Co., San Francisco, California, 3½" x 5", $350.00 – 400.00.

Courtesy of Alex & Marilyn Znaiden

Sally Clover by Clover Farm Stores, Cleveland, Ohio, 5¾" x 4½", $25.00 – 50.00.

Courtesy of Bob & Correna Anderson

Save-Way by Save-Way Super Markets, Toledo, Ohio, 3½" x 5", $1.00 – 25.00.

Courtesy of Tom & Lynne Sankiewicz

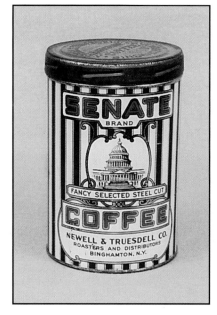

Senate by Newell & Truesdell Co., Binghamton, New York, 6¼" x 4", $200.00 – 250.00.

Courtesy of Grant Smith

Serv-Well by Twin City Wholesale Grocer Co., St. Paul & Minneapolis, Minnesota, marked A.C. Co. 68A, 4" x 5", $150.00 – 200.00.

Courtesy of Alex & Marilyn Znaiden

Severin Blend paper label by Keefer-Stewart Co., Indianapolis, Indiana, 6" x 4¼", no price available.

Courtesy of Mike & Sharon Hunt

Shasta by J.A. Folger & Co., San Francisco & Kansas City, marked A.C. Co., 7" x 5", $150.00 – 200.00.

Courtesy of Bob & Sherri Copeland

Silver Cup paper label by William Holt, 4" x 5",
$25.00 – 50.00.

Courtesy of Tom & Lynne Sankiewicz

Society sample by Bower & Bartlett,
Boston, Massachusetts, marked A.C. Co.,
2" x 2½", $250.00 – 300.00.

Courtesy of Ken & Nancy Jones

Spartan by Grand Rapids Coffee
Co., marked Continental Can Co.,
3½" x 5", $25.00 – 50.00.

Special Brand by Hulman Coffee
Co., Terre Haute, Indiana, marked
Columbia Can Co., St. Louis, MO.,
11½" x 7¼", $300.00 – 350.00.

Courtesy of Mike & Sharon Hunt

Square Deal by E-J Workers
Stores, marked Passaic Metalware Co., Passaic, New Jersey, 6"
x 4", $300.00 – 350.00.

Courtesy of Alex & Marilyn Znaiden

Steamboat by F.W. Hinz & Sons, Cincinnati, Ohio, 3½" x 5", $150.00 – 200.00.

Standard store bin by Steinwender Stoffregen Coffee Co's., 18½" x 17" x 13½", $600.00 – 700.00.

Courtesy of Alex & Marilyn Znaiden

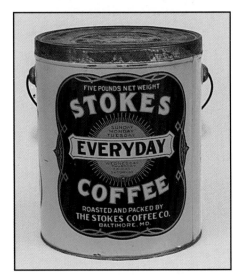

Summit by The Summit Wholesale Grocery Co., Akron Ohio, 3½" x 5", $50.00 – 75.00.

Courtesy of Bob & Sherri Copeland

Sunbeam by Francis H. Leggett & Co., New York, New York, 4" x 5", $50.00 – 75.00.

Courtesy of Tom & Lynne Sankiewicz

Stokes Everyday by Stokes Coffee Co., Baltimore, Maryland, 9" x 7½", $100.00 – 150.00.

Courtesy of Tom & Mary Lou Slike

Swansdown by Swansdown Coffee
Co. Inc., marked Interprise Stamping
Co., Pittsburgh, Pennsylvania, 6½"
x 4¼", $300.00 – 350.00. Note:
paper label less valuable.
Courtesy of Mike & Sharon Hunt

Swell Blend by Wilcox & Crissey Co. Inc.,
Jamestown, New York, marked A.C. Co. 27A,
4" x 5", $75.00 – 100.00.

Tac-Cut by Tolerton & Warfield Co., Sioux City, Iowa, left: 5½" x
4¼", $500.00 – 600.00; right: 4" x 5", $300.00 – 350.00.
Courtesy of Alex & Marilyn Znaiden

Tac-Cut by Wm. Tackaberry Co.,
Sioux City, Iowa, 9½" x 5½",
$1,000.00 – 1,250.00.
Courtesy of Alex & Marilyn Znaiden

Today's Coffee by California Packing Corp., San Francisco, California, 3½" x 5", $25.00 – 50.00.

Courtesy of Bob & Sherri Copeland

Ten Eyck by Bacon Stickney & Co. Inc., Albany, New York, left: 8" x 6", $450.00 – 500.00; right: 5½" x 4½", $250.00 – 300.00.

Courtesy of Alex & Marilyn Znaiden

Timur by A.J. Kasper Co., Chicago, Illinois, 5¾" x 4¼", $700.00 – 800.00.

Courtesy of Grant Smith

Tropical by C.A. Murdoch Mfg. Co., Kansas City, Missouri, 3¾" x 5", $300.00 – 350.00.

Courtesy of Alex & Marilyn Znaiden

Town Crier by Dukane Coffee Corp., Pittsburgh, 6" x 4¼", $1,000.00 – 1,250.00.

Courtesy of Grant Smith

Uncle Eph's paper label by Uncle Eph's Food Shop, Boston, 3½" x 5", $1.00 – 25.00.

Courtesy of Bob & Sherri Copeland

Turkey by A.J. Kasper Co., Chicago & Kansas City, left: 10¾" x 5½", $600.00 – 700.00; right: 5¾" x 4¼", $500.00 – 600.00.

Courtesy of Alex & Marilyn Znaiden

TVF (The Very Finest) by Charles & Company's, New York, New York, marked American Can Co. 50A, 5¾" x 4¼", $75.00 – 100.00.

Courtesy of Tom & Mary Lou Slike

United by United Distributing Co., marked Passaic Metalware Co., Passaic, N.J., 6" x 4", $100.00 – 150.00.

Courtesy of Grant Smith

Valina by Aragon Coffee Co. Inc., Richmond, Virginia, marked American Can Co. 43A, 10½" x 6", $800.00 – 900.00.

Courtesy of Tom & Mary Lou Slike

Venizelos by T. & A. Coffee Co., New York, New York, 3½" x 5", $75.00 – 100.00.

Valina by Aragon Coffee Co. Inc., Richmond, Virginia, marked A.C. Co. 50A, 5½" x 4", $600.00 – 700.00.

Courtesy of Alex & Marilyn Znaiden

Venizelos by Turkish & Arabian Coffee Co., New York, 5½" x 4", $350.00 – 400.00.

Courtesy of Alex & Marilyn Znaiden

Vienna by Woolson Spice Co., Toledo, Ohio, left: 3½" x 5", $1.00 – 25.00; center: 6" x 4", $25.00 – 50.00; center-top: sample, 2¾" x 3", $25.00 – 50.00; right: 3½" x 5", $1.00 – 25.00.

Courtesy of Tom & Lynne Sankiewicz

Wak-em Up by Andresen-Ryan Coffee Co., Duluth, Minnesota, 8¾" x 7½", $450.00 – 500.00.

Courtesy of Alex & Marilyn Znaiden

Wak-em Up by Andresen-Ryan Coffee Co., Boston, Massachusetts, 9" x 7½", $450.00 – 500.00.

Courtesy of Tom & Mary Lou Slike

Warrior by Magnolia Coffee Co., Boston, Massachusetts, marked Norton Bros., 7" x 5" x 5", $250.00 – 300.00.

Courtesy of Alex & Marilyn Znaiden

Wedding Breakfast by Pioneer Coffee & Spice Mills, Vancouver & Victoria, B.C., marked A.C. Co., 5¼" x 4¼", $500.00 – 600.00.

Courtesy of Grant Smith

Weideman by Weideman Co., Cleveland, Ohio, marked A.C. Co. 68A, 4" x 5", $50.00 – 75.00.

Welcome Guest by The Inter-State Coffee & Spice Co., Joplin, Missouri, left: 7½" x 5½", $600.00 – 700.00; right: 6" x 4¼", $1,000.00 – 1,250.00.

Courtesy of Alex & Marilyn Znaiden

White Bear by Durand-McNeil-Horner Co., Chicago, Illinois, 4" x 5", $150.00 – 200.00.

Courtesy of Alex & Marilyn Znaiden

White Bear cardboard with tin top & bottom by Durand & Kasper Co., Chicago, Illinois, 6" x 4½" x 3", $200.00 – 250.00.
Courtesy of Alex & Marilyn Znaiden

White Goose by Shuster-Gormly Co., Jeannette, Pennsylvania, 8" x 7½", $600.00 – 700.00.
Courtesy of Alex & Marilyn Znaiden

White Swan by White Swan Spices & Cereals, Toronto, 4½" x 5" x 3½", $100.00 – 150.00.
Courtesy of Ken & Nancy Jones

Widlar's Mocha and Java by Widlar Co., Cleveland, Ohio, 5½" x 4¼", $150.00 – 200.00.
Courtesy of Bob & Sherri Copeland

Wishbone by Bunn Capitol Grocery Co., marked C.C. Co., 6" x 4", $75.00 – 100.00.
Courtesy of Ken & Nancy Jones

Yellow Bonnet sample by Springfield Grocery Co., Springfield, Missouri, marked Missouri Can Co., 2¾" x 3", $350.00 – 400.00.
Courtesy of Ken & Nancy Jones

Zephyr by Swanson Bros. Inc., Chicago, Illinois, 4" x 5", $100.00 – 150.00.
Courtesy of Tom & Lynne Sankiewicz

COFFEE TINS NOT SHOWN:

Admiration, 3½" x 5", $25.00 – 50.00

After Dinner, 7" x 5" x 5", $100.00 – 150.00

Aladdin, 6" x 3½", $200.00 – 250.00

Alice May (woman w/hat), 4" x 5", $600.00 – 700.00

Alpine, 5½" x 4¼", $75.00 – 100.00

Alta, 3½" x 5", $1.00 – 25.00

Ambassador, 3½" x 5", $25.00 – 50.00

American Mills (man/lion), 3¾" x 6" x 4", $100.00 – 150.00

Amocat, 6" x 4", $600.00 – 700.00

Ben Hur (Berkley's), 6" x 4", $350.00 – 400.00

Big Rock paper label, 6" x 4", $200.00 – 250.00

Black Cross, 5" x 3½", $200.00 – 250.00

Blue Jay, 6" x 4", $150.00 – 200.00

Blue Pine, 5¾" x 4¼", $75.00 – 100.00

Blue Ribbon, 6" x 4", $100.00 – 150.00

Braid's Best, 6" x 4", $25.00 – 50.00

Brite-Mawnin, 5½" x 4¼", $100.00 – 150.00

Cafe London House, 3½" x 5", $25.00 – 50.00

Cafe President, 5¾" x 4¼", $250.00 – 300.00

Charter Oak (Williams), 6" x 4", $250.00 – 300.00

Choisa paper label, 6" x 4", $50.00 – 75.00

Chuck Wagon, 3½" x 5", $75.00 – 100.00

Circle Brand (cup), 6" x 4", $100.00 – 150.00

Club House Brand, 4" x 5", $25.00 – 50.00

Colonial Club, 3½" x 5", $25.00 – 50.00

Columbia, 6" x 4", $400.00 – 450.00

Cottage Brand paper label, 6" x 4", $200.00 – 250.00

Crescent Cream, 6" x 4", $100.00 – 150.00

Cumberland Club, 6" x 4", $1,000.00 – 1,250.00

Cumberland Club pail, 8" x 7½", $700.00 – 800.00

Dalton's, 5½" x 4¼", $75.00 – 100.00

Demi-Tasse, 6" x 4", $150.00 – 200.00

Dependon, 3½" x 5", $100.00 – 150.00

Diana, 6" x 4¼", $700.00 – 800.00

Eberhard's, 3½" x 5", $25.00 – 50.00

Ecco, 6" x 4", $75.00 – 100.00

Eclipse, 6" x 4", $500.00 – 600.00

Elba Queen, 3½" x 5", $50.00 – 75.00

Empire Mills, 8" x 4", $400.00 – 450.00

Essie, 6" x 4", $75.00 – 100.00

Excelsior, 4" x 5", $50.00 – 75.00

Federal Brand, 6" x 4", $100.00 – 150.00

Federal King, 4" x 5", $25.00 – 50.00

Festival, 3½" x 5", $100.00 – 150.00

Fireside Egg, 3½" x 5", $25.00 – 50.00

Flagstaff, 3½" x 5", $25.00 – 50.00

Foote's Flavorite (cup), 6" x 4", $75.00 – 100.00

Fort Pitt, 6" x 4", $350.00 – 400.00

Fox, 6" x 4", $200.00 – 250.00

Fred Harvey, 3½" x 5", $100.00 – 150.00

Fruitider, 6" x 4¼", $100.00 – 150.00

Gazelle Brand, 5¼" x 4½", $450.00 – 500.00

Georgia Bell (woman) pail, 7½" x 6", $300.00 – 350.00

Glendale, 6" x 4", $50.00 – 75.00

Gold Bar, 3½" x 5", $25.00 – 50.00

Gold Bond, 4" x 5", $25.00 – 50.00
Gold Coin, 4" x 5", $100.00 – 150.00
Golden Days, 7" x 5" x 5", $150.00 – 200.00
Golden Morn, 5¾" x 4¼", $50.00 – 75.00
Golden Rod, 6½" x 6", $100.00 – 150.00
Grand Union, 4" x 5", $50.00 – 75.00
Halligan's Pure Qill, 6" x 4", $100.00 – 150.00
Happy Hour, 3½" x 5", $25.00 – 50.00
Hazel, 6" x 4", $100.00 – 150.00
Home Garden, 3½" x 5", $75.00 – 100.00
Horseshoe Brand, 6" x 4", $250.00 – 300.00
House Party, 4" x 5", $150.00 – 200.00
Imperio (crown), 6" x 4", $100.00 – 150.00
Invitation, 6" x 4", $200.00 – 250.00
Jamoka, 6" x 4", $400.00 – 450.00
Jefferson Park (horse), 6" x 4", $400.00 – 450.00
Jevne's, 7" x 3½", $50.00 – 75.00
Justrite (Weikel's), $100.00 – 150.00
Kar-A-Van (Kiro), 6" x 4", $300.00 – 350.00
Kennedy's (hotel type), 3½" x 5", $25.00 – 50.00
King's Taste, 6" x 4", $75.00 – 100.00
Lady Betty, 3½" x 5", $50.00 – 75.00
Le Roi, 6" x 4", $50.00 – 75.00
Magnolia, 3½" x 5", $100.00 – 150.00
Mazon, 4" x 5", $25.00 – 50.00
Miss Carolina, 3½" x 5", $50.00 – 75.00
Mister Donut, 3½" x 5", $250.00 – 300.00
Momaja, 6" x 5" x 3", $100.00 – 150.00
Morning Glow, 3½" x 5", $100.00 – 150.00
Morning Star, 3½" x 5", $50.00 – 75.00
Morning Treat, 4" x 5", $50.00 – 75.00
Mother's, 4" x 5", $150.00 – 200.00
Motor, 6" x 4", $500.00 – 600.00
Much-More, 3½" x 5", $25.00 – 50.00
N.S.C., 3¾" x 5", $25.00 – 50.00
Nash's Jubilee, 9" x 6½", $300.00 – 350.00
Nathor's Best, 3½" x 5", $25.00 – 50.00
Old Glory, 6" x 4", $1,250.00 – 1,500.00

On Time (train), 6" x 4", rare, no price available
Orinoco, 10½" x 6", $300.00 – 350.00
Paul Bunyan, 4" x 5", $300.00 – 350.00
Pointer (red) pail, 7" x 5", $600.00 – 700.00
Pope, 4" x 5", $500.00 – 600.00
Porico Brand, 7" x 5" x 5", $500.00 – 600.00
Q-B, 6" x 4", $25.00 – 50.00
Re-Joyce, 3½" x 5", $25.00 – 50.00
Red Bird, 5½" x 4¼", $100.00 – 150.00
Red Hussar, 6" x 4", $700.00 – 800.00
Red Ribbon DeLuxe, 4" x 5", $50.00 – 75.00
Red Swan, 3½" x 5", $100.00 – 150.00
Reliance, 3½" x 5", $50.00 – 75.00
Roundup, 3½" x 5", $400.00 – 450.00
Royal M Brand, 6" x 4", $150.00 – 200.00
Sanico, 3½" x 5", $50.00 – 75.00
Sanico, 6" x 4", $150.00 – 200.00
Savoy, 4" x 5", $25.00 – 50.00
Silver Blend, 10½" x 5½", $200.00 – 250.00
Silver Cup, 4" x 5", $75.00 – 100.00
St. James, 9" x 8" x 5½", $250.00 – 300.00
Stuyvesant, 6¼" x 4", $3,000.00+
Success Brand paper label, 5½" x 4¼", $75.00 – 100.00
Sunland, 3½" x 5", $50.00 – 75.00
Superba, 5¾" x 4¼", $50.00 – 75.00
Superba, 7" x 5" x 5", $200.00 – 250.00
Terrace Club, 6" x 4", $700.00 – 800.00
Tops All, 6" x 4", $350.00 – 400.00
Torke, 3½" x 5", $75.00 – 100.00
Tudor, 5½" x 4½", $100.00 – 150.00
Value Brand, 5¾" x 4¼", $200.00 – 250.00
Vanity (peacock), 3½" x 5", $150.00 – 200.00
Vesper, 3½" x 5", $25.00 – 50.00
Vesta, 10" x 5", $400.00 – 450.00
Wedding Ring, 6" x 4", $300.00 – 350.00
Weis, 6" x 4", $150.00 – 200.00
White Star, 6" x 4", $100.00 – 150.00
Yale (ship), 8" x 5" x 5", $250.00 – 300.00

Above All by Satin Candy Co. Inc., Baltimore, Maryland, marked Platt Can Co., $100.00 – 150.00.
Courtesy of Schimpff's Confectionary

Angelus by Rueckheim Bros. & Eckstein, Chicago & Brooklyn, 9¾" x 5¼", $100.00 – 150.00.
Courtesy of Schimpff's Confectionary

Baur's marked Denver, Colo., 2¼" x 5" x 5", $1.00 – 25.00.
Courtesy of Schimpff's Confectionary

Billy Buster by Wm. Derrenbacher Inc., Brooklyn, New York, 7" x 6", $25.00 – 50.00.
Courtesy of Schimpff's Confectionary

Blome's, left: 9" x 5½"; right: 7¾" x 5½", $25.00 – 50.00 each.
Courtesy of Schimpff's Confectionary

Bunte by Bunte Bros., Chicago, marked Continental Can Co., Chicago, 14" x 10", $75.00 – 100.00 Note: two variations of reverse side, old and new factory.

Courtesy of Schimpff's Confectionary

Bunte Bros. by Bunte Bros., Chicago, 2" x 8" x 4¾", $1.00 – 25.00.

Courtesy of Joan Bunte

Bunte by Bunte Bros., Chicago, Illinois, left: 9" x 4½" x 4½", $1.00 – 25.00; center: 14" x 10", $50.00 – 75.00; right: 10¼" x 3½" x 3½", $1.00 – 25.00.

Courtesy of Schimpff's Confectionary

Bunte Chocolates by Bunte Bros., Chicago, 2" x 6½" x 4¼", $1.00 –
25.00 each.
Courtesy of Schimpff's Confectionary

Bunte Brothers by Bunte Bros., Chicago,
14" x 10", $50.00 – 75.00.
Courtesy of Joan Bunte

Bunte Diana by Bunte Bros., Chicago, left: 8½" x 5" x 3"; center: 6¾"
x 5" x 3"; right: 8½" x 5" x 3", $25.00 – 50.00 each.
Courtesy of Joan Bunte

Bunte Diana by Bunte Bros., Chicago, Illinois,
$25.00 – 50.00 each.
Courtesy of Schimpff's Confectionary

Bunte Diana by Bunte Bros., Chicago, Illinois, left: 10" x 4½" x 4½"; right: 10" x 3½" x 3½", $25.00 – 50.00 each.

Courtesy of Joan Bunte

Bunte Diana by Bunte Bros., Chicago, left: 3½" x 2¾"; right: 9¾" x 5¼". $50.00 – 75.00 each.

Courtesy of Schimpff's Confectionary

Cella's by Cella Inc., New York, New York, 3" x 6½" x 4¼", $1.00 – 25.00.

Courtesy of Schimpff's Confectionary

Butler's Radiant Morsels by Butler Candy Co., Waukegan, Illinois, 6¾" x 4½" x 4½", $25.00 – 50.00.

Courtesy of Schimpff's Confectionary

Butler's Radiant Morsels by Butler Candies Inc., Elgin, Illinois, marked A.C. Co. 70A, 10¼" x 4½" x 4½", $1.00 – 25.00.

Courtesy of Schimpff's Confectionary

Charms paper label by Charms Co., Newark, New Jersey, 5" x 1¾" x 1¾", $1.00 – 25.00.

Courtesy of Schimpff's Confectionary

Chase's Mintetts by Chase Manufacturing Co., St. Joseph, Missouri, 3" x 2" x 1", $1.00 – 25.00.
Courtesy of Schimpff's Confectionary

Chase's by G.W. Chase & Son Mercantile Co., St. Joseph, Missouri, marked Missouri Can Co., 10½" x 10", $25.00 – 50.00.
Courtesy of Schimpff's Confectionary

Christopher's Brownie marked American Can Co. 98A, 9" x 6", $75.00 – 100.00.
Courtesy of Schimpff's Confectionary

Crane's by The Crane Chocolate Co., Cleveland, Ohio, marked A.C. Co. 54A, 3½" x 3¼", $25.00 – 50.00.
Courtesy of Schimpff's Confectionary

Collins by Collins-Hencke Candy Co., San Francisco, California, marked Western Can Co., San Francisco, 10¾" x 12¼", $100.00 – 150.00. Note: other sizes exist.
Courtesy of Schimpff's Confectionary

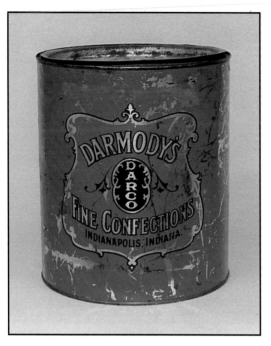

Dilling Confections by Dilling & Co., Indianapolis, Indiana, marked A.C. Co., 8" x 12¼", $25.00 – 50.00.
Courtesy of Schimpff's Confectionary

Darmody's from Indianapolis, Indiana, marked Continental Can Co., 8½" x 7½", $25.00 – 50.00.
Courtesy of Schimpff's Confectionary

Dilling's by Dilling & Co., Indianapolis, Indiana, marked Heekin Can Co., 14¼" x 12", $150.00 – 200.00.
Courtesy of Schimpff's Confectionary

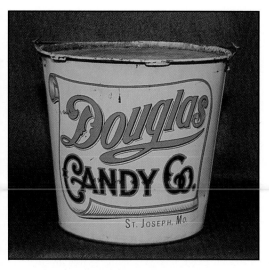

Douglas by Douglas Candy Co., St. Joseph, Missouri, marked American Can Co. 59A, 10½" x 11½", $50.00 – 75.00.
Courtesy of Schimpff's Confectionary

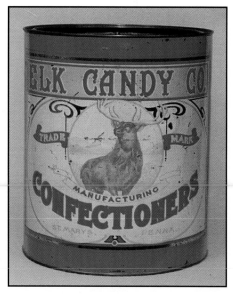

Elk by Elk Candy Co. Confectioners, St. Marys, Pennsylvania, 9¾" x 8¼", $100.00 – 150.00.
Courtesy of Schimpff's Confectionary

F.W. McNess' by Furst-McNess Co., Freeport, Illinois, marked A.C. Co. 70A, 7½" x 4½" x 4½", $25.00 – 50.00.
Courtesy of Schimpff's Confectionary

Farley's Tulip Brand by Farley Candy Co., Chicago, 14½" x 10", $100.00 – 150.00.
Courtesy of Schimpff's Confectionary

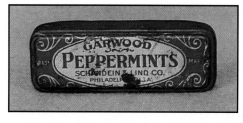

Garwood Peppermints by Schandein & Lind Co., Philadelphia, ½" x 2½" x 1", $1.00 – 25.00.
Courtesy of Schimpff's Confectionary

Gloss Candies by The George Close Co., Cambridge, Massachusetts, marked A.C. Co., 11 x 12½", $50.00 – 75.00.
Courtesy of Schimpff's Confectionary

Gottmann & Kretchmer marked Chicago, 7¼" x 5½", $25.00 – 50.00.
Courtesy of Schimpff's Confectionary

Grace Darling marked A.C. Co. 70A, 10¼" x 4½" x 4½", $25.00 – 50.00.
Courtesy of Schimpff's Confectionary

Greenland by Forkdipt Chocolates Co., Boston, marked Passiaic Metalware Co., California 1925, 6" x 4", $75.00 – 100.00.
Courtesy of Schimpff's Confectionary

Guth Caramels, right: 1" x 5" x 2"; left: 1" x 5" x 1", $25.00 – 50.00 each.
Courtesy of Schimpff's Confectionary

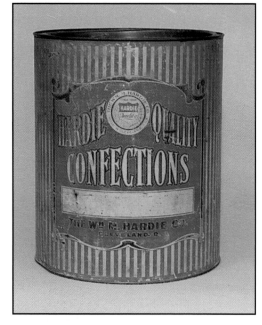

Hardie Quality Confections by The Wm. M. Hardie Co., Cleveland, Ohio, 9¾" x 8¼", $25.00 – 50.00.
Courtesy of Schimpff's Confectionary

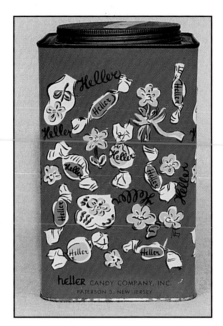

Heller by The Heller Candy Co. Inc., Paterson, New Jersey, 8½" x 5" x 5", $25.00 – 50.00.
Courtesy of Schimpff's Confectionary

Highland Confections by Hardie Brothers Co., Pittsburgh, Pennsylvania, 9¾" x 10½", $50.00 – 75.00.
Courtesy of Schimpff's Confectionary

Holtzman's sample by Holtzman Inc., Myerstown, Pennsylvania, 3" x 2", $50.00 – 75.00.
Courtesy of Mike & Sharon Hunt

Honeymoon by Francis H. Leggett Co., New York, 2¼" x 2¾", $1.00 – 25.00.
Courtesy of Schimpff's Confectionary

Honeymoon oval shaped by Francis H. Leggett Co., New York, 1¾" x 4" x 2¼", $1.00 – 25.00.
Courtesy of Schimpff's Confectionary

Hromada's by Hromada Candy Co., San Francisco, California, 8" x 6", $25.00 – 50.00.
Courtesy of Schimpff's Confectionary

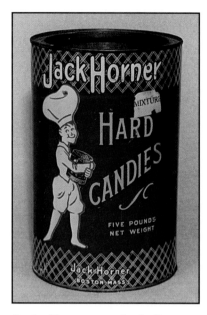

Hromada's by Hromada Candy Co., San Francisco, California, 8" x 6", $1.00 – 25.00.
Courtesy of Schimpff's Confectionary

Huyler's Washington Taffy, 5" x 4" x 5¾", $100.00 – 150.00.
Courtesy of Arnold & Cindy Richardson

Jack Horner marked Boston, MASS., 8½" x 5½", $50.00 – 75.00.
Courtesy of Schimpff's Confectionary

Jenny Lind by Colonial Candy Inc., New York, 1½" x 7", $25.00 – 50.00.
Courtesy of Schimpff's Confectionary

Joyful Hard Candies by The Tebbetts & Garland Store, Chicago, marked Channell Can Co., Chicago, 6¾" x 4½" x 4½", $50.00 – 75.00.
Courtesy of Schimpff's Confectionary

Keller's by Utica Candy Co, Utica, New York, marked A.C. Co. 11A, 7" x 6", $50.00 – 75.00.
Courtesy of Schimpff's Confectionary

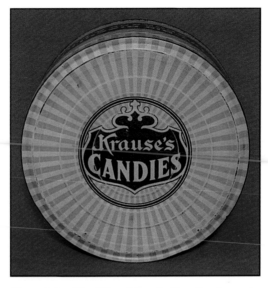

Krause's by Tru-Blue Biscuit Co., Spokane & Portland, marked Continental Can Co., 6" x 12¼", $25.00 – 50.00.
Courtesy of Schimpff's Confectionary

Laub's Nutty Twigs by E.R. Laub Candy Manufacturer, Chicago, Illinois, $1.00 – 25.00.
Courtesy of Schimpff's Confectionary

Lion paper label by Lion Specialty Co., Chicago, 10" x 4½" x 4½", $75.00 – 100.00.
Courtesy of Schimpff's Confectionary

Loft Midget Sticks marked New York, ¾" x 6" x 4", $150.00 – 200.00.
Courtesy of Schimpff's Confectionary

Long's Ox-Heart paper label by Oswego Candy Works Inc., Oswego, New York, marked Karle Litho Co. Rochester, N.Y., 9½" x 10½", $25.00 – 50.00.
Courtesy of Schimpff's Confectionary

Mellomints by Brandle & Smith Co., Philadelphia, left: 6½"
x 8½", $50.00 – 75.00; right: 1½" x 6¾" x 4¼", $1.00 – 25.00.
Courtesy of Schimpff's Confectionary

Mellomints by Brandle & Smith Co., Philadelphia,
left & right: 2" x 4" x 2¼", $1.00 – 25.00 each; center:
sample, 1½" x 2", $25.00 – 50.00.

Melvin's by Melvin Candy Co., Chicago, successor to Howard H. Hoyt Candy Co., 14¼" x
10½", $100.00 – 150.00.
Courtesy of Schimpff's Confectionary

Melvin's by Melvin Candy Co., Chicago, left: 10" x 4½"
x 4½"; right: 6¼" x 4½" x 4½", $75.00 – 100.00 each.
Courtesy of Schimpff's Confectionary

Monarch by Reid, Murdoch & Co., Chicago, 14½" x 12¾", $300.00 – 350.00.
Courtesy of Schimpff's Confectionary

Monarch by Reid, Murdoch & Co., Chicago, 3½"
x 5", $200.00 – 250.00.
Courtesy of Schimpff's Confectionary

Mrs. Steven's marked Heekin Can Co., 2½" x 10",
$50.00 – 75.00.
Courtesy of Schimpff's Confectionary

Mrs. Steven's marked Heekin Can Co., 2" x 10", $50.00 – 75.00.
Courtesy of Schimpff's Confectionary

Mulford Mints by H.K. Mulford Chemist, Philadelphia, ¾" x 2½" x ¾", $1.00 – 25.00.
Courtesy of Schimpff's Confectionary

Oriole Candies by Brown & Haley Co., Tacoma, U.S.A., 10" x 12¼", $150.00 – 200.00.
Courtesy of Schimpff's Confectionary

Necco Peach Blossoms paper label by Necco Sweets Confectionary, Boston, 8½" x 5½", $25.00 – 50.00.
Courtesy of Schimpff's Confectionary

Necco Snowflake Mixture by The Necco Sweets New England Confectionary Co., marked A.C. Co. of Mass., 10" x 4½" x 4½", $50.00 – 75.00.
Courtesy of Schimpff's Confectionary

Parisian by Parisian Candy Co., Seattle, marked A.C. Co. 92A, 11¼" x 12½", $50.00 – 75.00.
Courtesy of Schimpff's Confectionary

Patterkrisp by The Patterson Candy Co., Limited, Toronto, Canada, marked Macdonald MFG. Co., 7¾" x 7¾" x 7½", $75.00 – 100.00.
Courtesy of Schimpff's Confectionary

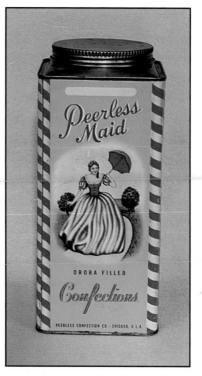

Peerless Maid by Peerless Confection Co., Chicago, 10¼" x 4½" x 4½", $25.00 – 50.00.
Courtesy of Schimpff's Confectionary

Peerless Maid by Peerless Confection Co., Chicago, 6½" x 4¼", $25.00 – 50.00.
Courtesy of Schimpff's Confectionary

Pig 'N Whistle marked Western Can Co., 7½" x 5", $75.00 – 100.00.
Courtesy of Schimpff's Confectionary

Plantation Daintes by Plantation Chocolate Co., Philadelphia, Pennsylvania, 5½" x 10", $1.00 – 25.00.
Courtesy of Schimpff's Confectionary

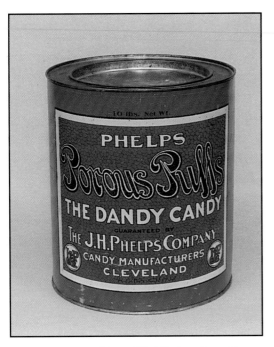

Porous Puffs by The J.H. Phelps Co., Cleveland, Ohio, marked A.C. Co., 9½" x 8¼", $50.00 – 75.00.
Courtesy of Schimpff's Confectionary

Punch by Ridenour-Baker Grocery Co., Kansas City, Missouri, 9" x 8½", $150.00 – 200.00.
Courtesy of Schimpff's Confectionary

Quality Candies by General Foods Products Co., Los Angeles, California, 13½" x 12½", $100.00 – 150.00.
Courtesy of Schimpff's Confectionary

Regennas Hard Candies by C. Fred Regennas & Sons Co. Inc., Lititz, Pennsylvania, 7" x 5½", $25.00 – 50.00.
Courtesy of Schimpff's Confectionary

Richardson's Mints by Thos. D. Richardson Co., Philadelphia, 2½" x 3½", $1.00 – 25.00.
Courtesy of Schimpff's Confectionary

Riley's Toffee by Riley Bros., Halifax, England, 5" x 6½" x 4¼", $100.00 – 150.00.
Courtesy of Bob & Sherri Copeland

Rex Confections by American Candy Co., Milwaukee, Wisconsin, 10" x 5¼", $25.00 – 50.00.
Courtesy of Schimpff's Confectionary

Royal Scarlet Mints paper label by R.C. Williams & Co. Inc., New York, 2" x 4" x 2¼", $1.00 – 25.00.
Courtesy of Schimpff's Confectionary

Robin Hood by Robin Hood Sweets Co., Brooklyn, New York, 2" x 6" x 6", $25.00 – 50.00.
Courtesy of Schimpff's Confectionary

Satin Finish by Brandle & Smith Co., Philadelphia, Pennsylvania, left & right: 1" x 3¾" x 2¼", $1.00 – 25.00 each; center: 4¾" x 4¾" x 4¾", $25.00 – 50.00.
Courtesy of Schimpff's Confectionary

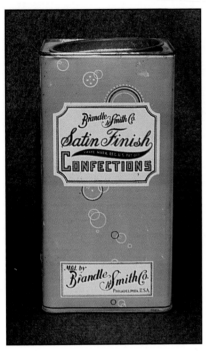

Satin Finish Confections by Brandle
& Smith Co., Philadelphia, 9¼" x
4¾" x 4¾", $1.00 – 25.00.
Courtesy of Schimpff's Confectionary

Satin Finish Madison Mixed Christmas tin by Ludens Inc., Read-
ing, Pennsylvania, 2¼" x 9½" x 5", $1.00 – 25.00.
Courtesy of Schimpff's Confectionary

Satin Finished Hard Candies & Marshmallows by General
Candy Co., San Francisco, California, 5½" x 12½",
$25.00 – 50.00.
Courtesy of Schimpff's Confectionary

Schwarz's Wafers by
Schwarz & Son, Newark,
New Jersey, 3" x 1", $25.00
– 50.00.
Courtesy of Schimpff's Confectionary

Société by Imperial Candy Co., Seattle, left: 10" x 12¼", $50.00 – 75.00; right bottom: 6½" x 9¾", $25.00 – 50.00; right top: 9¾" x 6", $25.00 – 50.00.
Courtesy of Schimpff's Confectionary

Société Confections by Imperial Candy Co., Seattle, 14½" x 10½", marked A.C. Co. 90A, $25.00 – 50.00.
Courtesy of Schimpff's Confectionary

Sunshine Daintifil by Loose-Wiles Co., 9" x 5½", $25.00 – 50.00.
Courtesy of Schimpff's Confectionary

Thinshell Candies by Thinshell Products, Chicago, Illinois, 10" x 4½" x 4½", $1.00 – 25.00 each.
Courtesy of Schimpff's Confectionary

Whitman's by Stephen F. Whitman & Son, Philadelphia, 3¾"
x 3½", $1.00 – 25.00.
Courtesy of Schimpff's Confectionary

Wayne Confections by Wayne Candies Inc., Fort Wayne,
Indiana, marked Heekin Can Co., Cinn. O., 6¾" x 12¼",
$25.00 – 50.00.
Courtesy of Schimpff's Confectionary

Y & S by National Licorice Co., Brooklyn, New York, left:
½" x 2" x 1¼"; right: ¼" x 2¼" x 1¾", $1.00 – 25.00 each.
Courtesy of Schimpff's Confectionary

Woodward by John G. Woodward & Co., Council Bluffs,
Iowa, 6¾" x 12½", $25.00 – 50.00.
Courtesy of Schimpff's Confectionary

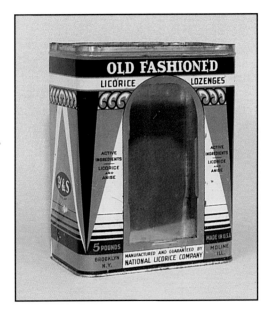

Y & S Old Fashioned Licorice Lozenges by National Licorice Co.,
marked A.C. Co. 10A, 7½" x 6" x 4", $75.00 – 100.00.
Courtesy of Schimpff's Confectionary

Yankee Doodle Dandy by Floriana Candy Co., Philadelphia,
Pennsylvania, 2½" x 5½", California 1928, $200.00 – 250.00.
Courtesy of Schimpff's Confectionary

Zavalla Confections by Sears, Roebuck and Co., Chicago, 6" x 4",
$1.00 – 25.00.
Courtesy of Schimpff's Confections

Zion by Zion Candy Co., Zion, Illinois, marked American Can Co. 60A, 9¼" x 12½", $25.00 – 50.00.
Courtesy of Schimpff's Confectionary

Zion by Zion Institutions & Industries,
Zion, Illinois, marked A.C. Co. 70A,
7½" x 4" x 4", $25.00 – 50.00.
Courtesy of Schimpff's Confectionary

American paper label by Manhattan Cocoa & Chocolate Mills, New York, 4" x 2¼" x 1¾", $25.00 – 50.00.

Courtesy of Bob & Sherri Copeland

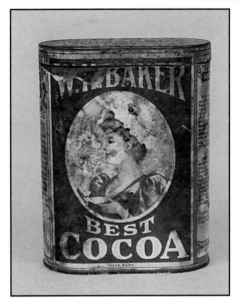

Baker Best by W.H. Baker, Winchester, 4¾" x 3¾" x 1¾", $50.00 – 75.00.

Courtesy of Hoby & Nancy Van Deusen

Baker's by Walter Baker & Co., Dorchester, Massachusetts, 6" x 3¼" x 3¼", $50.00 – 75.00.

Courtesy of Schimpff's Confectionary

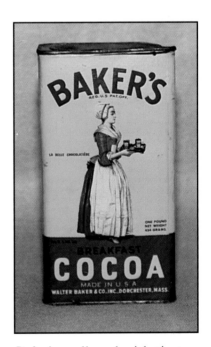

Baker's cardboard with tin top and bottom by Walter Baker & Co., Dorchester, Massachusetts, 7" x 3¾" x 2½", $1.00 – 25.00.

Barker's Hasty by Knickerbocker Chocolate Co., New York, 3¾" x 3", $1.00 – 25.00.

Courtesy of Hoby & Nancy Van Deusen

Benefit Brand paper label by Direct Importing Co. Inc., Boston, Massachusetts, 4½" x 3¼" x 2", $1.00 – 25.00.

Courtesy of Hoby & Nancy Van Deusen

Bensdorp marked Amsterdam, Holland, 6" x 3½" x 2¾", $75.00 – 100.00.
Courtesy of Hoby & Nancy Van Deusen

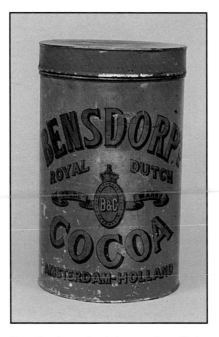

Bensdorp's marked Amsterdam-Holland, 9½" x 6", $25.00 – 50.00.
Courtesy of Hoby & Nancy Van Deusen

Bensdorp's paper label, 5" x 2¾", $1.00 – 25.00.
Courtesy of Hoby & Nancy Van Deusen

Boon by W.J. Boon & Comp., Wormerveer, Holland, 5" x 2¾" x 2¾", $25.00 – 50.00.
Courtesy of Ken & Nancy Jones

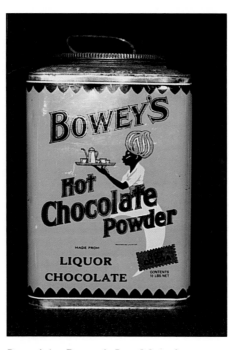

Bowey's by Bowey's Inc. Manufacturers, Chicago, Illinois, 10½" x 7" x 7", $100.00 – 150.00.
Courtesy of Richard & Ann Lehmann

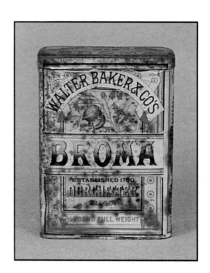

Broma paper label by Walter Baker & Co's., Dorchester, Massachusetts, 4" x 3" x 1¾", $1.00 – 25.00.
Courtesy of Hoby & Nancy Van Deusen

Bunte White House cardboard by Bunte Bros., Chicago, 5" x 2½" x 2½", $50.00 – 75.00.

Courtesy of Schimpff's Confectionary

Cherokee Maid cardboard with tin top and bottom by Griffin Mfg. Co., Muskogee, Oklahoma, 4¾" x 4½" x 3", $75.00 – 100.00.

Courtesy of Ken & Nancy Jones

Daisee Brand by Herrman Co., Paterson, New Jersey, marked A.C. Co. 15A, 6" x 4¼" x 3", $100.00 – 150.00.

Courtesy of Hoby & Nancy Van Deusen

Driessen's by A. Driessen, Rotterdam, left: 6" x 3½" x 2¾"; right: 4¾" x 3" x 2¼", $50.00 – 75.00.

Courtesy of Hoby & Nancy Van Deusen

Durkee-Mower's by Durkee-Mower Inc., Lynn, Massachusetts, 8½" x 6", $25.00 – 50.00.

Courtesy of Hoby & Nancy Van Deusen

Farmers Pride paper label by Hulman & Co., Terre Haute, Indiana, 4¼" x 7" x 4½", $75.00 – 100.00.

Courtesy of Mike & Sharon Hunt

French Maid Cocolat by French Maid Chocolate Co. Inc., New York, 4¼" x 3", $1.00 – 25.00.

Courtesy of Hoby & Nancy Van Deusen

Ghirardelli's by Ghirardelli Co., San Francisco, California, 7" x 5", $50.00 – 75.00.

Courtesy of Schimpff's Confectionary

Griffing's by Crave & Martin Co., New York, marked Passaic Metalware Co., 12¾" x 7¾" x 5½", $150.00 – 200.00.

Courtesy of Hoby & Nancy Van Deusen

Heberling's by G.C. Heberling Co., Bloomington, Illinois, 9¾" x 4¼" x 3", $50.00 – 75.00.

Courtesy of Bob & Sherri Copeland

Hershey's paper label, left & right: 4¾" x 3¼" x 2"; center: 5¼" x 3¼" x 2", $1.00 – 25.00 each.
Courtesy of Hoby & Nancy Van Deusen

Hershey's, 5" x 12½", $25.00 – 50.00. Note: a smaller reproduction exists.
Courtesy of Schimpff's Confectionary

Huyler's, 4¼" x 2½" x 2½", $50.00 – 75.00.
Courtesy of Hoby & Nancy Van Deusen

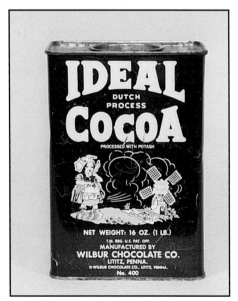

Ideal by Wilbur Chocolate Co., Lititz, Pennsylvania, 5¾" x 4" x 2½", $50.00 – 75.00.
Courtesy of Hoby & Nancy Van Deusen

Kwatta marked Kwatta Breeda, Holland, left: 6½" x 4" x 2½"; center: 5" x 3¼" x 2"; right: 4½" x 2½" x 1¾", $50.00 – 75.00 each.
Courtesy of Hoby & Nancy Van Deusen

Iona cardboard with tin top and bottom by The Great Atlantic & Pacific Tea Co., New York, 8¾" x 4¼", $1.00 – 25.00.
Courtesy of Hoby & Nancy Van Deusen

Iona cardboard with tin top and bottom by The Great Atlantic & Pacific Tea Co., New York, 9" x 4¼", $25.00 – 50.00.
Courtesy of Hoby & Nancy Van Deusen

La Belle paper label by Walter Baker & Co., left: 6" x 3¼" x 3¼", $25.00 – 50.00; right: 4½" x 3¼" x 2", $1.00 – 25.00.
Courtesy of Hoby & Nancy Van Deusen

Liberty cardboard with tin top and bottom by Runkel Bros. Inc., New York, 9¾" x 4½" x 3", $50.00 – 75.00.
Courtesy of Bob & Sherri Copeland

Loft by Loft Inc., New York, marked A.C. Co. 10A, 4¼" x 3" x 3", $25.00 – 50.00.
Courtesy of Hoby & Nancy Van Deusen

Lowney's paper label by Walter M. Lowney Co., Boston, Massachusetts, 4½" x 3¼" x 2", $25.00 – 50.00.

Courtesy of Bob & Sherri Copeland

Lowney's by Walter M. Lowney Co., Boston, Massachusetts, 4¾" x 3¼" x 2", $50.00 – 75.00.

Courtesy of Bob & Sherri Copeland

McNess' Champion cardboard with tin top & bottom by Furst-McNess Co., Freeport, Illinois, 5¼" x 3½" x 3½", $50.00 – 75.00.

Courtesy of Richard & Ann Lehmann

Monarch sample by Reid, Murdoch & Co., Chicago, Illinois, marked Pittsburgh, 3" x 1¾" x 1¾", $50.00 – 75.00.

Courtesy of Bob & Sherri Copeland

Millar's Magnet by E.B. Millar & Co., Chicago, 6" x 3¼" x 3¼", $50.00 – 75.00.

Courtesy of Bob & Sherri Copeland

Mogul paper label by Hooton Cocoa Co., Newark, New Jersey, 4¼" x 3¼" x 2¼", $25.00 – 50.00.

Courtesy of Hoby & Nancy Van Deusen

Our Mother's cardboard with tin top & bottom by E. & A. Opler Inc., New York, New York, 9¾" x 4¾" x 3¼", $25.00 – 50.00.

Ox-Heart by Longs Chocolate Works Inc., Oswego, New York, 9¼" x 6½", $100.00 – 150.00.
Courtesy of Hoby & Nancy Van Deusen

Puritan paper label by Puritan Co., New York, New York and Lititz, Pennsylvania, 4¼" x 3¼" x 2¼", $50.00 – 75.00.
Courtesy of Hoby & Nancy Van Deusen

Rockwood & Co's paper label by Rockwood & Co's., New York, 4" x 3" x 1½", $50.00 – 75.00.
Courtesy of Hoby & Nancy Van Deusen

Rockwood & Co's, New York, 4¾" x 2½" x 2½", $200.00 – 250.00.
Courtesy of Hoby & Nancy Van Deusen

Rock-Co cardboard with tin top and bottom by Rockwood & Co., Brooklyn, New York, 9" x 4", $50.00 – 75.00.

Courtesy of Schimpff's Confectionary

Runkel's sample by Runkel Bros. Inc., New York, 2½" x 1¾" x 1¼", $75.00 – 100.00.

Courtesy of Bob & Sherri Copeland

Runkel Brothers, New York, 4¾" x 2½" x 2½", $50.00 – 75.00.

Courtesy of Hoby & Nancy Van Deusen

Runkel's by Runkel Bros., New York, 5" x 2½" x 2½", $50.00 – 75.00.

Courtesy of Ken & Nancy Jones

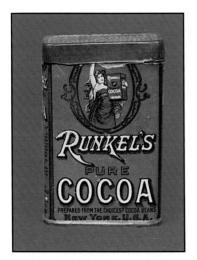

Runkel's paper label by Runkel Bros., New York, 4" x 2¾" x 1¼", $1.00 – 25.00.

Courtesy of Hoby & Nancy Van Deusen

Runkel's by Runkel Bros., New York, 6½" x 4" x 2½", $25.00 – 50.00.

Courtesy of Hoby & Nancy Van Deusen

Runkel's Chocolatina by Runkel Bros. Inc., New York, 11" x 7" x 7", $100.00 – 150.00.

Courtesy of Hoby & Nancy Van Deusen

Soluble Cocoa by J.P. Mott & Co., Halifax, Canada, 10¾" x 8½", $200.00 – 250.00.
Courtesy of Hoby & Nancy Van Deusen

Stollwerck by Stollwerck Bros. Inc., New York and Chicago, left:
6" x 6" x 2¼"; right: 4½" x 4½" x 1¾", $1.00 – 25.00 each.
Courtesy of Schimpff's Confectionary

Watkins by The J.R. Watkins Co.,
Winona, Minnesota, 6" x 3½" x 3½",
$50.00 – 75.00.
Courtesy of Tom & Mary Lou Slike

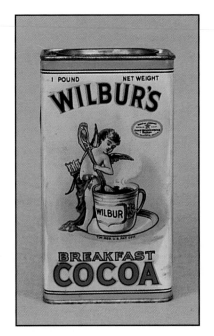

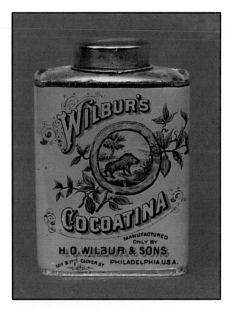

Weis cardboard with tin top and bottom by Pure Foods Stores, 9½" x 4½" x 3", $50.00 – 75.00.

Wilbur's (cherub) cardboard with tin top and bottom by Wilbur-Suchard Chocolate Co., Philadelphia and Lititz, Pennsylvania, 7" x 3¾" x 2½", $100.00 – 150.00.

Courtesy of Hoby & Nancy Van Deusen

Wilbur's Cocoatina by H.O. Wilbur & Sons, Philadelphia, marked Ginna & Co., New York, 5" x 3¼" x 2", $150.00 – 200.00.

Courtesy of Hoby & Nancy Van Deusen

Yacht Club cardboard with tin top and bottom by Reid, Murdoch & Co., 5½" x 3½" x 3½", $75.00 – 100.00.

Courtesy of Alex & Marilyn Znaiden

Zanzibar-Brand paper label by B. Heller & Co., Chicago, Illinois, 5½" x 3½" x 3½", $150.00 – 200.00.

Courtesy of Hoby & Nancy Van Deusen

POPCORN TINS

1 Minute by Hales Milling Co., Milwaukee, Wisconsin, 4½" x 2½", $350.00 – 400.00.

Courtesy of Mike & Sharon Hunt

3 Minute by National Oats Co., Cedar Rapids, Iowa, left: 4½" x 2½"; right: 4¾" x 2½"; $50.00 – 75.00 each.

Courtesy of Mike & Sharon Hunt

American Beauty paper label by American Pop Corn Co., Sioux City, Iowa, 5" x 2½", $100.00 – 150.00.

Courtesy of Mike & Sharon Hunt

American Beauty paper label by American Pop Corn Co., Sioux City, Iowa, 5" x 2½", $100.00 – 150.00.

Courtesy of Mike & Sharon Hunt

Baby Rice by Baby Rice Pop Corn Co., Waterloo, Wisconsin, left: paper label, 4½" x 3½", $250.00 – 300.00; center: 5" x 2½", $100.00 – 150.00; right: 4½" x 3½", $400.00 – 450.00.

Baby Rice by Baby Rice Pop Corn Co., Waterloo, Wisconsin, 3" x 3½", $400.00 – 450.00.

Courtesy of Hoby & Nancy Van Deusen

Bang-o by Central Pop Corn Co., Schaller, Iowa, 5" x 2½", $75.00 – 100.00 each.

Courtesy of Mike & Sharon Hunt

Betty Zane by Betty Zane Corn Products Inc., Marion, Ohio, 5¼" x 2½", $50.00 – 75.00 each.

Big Buster by Albert Dickinson Co., marked Continental Can Co., 4½" x 2½", $75.00 – 100.00.

Big Buster, left: by Albert Dickinson Co., Chicago, Illinois; right: by W.R. Grace & Co., Princeton, Illinois, 4¾" x 2½", $75.00 – 100.00 each.
Courtesy of Mike & Sharon Hunt

Blitz by Red River Valley Pop Corn Co., Hugo, Oklahoma, 5" x 2½", $150.0 – 200.00.
Courtesy of Mike & Sharon Hunt

Blue Diamond paper label by Elmer Schroeder, Buhl, Idaho, 4" x 2½", $100.00 – 150.00.
Courtesy of Mike & Sharon Hunt

Bomb-Buster paper label by Ray's Farm Foods, Mattoon, Illinois, 5" x 2½", $25.00 – 50.00.
Courtesy of Mike & Sharon Hunt

Bonnie Lee by B & L Pop Corn Co., Van Buren, Indiana, left: cardboard with tin top and bottom, 5½" x 3" x 1¾", $50.00 – 75.00; right: 5" x 2½", $100.00 – 150.00.
Courtesy of Mike & Sharon Hunt

Buddy Boy by Buddy Boy Pop Corn Co., Watseka, Illinois, 4½" x 2½", $200.00 – 250.00.
Courtesy of Mike & Sharon Hunt

Butter Boy paper label by Ray
G. Redding, Mattoon, Illinois,
4" x 2¾", $25.00 – 50.00.
Courtesy of Mike & Sharon Hunt

Chesty by Chesty Foods Inc.,
Terre Haute, Indiana,
marked Canco, 5½" x 3",
$400.00 – 450.00.
Courtesy of Mike & Sharon Hunt

Corn Sure Pop by Hart & Howell Co., Brooklyn, Michigan,
4¾" x 2½", $100.00 – 150.00.
Courtesy of Mike & Sharon Hunt

Curtiss by Curtiss Candy Co,
Chicago, Illinois, 4¾" x 2½",
$75.00 – 100.00.

Danny Boy by Albert Dickinson
Co., Chicago, Illinois, 4" x 2¾",
$300.00 – 350.00.
Courtesy of Mike & Sharon Hunt

Davis paper label by Better
Taste Popcorn Co., Anderson,
Indiana, 5¼" x 2½", $50.00 –
75.00.
Courtesy of Hoby & Nancy Van Deusen

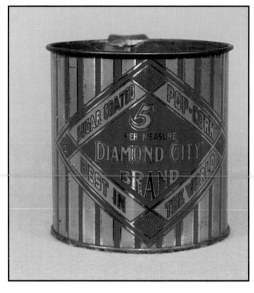

Defiance cardboard with tin tip and bottom by Associated Food Dist. Inc., Cold Water, Michigan, 5½" x 2½", $100.00 – 150.00.
Courtesy of Mike & Sharon Hunt

Del Monico cardboard with tin tip and bottom by Audubon Food Co., Louisville, Kentucky, 6" x 2¼", $75.00 – 100.00.
Courtesy of Mike & Sharon Hunt

Diamond City cup, 4" x 4", $75.00 – 100.00. Note: handle on reverse side.
Courtesy of Hoby & Nancy Van Deusen

Dolly Madison (After School) by Interstate Bakeries Corp., Chicago, Illinois, 11½" x 7½", $25.00 – 50.00.
Courtesy of Hoby & Nancy Van Deusen

Donald Duck by Popcorn Sales Inc., Carnarvon, Iowa, 5" x 2½", $300.00 – 350.00.

Festival cardboard with tin top and bottom by The Bagnall Co., Kansas City, Missouri, 5¼" x 2¾", $300.00 – 350.00.
Courtesy of Hoby & Nancy Van Deusen

Georgie Porgie by Georgie Porgie Co., Council Bluffs, Iowa, 5" x 2½", $100.00 – 150.00.

Courtesy of Mike & Sharon Hunt

Glancy's cardboard with tin tip and bottom by Fred F. Glancy & Sons, Hartford City, Indiana, 5½" x 2½", $25.00 – 50.00.

Gloria Jean by Hart & Howell Co., Brooklyn, Michigan, 5" x 2½", left: $100.00 – 150.00; right: $250.00 – 300.00.

Courtesy of Mike & Sharon Hunt

Gloria Jean cardboard with tin top and bottom by Hart & Howell, Brooklyn, Michigan, 5" x 2½", $150.00 – 200.00.

Home Brand paper label by Griggs, Cooper & Co., St. Paul, Minnesota, 5" x 2½", $100.00 – 150.00.

Courtesy of Mike & Sharon Hunt

Hopalong Cassidy's by John L. Srtickland Co. Inc., 5" x 2¾", $200.00 – 250.00.

IGA by Independent Grocers Alliance Dist. Co., Chicago, Illinois, 4½" x 2¾", $150.00 – 200.00.

Courtesy of Mike & Sharon Hunt

Jays by Special Foods Co., Chicago, Illinois, marked National Can Corp., 11½" x 7½", $1.00 – 25.00.

Courtesy of Hoby & Nancy Van Deusen

Jiffy by American Pop Corn Co., Sioux City, Iowa, 4¾" x 2½", $150.00 – 200.00.

Courtesy of Mike & Sharon Hunt

Jolly Time by American Pop Corn Co., Sioux City, Iowa, 4¾" x 2½", left to right: #1, $50.00 – 75.00; #2, $50.00 – 75.00; #3, $100.00 – 150.00; #4, cardboard with tin top and bottom, $25.00 – 50.00.

Courtesy of Mike & Sharon Hunt

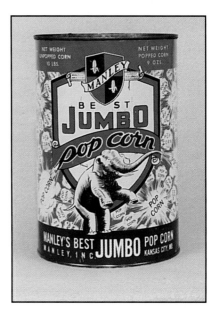

Jumbo by Manley Inc., Kansas City, Missouri, 9½" x 6¾", $100.00 – 150.00.

Courtesy of Hoby & Nancy Van Deusen

Krinx by A.A. Walter & Co., Albany, New York, 7½" x 12½", $25.00 – 50.00.
Courtesy of Hoby & Nancy Van Deusen

Little Badger by Wisconsin Pop Corn Co., Waterloo, Wisconsin, 4½" x 2¾", $200.00 – 250.00.
Courtesy of Mike & Sharon Hunt

Little Buster by Albert Dikinson Co., marked Continental Can Co., 4½" x 2½", $75.00 – 100.00.

Loft, marked A.C. Co. 10A, 6½" x 5", $1.00 – 25.00.
Courtesy of Hoby & Nancy Van Deusen

Lucky Jim by J.A. McCarty Seed Co., Evansville, Indiana, marked Crown Can Co., 4½" x 2½", $200.00 – 250.00.
Courtesy of Mike & Sharon Hunt

Midget by Hales Milling Co., Milwaukee, Wisconsin, marked A.C. Co. 68A, 4½" x 3½", $150.00 – 200.00.
Courtesy of Mike & Sharon Hunt

Monarch, left: paper label by Reid Murdoch & Co., Chicago, Illinois, 5" x 2½", $200.00 – 250.00; right: by Consolidated Grocers Inc., Chicago, Illinois, 4¾" x 2½", $250.00 – 300.00.
Courtesy of Mike & Sharon Hunt

Monarch by Reid Murdoch & Co., Chicago, Illinois, 3¾" x 3½", $250.00 – 300.00.
Courtesy of Hoby & Nancy Van Deusen

Monarch by Consolidated Food Distributors, Chicago, Illinois, 5½" x 6", $50.00 – 75.00.
Courtesy of Hoby & Nancy Van Deusen

Mor-Zip cardboard by Ronald Meyer Pop Corn, Carnarvon, Iowa, 7½" x 2", $50.00 – 75.00.

Mother Jackson's by Jackson Newport Foods Co., Longueuil, Providence of Quebec, 4½" x 2½", $200.00 – 250.00.
Courtesy of Mike & Sharon Hunt

Mrs. Klein's, Chicago, Illinois, 11½" x 7½", $1.00 – 25.00.
Courtesy of Hoby & Nancy Van Deusen

"OK" Pop paper label by H.T. Beck, Lewisburg, Pennsylvania, 11" x 7¾", $25.00 – 50.00.
Courtesy of Hoby & Nancy Van Deusen

Peggy Kellogg paper label by Sears, Roebuck & Co., Chicago, Illinois, 5" x 2½", $100.00 – 150.00.
Courtesy of Mike & Sharon Hunt

Pep-Pop by Peppard Sedd Co., Kansas City, Missouri, marked Canco, 5" x 2½", $100.00 – 150.00 each.
Courtesy of Mike & Sharon Hunt

Pickwick paper label by Kansas City Wholesale Grocery Co., 5" x 2½", $100.00 – 150.00.
Courtesy of Mike & Sharon Hunt

Plee-zing by Hart & Howell Co., Brooklyn, Michigan, marked Canco, 5" x 2½", $100.00 – 150.00.
Courtesy of Mike & Sharon Hunt

Polly-Pops paper label by National Quality Foods, Chicago, Illinois, 7" x 6¼", $50.00 – 75.00.

Courtesy of Hoby & Nancy Van Deusen

Popeye by Purity Mills Inc., Dixon, Illinois, 5" x 2½", left: cardboard with tin top and bottom, $25.00 – 50.00; center and right: $150.00 – 200.00 each.

Courtesy of Mike & Sharon Hunt

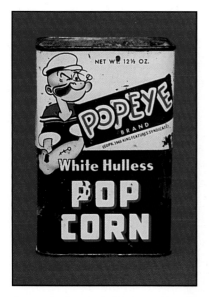

Popeye by Purity Mills Inc., Dixon, Illinois, 4¾" x 3¼" x 2", $75.00 – 100.00.

Courtesy of Hoby & Nancy Van Deusen

Poppy by Sac City Canning Co., Sac City and Storm Lake, Iowa, marked C.C. Co., 4½" x 3", $350.00 – 400.00.

Courtesy of Mike & Sharon Hunt

Poppy by Iowa Canning Co., Vinton, Iowa, 5" x 2¾", $200.00 – 250.00.

Courtesy of Mike & Sharon Hunt

Pops-Rite by Blevins Pop Corn Co., Nashville, Tennessee, marked Heekin Can Co., left: 5" x 2½", $100.00 – 150.00; right: cardboard with tin top and bottom, 4¾" x 2¾", $50.00 – 75.00.
Courtesy of Mike & Sharon Hunt

Popswell cardboard with tin top and bottom by Bernau Processing Plant, Lake City, Iowa, 5¼" x 3" x 1¾", $50.00 – 75.00.
Courtesy of Mike & Sharon Hunt

Princeton Farms, Princeton, Indiana, 4¾" x 2½", left: $150.00 – 200.00; right: $100.00 – 150.00.
Courtesy of Mike & Sharon Hunt

Richelieu by Sprague Warner, Chicago, Illinois, 4¾" x 2¾", $150.00 – 200.00.
Courtesy of Mike & Sharon Hunt

RoseKist by Rose Kist Foods Inc., Thomasville, Georgia, marked Crown Can Co., 5" x 2¾", $100.00 – 150.00.
Courtesy of Mike & Sharon Hunt

Savoy embossed paper label by Steele-Wedeles Co., Chicago, Illinois, 5" x 2½", $50.00 – 75.00.

Courtesy of Mike & Sharon Hunt

Sūp R popt paper label by Dwight Hamlin Co., Pittsburgh, Pennsylvania, 10" x 8", $25.00 – 50.00.

Courtesy of Hoby & Nancy Van Deusen

Sweet Brier by Midland Grocery Co. of Ohio, 4¾" x 2½", $150.00 – 200.00.

Courtesy of Mike & Sharon Hunt

Target paper label by Target Pop Corn Co., Blue Springs, Missouri, 5" x 2½", $150.00 – 200.00.

Courtesy of Mike & Sharon Hunt

Thunderbolt by American Pop Corn Co., Souix City, Iowa, left: cardboard with tin top and bottom, 7½" x 2", $75.00 – 100.00; right: 5" x 2½", $100.00 – 150.00.

Courtesy of Mike & Sharon Hunt

TNT by The Barteldes Seed Co., Lawrence, Kansas and Denver, Colorado, 5" x 2¾", $100.00 – 150.00.

TNT, left: by Food Products Inc., 4¾" x 2½"; right: by Barteldes Seed Co., 5" x 2½", $100.00 – 150.00 each.

Courtesy of Mike & Sharon Hunt

TNT by Barteldes Seed Co., Lawrence, Kansas, and Denver, Colorado, 5½" x 2½", $100.00 – 150.00.

Courtesy of Hoby & Nancy Van Deusen

Weideman by Weideman Co., Cleveland, Ohio, 4¾" x 2¾", $300.00 – 350.00.

Courtesy of Mike & Sharon Hunt

White Swan cardboard with tin top and bottom by Waples-Platter Co., Denison-Fort Worth-Dallas, Texas, 3" x 2¼" x 1½", $50.00 – 75.00.

Courtesy of Mike & Sharon Hunt

Young America by Certified Brands Inc., Kansas City, Missouri, 5" x 2½", $300.00 – 350.00.

Courtesy of Mike & Sharon Hunt

Air-Float Rose by Talcum Puff Co., New York, 4¾" x 2½" x 1¼", $25.00 – 50.00 each.
Courtesy of Bill & June Mason

Air Float (medicated) by Talcum Puff Co., 5" x 1¾", ca. 1932, $25.00 – 50.00.
Courtesy of Bob & Sherri Copeland

Air-Float baby powder by Talcum Puff Co., New York, 6" x 2¼" x 1¼", $75.00 – 100.00.
Courtesy of Bill & June Mason

April Showers marked Paris, New York, 4¼" x 1¾" x 1", $25.00 – 50.00.
Courtesy of Bob & Sherri Copeland

Arthur's Corylopsis of Japan by The Arthur Chemical Co., New Haven, Connecticut, 5½" x 3" x 1½", $350.00 – 400.00.
Courtesy of Alex & Marilyn Znaiden

Baker's Talcum by L.M. Leiverman's Sons Inc., Philadelphia, Pennsylvania, 4" x 1¾", $100.00 – 150.00.
Courtesy of Grant Smith

Borated Talcum (perfumed) marked American Stopper Co., Brooklyn, New York, 4" x 1¾", $100.00 – 150.00.
Courtesy of Grant Smith

Borated Talcum (perfumed) by Boerner-Fry Co., Iowa City, Iowa, marked Norton Bros., Chicago, 4" x 1¾", $200.00 – 250.00.
Courtesy of Grant Smith

Borated Talcum (perfumed) marked American Stopper Co., Brooklyn, New York, 4" x 1¾", $100.00 – 150.00.
Courtesy of Grant Smith

Brunswick's Cueglide by Brunswick-Balke-Collender Co., 5½" x 3" x 1½", rare, no price available.
Courtesy of Mike & Sharon Hunt

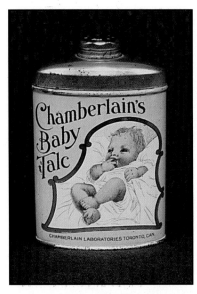

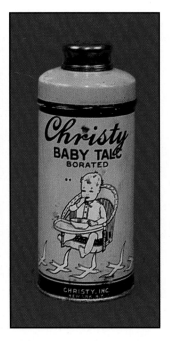

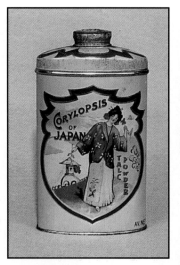

Chamberlain's by Chamberlain Laboratories, Toronto, Canada, 4¾" x 3" x 1½", $2,500.00 – 3,000.00.
Courtesy of Grant Smith

Christy by Christy Inc., Newark, New York, 5" x 2", $50.00 – 75.00.
Courtesy of Mike & Sharon Hunt

Corylopsis of Japan by Talcum Puff Co., New York, 5½" x 3" x 1½", $75.00 – 100.00.
Courtesy of Bill and June Mason

CPC by California Perfume Co., New York, 4½" x 1¾", $350.00 – 400.00.
Courtesy of Grant Smith

Danity Violet, borated, by White Chemical Co., Chicago, marked American Can Co., 4" x 1¾", $100.00 – 150.00.

Courtesy of Bob & Sherri Copeland

De Parma Violet by Northrop & Lyman Co. Limited, Toronto, Canada, 4½" x 2½" x 1¼", $25.00 – 50.00.

Courtesy of Bill & June Mason

Dilnorpa by The Dill Co., Norristown, Pennsylvania, 6½" x 2¼" x 1¼", $500.00 – 600.00.

Courtesy of Grant Smith

Dorothy Vernon by Jennings Co., Grand Rapids, Michigan, marked American Stopper Co., 4¾" x 2" x 1", $200.00 – 250.00.

Courtesy of Grant Smith

Dr. Sayman's cardboard with tin top and bottom by Dr. T.M. Sayman, St. Louis, Missouri, 5" x 2¼", $50.00 – 75.00.

Courtesy of Tom & Mary Lou Slike

Drees' Sweet Violet by Con. F. Drees, Covington, Ohio, 4½" x 2½" x 1¼", $25.00 – 50.00.

Courtesy of Bob & Sherri Copeland

Elysian by Elysian Manufacturing Co., Detroit, 4" x 1¾", $75.00 – 100.00.

Courtesy of Grant Smith

Fehr's by Dr. Julius Fehr, marked American Stopper Co., 4¼" x 2½" x 1½", $100.00 – 150.00.

Courtesy of Grant Smith

Florentine by Wilbert Co., Philadelphia, Pennsylvania, 4" x 1¾", $150.00 – 200.00.
Courtesy of Grant Smith

Flores del Campo, 6¼" x 3" x 1½", $100.00 – 150.00.
Courtesy of Bob & Sherri Copeland

Franco by Franco American Hygienic Co., Chicago, 4¾" x 2½" x 1¼", $25.00 – 50.00.
Courtesy of Bob & Sherri Copeland

French Talcum by Durant Et Rue Lafitte, Paris, 4" x 1¾", $75.00 – 100.00.
Courtesy of Grant Smith

Frescodor by The Sydney Ross Co. Inc., 5½" x 3" x 1", $450.00 – 500.00.

Harmony Carnation by Harmony of Boston, 5" x 2½" x 1½", $50.00 – 75.00.
Courtesy of Ken & Nancy Jones

Hawley's by Hawley Manufacturing Co., New York, 4" x 1¾", $100.00 – 150.00.
Courtesy of Alex & Marilyn Znaiden

Hemstreet's foot powder by Dr. Hemstreet Co., Glen Falls, New York, 4½" x 2" x 1¾", no price available.

Courtesy of Grant Smith

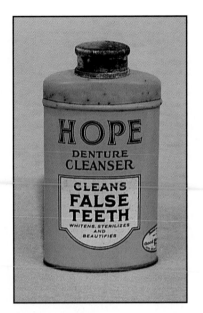

Hope by Hope Inc., New York, New York, marked C.C. Co., 4" x 2¼" x 1¼", $1.00 – 25.00.

Courtesy of Dave Garland

Imperial by Imperial Manufacturing Co., Detroit, Michigan, 4" x 1¾", $50.00 – 75.00.

Courtesy of Grant Smith

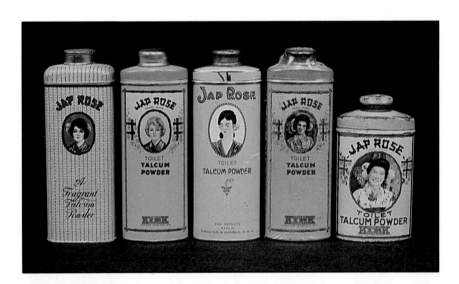

Jap Rose by Kirk Products, Chicago, Illinois, left to right: #1, 6" x 2¼" x 1½", $150.00 – 200.00; #2, #3, #4, 6" x 2¼" x 1½", $100.00 – 150.00 each; #5, 4¾" x 2½" x 1¼", $75.00 – 100.00.

Courtesy of Bill & Amy Vehling

Kimball's by Kimball Bros. & Co., Enosburg Falls, Vermont, marked Continental Can Co., 6¾" x 2" x 1½", no price available.

Courtesy of Bill & June Mason

"La Creole" by La Creole Laboratories, Memphis, Tennessee, 6" x 2" x 1¼", $1.00 – 25.00.
Courtesy of Bill & June Mason

Lander Baby Borated by Lander, New York, New York, 8" x 2", $50.00 – 75.00.
Courtesy of Mike & Sharon Hunt

Larkin Baby Talcum by Larkin Co. Inc., Buffalo, 6" x 2½" x 1¼", $100.00 – 150.00.
Courtesy of Mike & Sharon Hunt

Larkin Orange Blossom by Larkin Co. Inc., Buffalo, 6" x 2¼" x 1¼", $25.00 – 50.00.
Courtesy of Bill & June Mason

Lilac Belle by Wm. Waltke & Co., St. Louis, Missouri, 4¾" x 2½" x 1¼", $50.00 – 75.00.
Courtesy of Bob & Sherri Copeland

Little Lady by Helene Pessl Inc., New York, 6" x 2", $25.00 – 50.00.
Courtesy of Mike & Sharon Hunt

Lov'me by Melba, 6¼" x 2¼" x 1¼", $25.00 – 50.00.
Courtesy of Bill & June Mason

Maxim's by Maxim, Pringle & Brush Co., New York, marked A.C. Co., 4" x 1¾", $100.00 – 150.00.
Courtesy of Grant Smith

Mennen Baby Powder by The Mennen Co., Morristown, New Jersey, and Toronto, Canada, 4" x 1¼" x 1¼", $1.00 – 25.00.
Courtesy of Bill & June Mason

Mennen's (violet talcum) by Gerhard Mennen Chemical Co., Newark, New Jersey, marked A.C. Co. 11A, 4" x 1¾", $75.00 – 100.00.
Courtesy of Grant Smith

Mennen's borated talcum by Gerhard Mennen Chemical Co., Newark, New Jersey, 4" x 1½", $75.00 – 100.00 each.
Courtesy of Bob & Sherri Copeland

Mother Goose baby powder by Baby Health Products, New York, New York, 6½" x 2½" x 1¾", $1,500.00 – 1,750.00.
Courtesy of Grant Smith

Nelson's Baby Powder by The Penslar Co., Detroit, Michigan and Wakerville, Ontario, 4½" x 3" x 1½", $100.00 – 150.00.
Courtesy of Bill & June Mason

Newton by Paul D. Newton & Co. Inc., Newark, New Jersey, 5" x 2", $50.00 – 75.00.

Old English by Edward J. Moore, New York, 4" x 1¾", $75.00 – 100.00.
Courtesy of Alex & Marilyn Znaiden

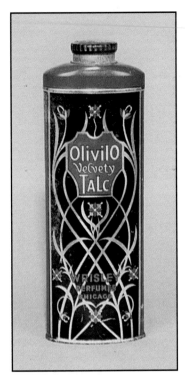

Orchid Corson's Ideal by Sovereign Perfumes Ltd., Toronto, Canada, 4½" x 2½" x 1¼", $100.00 – 150.00.
Courtesy of Bill & June Mason

Palmer by Solon Palmer Perfumer, New York, marked American Stopper Co., 4¾" x 2½" x 1½", $50.00 – 75.00.
Courtesy of Bill & June Mason

OlivilO by Wrisley perfumer, Chicago, 6½" x 2¼" x 1¼", $1.00 – 25.00.
Courtesy of Bill & June Mason

Oriole by Foley & Co., Chicago, 6" x 2¼" x 1¼", $75.00 – 100.00.
Courtesy of Bill & June Mason

Palmolive after shaving powder by Colgate-Palmolive-Peet Co., left: 6" x 2¼" x 1¼", $1.00 – 25.00; right: sample, 3½" x 1½" x 1", $25.00 – 50.00.
Courtesy of Dave Garland

"Pebete" by Hispano Laboratories, Argentino, 3½" x 2½" x 1¼", no price available.

Perfumed Talcum by Billings, Clapp Co., Boston, marked A.C. Co., 4" x 1¾", $75.00 – 100.00.
Courtesy of Grant Smith

Perfumed Talcum (violet) marked American Stopper Co., Brooklyn, New York, 4" x 1¾", $100.00 – 150.00.
Courtesy of Grant Smith

Perfumed Talcum, borated, marked American Stopper Co., Brooklyn, New York, 4" x 1¾", $100.00 – 150.00.
Courtesy of Grant Smith

Perfumed Talcum by Mace Perfumer, Philadelphia, Pennsylvania, marked American Stopper Co., 4" x 1¾", $75.00 – 100.00.
Courtesy of Grant Smith

Perfumed Talcum by Herman Chemical Co., Brooklyn, New York, 4" x 1¾", $75.00 – 100.00.
Courtesy of Grant Smith

Red Cross by H.S. Peterson & Co., Chicago, Illinois, 1¼" x 2¾", $200.00 – 250.00.
Courtesy of Alex & Marilyn Znaiden

Police foot powder by The Purity Laboratories, Brooklyn, New York, 5" x 2½" x 1¼", $800.00 – 900.00.
Courtesy of Grant Smith

Pussy Scat by Sudbury Laboratory, So. Sudbury, Massachusetts, 3" x 2" x 1", $25.00 – 50.00.
Courtesy of Tom Sankiewicz

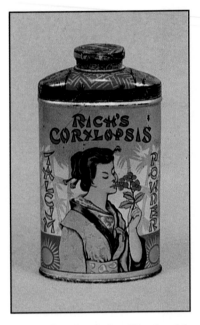

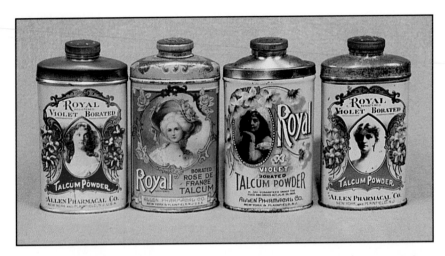

Royal by Allen Pharmacal Co., New York and Plainfield, New Jersey, left to right: #1, $250.00 – 300.00; #2, $400.00 – 450.00; #3, $350.00 – 400.00; #4, $250.00 – 300.00.
Courtesy of Grant Smith

Rich's Corylopsis by Charles M. Rich, marked American Stopper Co., 4¾" x 2½" x 1¼", $400.00 – 450.00.
Courtesy of Grant Smith

Royal by The Allen Pharmacal Co., New York and Plainfield, New Jersey, 4" x 2¼" x 1¼", $300.00 – 350.00.
Courtesy of Grant Smith

Sanadora by Winifred Darrow Co., Three Rivers, Michigan, 5¾" x 2½", $50.00 – 75.00.
Courtesy of Mike & Sharon Hunt

Sanitol by Sanitol Chemical Laboratory Co., St. Louis, 4½" x 2½" x 1½", $350.00 – 400.00.
Courtesy of Grant Smith

Smith's Rosebud by Rosebud Perfume Co., Woodsboro, Maryland, 5" x 2¼" x 1¼", $350.00 – 400.00.

Courtesy of Grant Smith

Sozodont tooth powder by Hall & Ruckel, New York, 3½" x 2¼" x 1¼", $100.00 – 150.00.

Courtesy of Dave Garland

Squibb's by E.R. Squibb & Sons, marked American Stopper Co., 4¾" x 1½", $25.00 – 50.00.

Courtesy of Bob & Sherri Copeland

Stearn's by Stearn's Perfumer, Detroit, 5¼" x 3" x 1½", $500.00 – 600.00.

Courtesy of Grant Smith

Sweet Pea embossed tin by Lazell Perfumer, marked American Stopper Co., 4½" x 2½" x 1½", $75.00 – 100.00.

Courtesy of Bob & Sherri Copeland

Talc Egyptian by Palmolive, 6" x 2¼" x 1¼", $1.00 – 25.00.

Courtesy of Bill & June Mason

Tally-Ho by Tally-Ho Distributor, New York, 4¾" x 2¾" x 1", $1.00 – 25.00.

Courtesy of Bob & Sherri Copeland

Taylor's Blue Bird by John Taylor & Co., Toronto, 4½" x 2½" x 1¼", $300.00 – 350.00.
Courtesy of Bill & June Mason

Tooth Powder, manufacturer unknown, marked American Can Co., 4" x 1¾", $75.00 – 100.00.
Courtesy of Dave Garland

Violet talcum & toilet powder by F.F. Dalley Co., Hamilton, Canada, marked Thos Davidson Co., 4½" x 2½" x 1¼", $25.00 – 50.00.
Courtesy of Bill & June Mason

Violet Borated embossed paper label by VanGorder-Hapgood Drug and Seed Store, Warren, Ohio, 4½" x 2½" x 1¼", $25.00 – 50.00.
Courtesy of Bill & June Mason

Violet Talcum Powder, manufacturer unknown, 4" x 1¾", $75.00 – 100.00.
Courtesy of Grant Smith

Vision d'Eden by American Company Dist., Memphis, Tennessee, 5" x 2", $50.00 – 75.00.
Courtesy of Mike & Sharon Hunt

Waltz Dream, marked Mozart, New York, 6" x 2¼" x 1¼", $75.00 – 100.00.
Courtesy of Bill & June Mason

Watkins by J.R. Watkins Medical Co., Winona, Minnesota, 4" x 1¾", $150.00 – 200.00.
Courtesy of Grant Smith

POWDER SAMPLE TINS

Amami by Prichard & Constance, London–New York, left: 2¼" x 1" ; right: 2" x 1¼" x ¾", $100.00 – 150.00 each.

Amolin by The Amolin Co., New York, New York, 2¾" x 1", $1.00 – 25.00.

Armand by The Armand Co., Des Moines, 2" x 1¼" x ¾", $75.00 – 100.00 each.

As The Petals by Lazell Perfumers, 2" x 1¼" x ¾", $100.00 – 150.00. Note: another sample variation exists, the full-size version is known as Cloth of Gold.

B & B baby talc by Bauer & Black, Chicago–New York–Toronto, 2¼" x 1½" x ¾", $75.00 – 100.00.

B.F.I. by H.K. Mulford Co., Philadelphia, 2" x 1", $1.00 – 25.00.

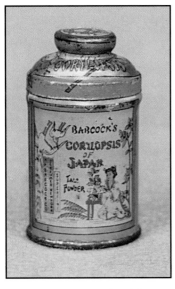

Babcock's Corylopsis of Japan, 2" x 1" x ¾", $100.00 – 150.00.

Bel Bon by Bruguier Chemical Co., Newark, New Jersey, 2" x 1¼" x ¾", $50.00 – 75.00.

Cashmere Bouquet by Colgate & Co., New York, 2" x 1¼" x ¾", $25.00 – 50.00.

Cashmere Bouquet (wreath) by Colgate & Co., New York, 2" x 1¼" x ¾", $25.00 – 50.00.

Cha Ming by Colgate & Co., New York, 2" x 1¼" x ¾", $50.00 – 75.00.

Co-Re-Ga tooth powder by Corega Chemical Co., Cleveland, Ohio, 2¼" x 1¼" x ¾", $1.00 – 25.00.

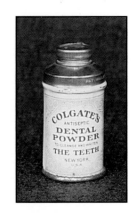

Colgate's dental powder by Colgate & Co., 2" x 1", $25.00 – 50.00.

Courtesy of Bob & Sherri Copeland

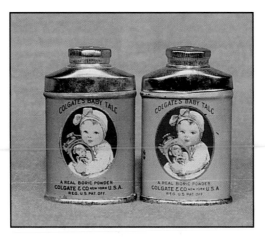

Colgate's Rapid Shave Powder, 2¼" x 1¼" x ¾", $50.00 – 75.00.

Courtesy of Dave Garland

Colgate's Baby Talc by Colgate & Co., New York, 2" x 1¼" x ¾", $100.00 – 150.00 each.

Colgate's Dactylis by Colgate & Co., New York, 2" x 1¼" x ¾", $100.00 – 150.00.

Colgate's Monad talc by Colgate & Co., New York, 2¼" x 1¼" x ¾", $75.00 – 100.00.

Courtesy of Bob & Sherri Copeland

Colgate's La France Rose by Colgate & Co., New York, 2" x 1¼" x ¾", $75.00 – 100.00.

Colgate's Monad by Colgate & Co., New York, 2" x 1¼" x ¾", $75.00 – 100.00.

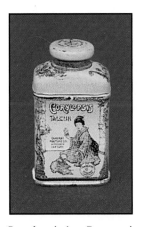

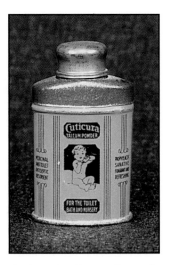

Colgate's Violet by Colgate & Co., New York, 2" x 1¼" x ¾", $75.00 – 100.00.

Corylopsis by Samurai Perfume Co., 2" x 1" x ¾", $150.00 – 200.00.
Courtesy of Grant Smith

Cuticura by Potter Drug & Chemical Corp., Boston, 2¼" x 1¼" x ¾", $100.00 – 150.00.

Deodo by H.K. Mulford Co., Philadelphia, 3" x 1¼" x ¾", $50.00 – 75.00.

Dr. Wernet's tooth powder by Wernet Dental Mfg. Co., Brooklyn, New York, 2¼" x 1¼" x ¾", $25.00 – 50.00.

Dr. I.W. Lyon's tooth powder, R.L. Watkins Co., Cleveland, Ohio, 2½" x 1¼", $50.00 – 75.00.

Erasmic marked London–Paris, 2½" x ¾" x ¾", $200.00 – 250.00.

Eutaska by Jergens, Cincinnati, Ohio, 2¼" x 1¼" x ¾", $100.00 – 150.00.

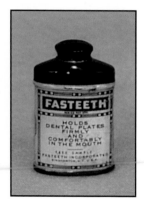

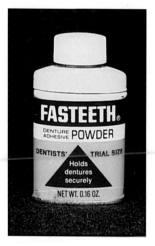

Euthymol Violet by Parke, Davis & Co., Detroit, Michigan, 2¼" x 1¾" x ¾", $75.00 – 100.00.

Fasteeth by Fasteeth Inc., Binghamton, New York, 2" x 1¼" x ¾", $25.00 – 50.00.

Courtesy of Bob & Sherri Copeland

Fasteeth tooth powder by Vick Chemical Co., New York, New York, 2¼" x 1¼" x ¾", $1.00 – 25.00.

Florient by Colgate & Co., New York, 2" x 1¼" x ¾", $50.00 – 75.00.

Gardenia by Richard Hudnut, New York–Paris, 2¼" x 1¾" x ¾", $100.00 – 150.00.

Gibbs made in Great Britain, 2½" x ¾" x ¾", $300.00 – 350.00.

Courtesy of Grant Smith

Hinds by A.S. Hinds, Portland, Maine, 2¼" x 1¼" x ¾", $100.00 – 150.00.

Courtesy of Grant Smith

Hope denture powder by Hope Denture Co., 2" x 1¼" x ¾", $25.00 – 50.00.

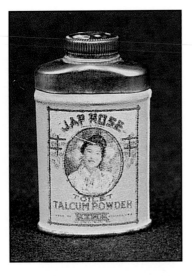

Ideal Talcum by Larkin Co.
Inc., Buffalo, 2" x 1¼" x
¾", $100.00 – 150.00.

Jap Rose, 2¼" x 1¼" x ¾",
$75.00 – 100.00.

Larkin Orange Blossom by
Larkin Co. Inc., Buffalo,
2" x 1¼" x ¾", $75.00 –
100.00.

Lilas DeFrance by Ed Pin-
aud, Paris, 2" x 1¼" x ¾",
$150.00 – 200.00.
Courtesy of Bob & Sherri Copeland

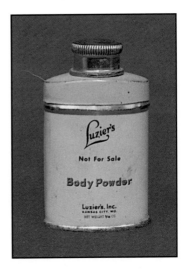

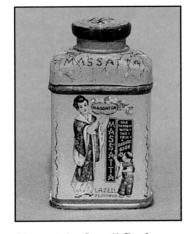

Marathon foot powder by
McKesson & Robbins
Inc., 2¼" x 1¼" x 1",
$1.00 – 25.00.
Courtesy of Bob & Sherri Copeland

Massatta by Lazell Perfumer,
2" x 1¼" x ¾", $50.00 – 75.00.

Luzier's by Luzier's Inc.,
Kansas City, Missouri, 2¼" x
1¼" x ¾", $25.00 – 50.00.
Courtesy of Jill & Warren Schimpff

Mennen by The Mennen Co., Newark, New
Jersey, 2" x 1", $1.00 – 25.00 each.

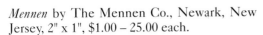

Mennen Borated Talcum by The Mennen Co., Newark, New Jersey, left: 2" x 1"; right: 1¾" x 1", $25.00 – 50.00. each.

Mennen talcum for men by The Mennen Co., Newark, New Jersey, 2¼" x 1¼" x ¾", $50.00 – 75.00.

Mennen Antiseptic Borated by The Mennen Co., Newark, New Jersey, 2½" x ¾" x ½", $50.00 – 75.00.

Courtesy of Bob & Sherri Copeland

Mennen for Men by The Mennen Co., Newark, New Jersey, 2" x 1" x 1", $25.00 – 50.00.

Courtesy of Bob & Sherri Copeland

Mennen's Borated Talcum by Gerhard Mennen Chemical Co., Newark, New Jersey, 2" x 1¼" x ¾", $100.00 – 150.00.

Mennen's Flesh Tint by Gerhard Mennen Chemical Co., Newark, New Jersey, 2" x 1¼" x ¾", $75.00 – 100.00.

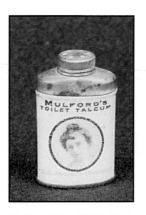

Mulford's by H.K. Mulford Co., Philadelphia, 2¼" x 1¼" x ¾", $100.00 – 150.00.
Courtesy of Grant Smith

Na-Dru-Co Royal Rose by National Drug and Chemical Co. of Canada, 2¼" x 1¾" x ¾", $150.00 – 200.00.
Courtesy of Bill & June Mason

Mennen's Violet Talcum by Gerhard Mennen Co., Newark, New Jersey, 2" x 1¼" x ¾", $50.00 – 75.00.

Mirelle marked Kleinert's, 2" x 1¼" x ¾", $100.00 – 150.00.

Natoma by California Perfume Co., New York, 2" x 1¼" x ¾", $450.00 – 500.00.

Odorono deodorant powder, 1¾" x 1¼" x ¾", $1.00 – 25.00.

Perma Grip by The Prophylactic Brush Co., Florence, Massachusetts, 2¼" x 1¼" x ¾", $1.00 – 25.00.

Qualitol tooth powder by Qualitol Chemical Co., Buffalo, New York, 2¼" x 1¼" x ¾", $25.00 – 50.00.

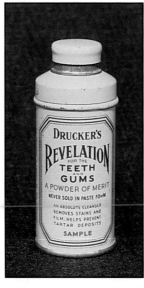

Revelation tooth powder by August E. Drucker Co., San Francisco, California, 2½" x 1", $1.00 – 25.00.

Rexall tooth powder by United Drug Co., Boston, Massachusetts, 2" x 1", $75.00 – 100.00.

Royal Vinolia by Vinolia Co. Ltd., London, Paris, Toronto, 2¼" x 1¼" x ¾", $200.00 – 250.00.

San Toy by The Wrisley Co., 2" x 1", $75.00 – 100.00.

Sana Balm by The Sana Balm Co., Philadelphia, Pennsylvania, 2½" x 1", $50.00 – 75.00.
Courtesy of Grant Smith

Sanitol by The Sanitol Chemical Laboratory Co., St. Louis, 2" x 1¼" x ¾", $150.00 – 200.00.
Courtesy of Grant Smith

Squibb's Bouquet by E.R. Squibb & Sons, 2¼" x 1¾" x ¾", $50.00 – 75.00.

Syke's Comfort by The Comfort Powder Co., Boston, Massachusetts, 1½" x 1¼" x 1", $500.00 – 600.00.

Sylvan Violet by Armour & Co., Chicago, 2" x 1¼" x ¾", $150.00 – 200.00.

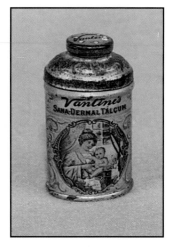

Taylor's Blue Bird by John Taylor & Co., Toronto, Canada, 2" x 1¼" x ¾", $500.00 – 600.00.

Taylor's Valley Violet, 2¼" x 1¾" x ¾", $75.00 – 100.00.
Courtesy of Bill & June Mason

Vantine's Kutch Sandalwood by A.A. Vantine & Co., New York, 2" x 1¼" x ¾", $150.00 – 200.00.

Vantine's Sana-Dermal by A.A. Vantine & Co., New York, 2" x 1", $500.00 – 600.00.

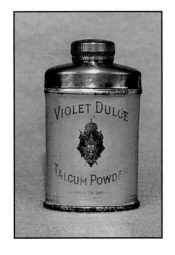

Violet Talc Powder by Colgate & Co., New York, 2" x ¾", $100.00 – 150.00.

Violet Dulce talcum powder marked Harmony of Boston, 2" x 1¼" x ¾", $50.00 – 75.00.

Violet Sec by Richard Hudnut, New York–Paris, 2" x 1¼" x ¾", $75.00 – 100.00.

Violet Talcum Brut by Hanson-Jenks Co., New York, New York, 2¼" x 1¼" x ¾", $100.00 – 150.00.

Wernet's tooth powder by Block Drug Co. Inc., Jersey City, New Jersey, 2¼" x 1¼" x ¾", $1.00 – 25.00.

White Witch by North American Dye Corp., Mount Vernon, New York, 2¼" x 1¼" x ¾", $150.00 – 200.00.

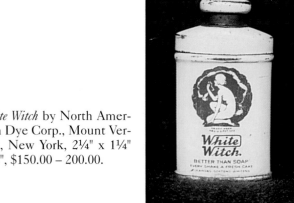

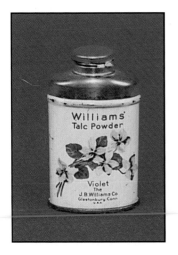

Williams' by J.B. Williams Co., Glastonbury, Connecticut, 2¼" x 1¼" x ¾", $75.00 – 100.00.

Courtesy of Grant Smith

Williams' baby talc by J.B. Williams Co., Glastonbury, Connecticut, 2¼" x 1¼" x ¾", $500.00 – 600.00.

Williams', left: La Tosca Rose; right: Carnation by J.B. Williams, Glastonbury, Connecticut, 2" x 1¼" x ¾", $75.00 – 100.00 each.

Williams' shaving powder by The J.B. Williams Co., Glastonbury, Connecticut, 2" x 1", $50.00 – 75.00.

Courtesy of Dave Garland

Williams' by J.B. Williams, Glastonbury, Connecticut, 2¼" x 1¼" x ¾", $75.00 – 100.00.

Williams' Carnation by J.B. Williams, Glastonbury, Connecticut, 2¼" x 1¼" x ¾", $75.00 – 100.00.

Williams' English Lilac by J.B. Williams Glastonbury, Connecticut, 2¼" x 1¼" x ¾", $75.00 – 100.00.

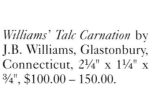

Williams' Talc Carnation by J.B. Williams, Glastonbury, Connecticut, 2¼" x 1¼" x ¾", $100.00 – 150.00.

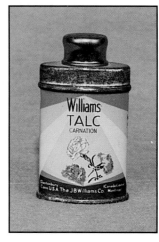

3 Merry Widows, aluminum, manufacturer unknown, ½" x 1½", $50.00 – 75.00.
Courtesy of Dave Fry

3 Merry Widows, aluminum, manufacturer unknown, ½" x 1½", $25.00 – 50.00 each.
Courtesy of Dave Fry

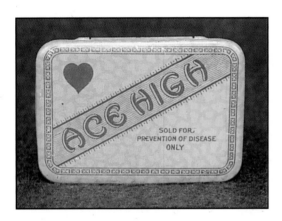

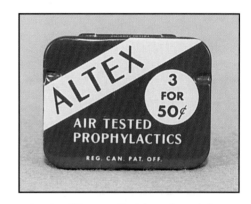

Ace High, manufacturer unknown, ¼" x 2¾ x 1¾", rare, no price available.
Courtesy of Dave Fry

Altex by Western Rubber Co. of Canada, ¼" x 2" x 1½", $500.00 – 600.00.
Courtesy of Dave Fry

Apris by Killian Manufacturing Co., Akron, Ohio, ¼" x 2¼" x 1¾", $500.00 – 600.00.
Courtesy of Dave Fry

Aristocrat by Midwest Drug Co., Minneapolis, Minnesota, ¼" x 2¼" x 1¾", $800.00 – 900.00. Note: a round variation exists.
Courtesy of Dave Fry

Blue Ribbon Brand by American Hygienic Co., Baltimore, Maryland, ¼" x 2¼" x 1¾", $500.00 – 600.00. Note: another variation exists.
Courtesy of Dave Fry

Crest by Killian Manufacturing Co., Akron, Ohio, ¼" x 2½" x 1¾", $350.00 – 400.00.
Courtesy of Dave Fry

Derbies by Killian Manufacturing Co., Akron, Ohio, ¼" x 2½" x 1¾", $450.00 – 500.00.
Courtesy of Dave Fry

Double AA, manufacturer unknown, ¼" x 2¾" x 1¾", $500.00 – 600.00.
Courtesy of Dave Fry

Drug-Pak by Nutex, Philadelphia, Pennsylvania, ¼" x 2¼" x 1¾", $500.00 – 600.00.
Courtesy of Dave Fry

Le Transparent by Youngs Rubber Corp. Inc., New York, New York, ¼" x 2¾" x 1¾", $150.00 – 200.00.
Courtesy of Dave Fry

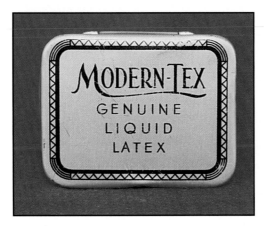

Modern-Tex by Modern Dist. Co., Detroit, Michigan, ¼" x 2¼" x 1¾", $250.00 – 300.00.
Courtesy of Dave Fry

Monarch by Reid Murdoch & Co., Chicago, ¼" x 2¼" x 1¾", rare, no price available.
Courtesy of Dave Fry

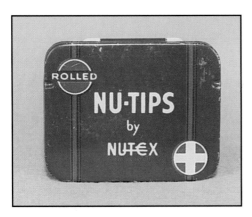

Nu-Tips by Nutex Corp. of America, Philadelphia, Pennsylvania, ¼" x 2¼" x 1¾", $300.00 – 350.00.
Courtesy of Dave Fry

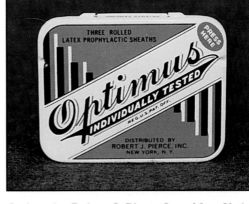

Optimus by Robert J. Pierce Inc., New York, New York, ¼" x 2" x 1¾", $300.00 – 350.00.
Courtesy of Dave Fry

Parisians, manufacturer unknown, ¼" x 2¾" x 1¾", $800.00 – 900.00.
Courtesy of Dave Fry

Peaches, manufacturer unknown, ¼" x 2¾" x 1¾", rare, no price available.
Courtesy of Dave Fry

Peacock, ½" x 1½", $100.00 – 150.00.
Courtesy of Bob & Sherri Copeland

Peacocks by Dean Rubber Manufacturing Co., Kansas City, Missouri, ¼" x 2¼" x 1¾", left: $25.00 – 50.00; right: $150.00 – 200.00.
Courtesy of Dave Fry

Ramses by Julius Schmid Inc., New York, New York, ¼" x 2¼" x 1¾", $150.00 – 200.00.
Courtesy of Bob & Sherri Copeland

Princess Pat Selectos, aluminum, manufacturer unknown, ½" x 1½", $25.00 – 50.00
Courtesy of Dave Fry

Rainbow Brand, manufacturer unknown, ½" x 1½", $1,000.00 – 1,250.00.
Courtesy of Dave Fry

Ramses by Julius Schmid Inc., New York, New York, ¼" x 2¾" x 2"; left: $150.00 – 200.00; center: $250.00 – 300.00; right: $250.00 – 300.00.
Courtesy of Dave Fry

Romeos by Aronab Products Co., San Francisco, California, ¼" x 2¼" x 1¾", $600.00 – 700.00.

Courtesy of Dave Fry

Romeos by Aronab Products Co., San Francisco, California, ¼" x 2¼" x 1¾", $450.00 – 500.00 each.

Courtesy of Dave Fry

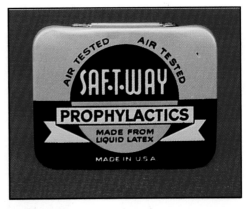

Rx 96 by Gotham Rubber Co., Chicago–New York, ¼" x 2" x 1½", $450.00 – 500.00.

Courtesy of Dave Fry

Saf.T.Way by Gotham Rubber Co., Chicago, Illinois, ¼" x 2¼" x 1¾", $350.00 – 400.00.

Courtesy of Dave Fry

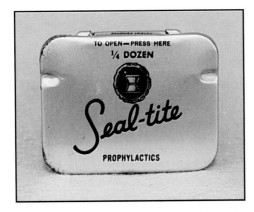

Seal-Tite by Allied Latex Corp., Newark, New Jersey, ¼" x 2¼" x 1¾", $500.00 – 600.00.

Courtesy of Dave Fry

Shadows by Young's Rubber Corp., ¼" x 2¼" x 1¾", $150.00 – 200.00.

Courtesy of Dave Fry

Sheik by Julius Schmid Inc., New York, New York, left: ¼" x 2¼" x 1¾",
$50.00 – 75.00; center: ½" x 1¾" x 1¾", $150.00 – 200.00; right: ¼" x 2¼" x
1¾", $50.00 – 75.00.
Courtesy of Dave Fry

Sheik by Julius Schmid Inc., New York, New York, ¼" x 2¼" x 1¾", $100.00 –
150.00 each.
Courtesy of Dave Fry

Silk-Skin, manufacturer unknown,
¼" x 2½" x 1¾", $400.00 – 450.00.
Courtesy of Bob & Sherri Copeland

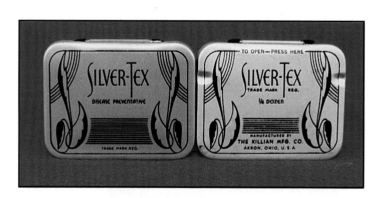

Silver-Tex by The Killian Mfg. Co., Akron, Ohio, ¼" x 2¼" x
1¾", $75.00 – 100.00.
Courtesy of Dave Fry

Silver Tex Deluxe by L.E. Shunk Latex
Products Inc., Akron, Ohio, ¼" x 2¼" x
1½", $450.00 – 500.00.
Courtesy of Dave Fry

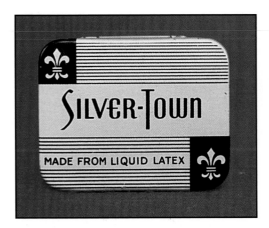

Silver-Town by Mayfair Chemical Corp.,
New York, New York, ¼" x 2¼" x 1¾",
$400.00 – 450.00.
Courtesy of Dave Fry

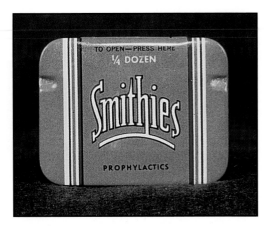

Smithies by Allied Latex Corp., Newark,
New Jersey, ¼" x 2¼" x 1½", $250.00 –
300.00.
Courtesy of Tom & Lynne Sankiewicz

Sovereigns by Excello Hygienic Products Corp.,
New York, New York, ¼" x 2¾" x 1½", $800.00 –
900.00.
Courtesy of Dave Fry

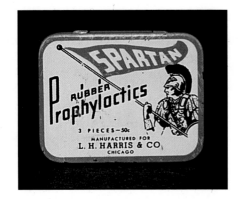

Spartan by L.H. Harris & Co., Chicago, ¼" x 2" x 1½", $800.00 – 900.00.
Courtesy of Dave Fry

Sphinx by Julius Schmid Inc., New York,
New York, ¼" x 2¼" x 1¾", $1,000.00 –
1,250.00.
Courtesy of Dave Fry

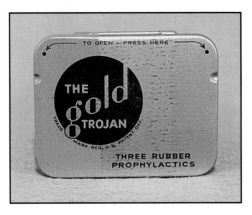

The Gold Trojan by Young's Rubber Corp.,
New York, New York and Trenton, New
Jersey, ½" x 2¼" x 1¾", $350.00 – 400.00.
Courtesy of Dave Fry

Three Cadets, manufacturer unknown,
½" x 1¾", $350.00 – 400.00.
Courtesy of Dave Fry

Three Cadets, manufacturer unknown,
½" x 1¾", $350.00 – 400.00.
Courtesy of Dave Fry

Trojans by Young's Rubber Corp., ¼" x 2¼" x 1¾", left:
$50.00 – 75.00; right: $100.00 – 150.00.
Courtesy of Dave Fry

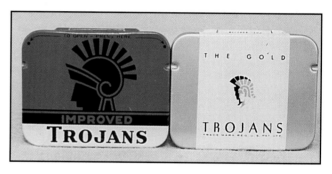

Trojans by Young's Rubber Corp., ¼" x 2¼" x 1¾", left:
$100.00 – 150.00; right: $150.00 – 200.00.
Courtesy of Dave Fry

Trojans The Transparent by Young's Rubber Corp., ¼" x 2½" x 1¾", $250.00 –
300.00.
Courtesy of Dave Fry

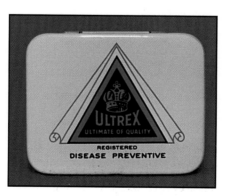

Ultrex by Ultrex Corp., Minneapolis,
Minnesota, ¼" x 2" x 1¾", $250.00 –
300.00.
Courtesy of Dave Fry

X Cello's by Killian Manufacturing
Co., Akron, Ohio, ¼" x 2" x 1¾",
$100.00 – 150.00.
Courtesy of Dave Fry

Note: Safety razor tins are priced without razors.

Anticor safety razor by Anticor Mfg. Co., New York, ¾" x 2¾" x ¾", $25.00 – 50.00.
Courtesy of Don Perkins

Allen's shaving stick by Allen Pharmacal Co., New York and Plainfield, New Jersey, marked American Stopper Co., 3½" x 1½", $25.00 – 50.00.
Courtesy of Dave Garland

Anticor safety razor by Anticor Mfg. Co., New York, marked American Stopper Co., 3¼" x 1" x 1", $50.00 – 75.00.
Courtesy of Don Perkins

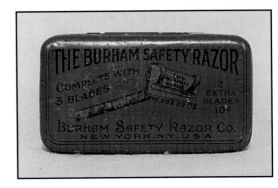

Burham safety razor by Burham Safety Razor Co., New York, New York, ¾" x 3¼" x 2", $100.00 – 150.00.
Courtesy of Don Perkins

Benedict safety razor, marked Somers Bros., Brooklyn, New York, ½" x 2¼" x 1¼", $200.00 – 250.00.
Courtesy of Don Perkins

Best British safety razor made in Australia, ¾" x 2¾" x 1¾", $100.00 – 150.00.
Courtesy of Don Perkins

Avon shaving stick by California Perfume Co. Inc., 3½" x 1½", $1.00 – 25.00.
Courtesy of Dave Garland

Burham (Latherette) shaving stick by Burham Safety Razor Co., New York City, 3½" x 1½", $25.00 – 50.00.
Courtesy of Dave Garland

Cadia shaving stick, 3½" x 1½", $25.00 – 50.00.
Courtesy of Dave Garland

Carmé shave stick, marked Omer Thomas Waterloo, 3½" x 1½", $75.00 – 100.00.
Courtesy of Don Perkins

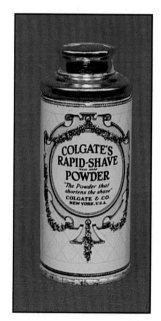

Colgate & Co. shaving sticks, left: 3½" x 1½"; center: 2½" x 1¼"; right: 1¾" x 1¼", $1.00 – 25.00 each.
Courtesy of Dave Garland

Colgate & Co's shaving sticks, marked Hasker & Marcuse, left: 3½" x 1½", $25.00 – 50.00; right: sample, 2" x 1¼", $50.00 – 75.00.
Courtesy of Dave Garland

Colgate's shave powder by Colgate & Co., New York, 4" x 1¾", $25.00 – 50.00.
Courtesy of Dave Garland

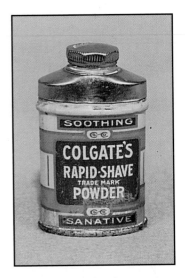

Colgate's sample shave powder, 2¼" x 1¼" x ¾", $50.00 – 75.00.

Courtesy of Dave Garland

Colgate's barbers' shaving powder, 8¼" x 4¼", left: $25.00 – 50.00; right: $1.00 – 25.00.

Courtesy of Dave Garland

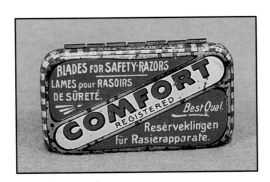

Comfort razor blade case made in Germany, ¼" x 2¼" x 1¼", $100.00 – 150.00.

Courtesy of Don Perkins

Comfort German safety razor by Ges Geschutzf, 2½" x 1½", $300.00 – 350.00.

Courtesy of Don Perkins

Comfort safety razor, 2½" x 1½", $250.00 – 300.00.

Courtesy of Dave Garland

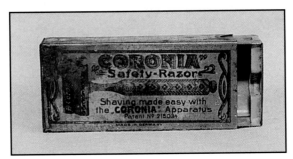

"Coronia" German safety razor with slide opening, 1¼" x 4½" x 2", $250.00 – 300.00.

Courtesy of Don Perkins

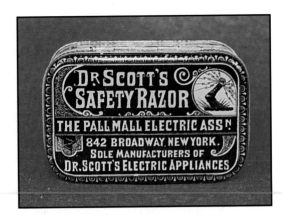

Dr. Scott's safety razor by Pall Mall Electric Assn., New York, marked Mersereau Mfg. Co., Brooklyn, N.Y., 1¼" x 3" x 2", $400.00 – 450.00.
Courtesy of Don Perkins

Cuticura shaving sticks by Potter Drug & Chemical Corp., Malden, Massachusetts, left: 3¼" x 1½"; right; 3" x 1½", $1.00 – 25.00 each.
Courtesy of Dave Garland

Dime safety razor by International Safety Razor Co., New York, 3¼" x 1", $50.00 – 75.00.
Courtesy of Don Perkins

Ever-Ready used razor blade retainer, 2" x 2" x 1", $25.00 – 50.00.
Courtesy of Bob & Sherri Copeland

Fox safety razor & strop by E. Lothar Schmitz, New York, 2¼" x 5" x 4½", $1,750.00 – 2,000.00.
Courtesy of Don Perkins

Fox safety razor by E. Lothar Schmitz, New York, 1½" x 3½" x 1½", $700.00 – 800.00.
Courtesy of Dave Garland

Gem (American) razor blade case by Gem Cutlery Co., New York, ¼" x 2¼" x ¼", $75.00 – 100.00.
Courtesy of Don Perkins

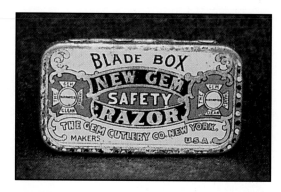

Gem (new) razor blade case by Gem Cutlery Co., New York, ¼" x 2¼" x 1¼", $75.00 – 100.00.
Courtesy of Don Perkins

Gem (American Crowned) safety razor, 1½" x 2¼" x 1¼", $150.00 – 200.00.
Courtesy of Don Perkins

Gem safety razor by Gem Cutlery Mfg. Co., New York, 2¼" x 1¼", $200.00 – 250.00.
Courtesy of Dave Garland

Gem razor blade cases by Gem Cutlery Co., New York, ¼" x 2¼" x 1¼", $75.00 – 100.00 each.
Courtesy of Dave Garland

Gem used razor blade retainer, 2" x 1¾" x 1", $25.00 – 50.00 each.

Gillette Service Set safety razor, ½" x 3½" x 2", $50.00 –
75.00.
Courtesy of Don Perkins

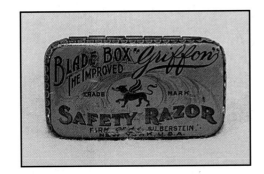

"Griffon" razor blade case by A.L. Silberstein, New York, ¼" x 2¼" x 1¼", $100.00
– 150.00.
Courtesy of Don Perkins

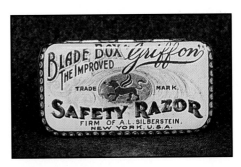

"Griffon" (white) razor blade case by
A.L. Silberstein, New York, ¼" x 2¼" x
1¼", $75.00 – 100.00.
Courtesy of Don Perkins

"Griffon" safety razors, 2¼" x 1¼", left: $200.00 –
250.00; center: $150.00 – 200.00; right: $200.00 –
250.00.
Courtesy of Don Perkins

"Griffon" safety razors, left: by A.L. Silberstein;
right: by Griffon Cutlery Co., 2½" x 1¾" x 1¼",
$150.00 – 200.00 each.
Courtesy of Don Perkins

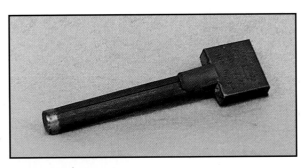

"Griffon" Corn Parer safety razor, made in Germany,
½" x 4" x 1", $25.00 – 50.00.
Courtesy of Don Perkins

Ingram's shaving cream by Ingram Co., Detroit, left: ¼" x 1¼"; right: ¼" x 1", $1.00 – 25.00 each.
Courtesy of Dave Garland

Hygienic shaving stick by Franco-American Hygienic Co., Chicago, Illinois, marked A.C. Co. 70A, 3¼" x 1½", $25.00 – 50.00.
Courtesy of Dave Garland

Hygienic after shaving powder by Franco-American Hygienic Co., Chicago, 4" x 1¾", $25.00 – 50.00.
Courtesy of Dave Garland

John Wanamaker razor blade case, ¼" x 2¼" x 1¼", $300.00 – 350.00.
Courtesy of Don Perkins

Kampfe safety razor by Kampfe Bros., New York, 1½" x 2¼" x 1¼", $75.00 – 100.00.
Courtesy of Dave Garland

Jergens shaving stick, marked Cincinnati, U.S.A., 3½" x 1½", $1.00 – 25.00.
Courtesy of Dave Garland

Kampfe safety razors by Kampfe Bros., 2¼" x 1½", $300.00 – 350.00.
Courtesy of Dave Garland

Kampfe's safety razor, marked Mersereau Mfg. Co., Brooklyn, New York, 2¼" x 1½", $250.00 – 300.00.

Courtesy of Dave Garland

Kampfe's razor blade cases by Kampfe Bros., New York City, New York, ¼" x 2¼" x 1¼", $75.00 – 100.00.

Courtesy of Dave Garland

Laurel lady's safety razor made in England, ½" x 1½" x 1", $75.00 – 100.00.

Courtesy of Don Perkins

Kampfe's Star razor strop tin by Kampfe Bros., New York, 6" x 2" x 1½", $150.00 – 200.00.

Courtesy of Dave Garland

Knight's Castle shaving soap by John Knight, London, England, 3½" x 1½", $50.00 – 75.00.

Courtesy of Dave Garland

"Laurel" (1934) safety razor made in England, 1" x 3" x 2¼", $75.00 – 100.00.

Courtesy of Don Perkins

237

Mennen used razor blade retainer, 2½" x 2½" x 1¾", $1.00 – 25.00.
Courtesy of Bob & Sherri Copeland

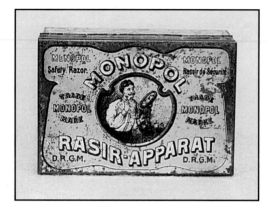

Monopol safety razor made in Germany, 1¼" x 2¾" x 1¾", $300.00 – 350.00.
Courtesy of Don Perkins

Magic cardboard shaving powder with tin top and bottom by The Shaving Powder Co., Savannah, Georgia, 4¼" x 2¼", $1.00 – 25.00.
Courtesy of Dave Garland

Raspail shaving stick, 3½" x 1½", $25.00 – 50.00.
Courtesy of Dave Garland

Monopol German safety razor by Schutz Monopol, 2¼" x 1½", $250.00 – 300.00.
Courtesy of Don Perkins

Palmolive after shaving talc by Colgate-Palmolive-Peet Co., left: 6" x 2¼" x 1¼", $1.00 – 25.00; right: sample, 3½" x 1½" x 1", $25.00 – 50.00.
Courtesy of Dave Garland

Razorette lady's safety razor by St. Clair Mfg. Co., Detroit, Michigan, ¼" x 1¾" x 1¼", $25.00 – 50.00.
Courtesy of Don Perkins

Razorette by St. Clair Mfg. Co., Detroit, Michigan, ¼" x 1¾" x 1½", $25.00 – 50.00.

Courtesy of Dave Garland

Reppenhagen razor paste by M.E. Reppenhagen Co., Highland Falls, New York, 2" x 1¼", $1.00 – 25.00.

Courtesy of Dave Garland

Rexall shave stick by United Drug Co., Toronto, Canada, 3½" x 1½", $25.00 – 50.00.

Courtesy of Dave Garland

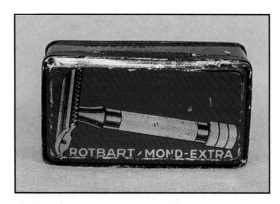

Rotbart German safety razor, 1½" x 3½" x 1¼", $75.00 – 100.00.

Courtesy of Don Perkins

Sicherheits safety razor, 2½" x 1½", $300.00 – 350.00.

Courtesy of Dave Garland

Star (yellow) razor blade case by Kampfe Bros., New York, ¼" x 2¼" x 1¼", $75.00 – 100.00.

Courtesy of Don Perkins

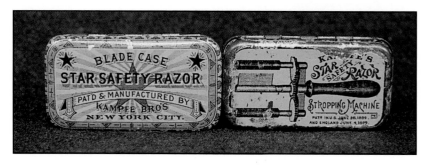

Star safety razors by Kampfe Bros., left: 2¼" x 1½", $200.00 – 250.00; right: 2¼" x 1¼", $300.00 – 350.00.
Courtesy of Don Perkins

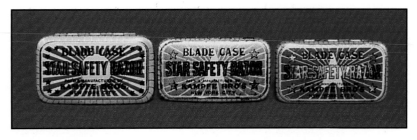

Star razor blade cases by Kampfe Bros., ¼" x 2¼" x 1¼", $50.00 – 75.00 each.
Courtesy of Dave Garland

Star razor blade cases by Kampfe Bros., ¼" x 2¼" x 1¼", $75.00 – 100.00 each.
Courtesy of Dave Garland

Star safety razors by Kampfe Bros., 2¼" x 1¼", $300.00 – 350.00 each.
Courtesy of Dave Garland

Star tin advertising signs by Kampfe Bros., no price available.
Courtesy of Don Perkins

Star (blue) safety razor by Kamfpe Bros., 2¼" x 1¼", $400.00 – 450.00.
Courtesy of Dave Garland

Star safety razors by Kampfe Bros., Brooklyn, New York, 1¾" x 2¼" x 1¼", $75.00 – 100.00 each.

Star French safety razor, 1¾" x 2¼" x 1½", $250.00 – 300.00.
Courtesy of Don Perkins

Star safety razors by Kampfe Bros., 2¼" x 1½", $250.00 – 300.00 each.
Courtesy of Dave Garland

Star safety razors by Kampfe Bros., 2½" x 1½", $350.00 – 400.00 each.
Courtesy of Dave Garland

Star safety razors by Kampfe Bros., Brooklyn, New York, 1¾" x 2¼" x 1¼", $75.00 – 100.00 each.
Courtesy of Don Perkins

Star (obverse & reverse) French razor blade cases by Kampfe Bros., ¼" x 1¾" x 1¼", $50.00 – 75.00 each.
Courtesy of Don Perkins

Torrey sharpening dressing by J.R. Torrey & Co., Worcester, Massachusetts, ¾" x 1¾" x 1", $25.00 – 50.00.
Courtesy of Don Perkins

Wilbert razor blade case, ¼" x 2¼" x 1¼", $250.00 – 300.00.
Courtesy of Don Perkins

Torrey's oil edge dressing by J.R. Torrey & Co., Worcester, Massachusetts, 2" x 1¼", $1.00 – 25.00.
Courtesy of Dave Garland

Torrey's Comet safety razor by J.R. Torrey Razor Co., Worcester, Massachusetts, marked Somers Bros., 1" x 3¼" x 2¼", $400.00 – 450.00.
Courtesy of Don Perkins

Wilbert safety razor by Sears, Roebuck & Co., Chicago, Illinois, marked American Can Co., $350.00 – 400.00.
Courtesy of Don Perkins

Wilbert safety razor by Wilbert Cutlery Co., Chicago, Illinois, 1½" x 2½" x 1¾", $350.00 – 400.00.
Courtesy of Don Perkins

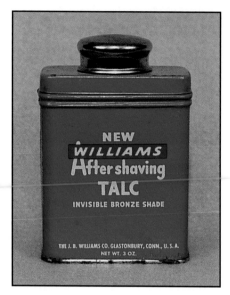

Williams after shaving talc by J.B. Williams Co., Glastonbury, Connecticut, 3¾" x 2½" x 1½", $1.00 – 25.00.
Courtesy of Don Perkins

Williams shave stick by J.B. Williams Co., Glastonbury, Connecticut, 2¾" x 1½", $1.00 – 25.00.
Courtesy of Don Perkins

Williams shaving powder by J.B. Williams Co., Glasonbury, Connecticut, 4" x 1¾", $25.00 – 50.00.
Courtesy of Dave Garland

Williams sample shaving powder by J.B. Williams Co., Glasonbury, Connecticut, 2" x 1", $50.00 – 75.00.
Courtesy of Dave Garland

Witch Hazel shaving stick by The Larkin Soap Mfg. Co., Buffalo, New York, 3½" x 1½", $25.00 – 50.00.
Courtesy of Dave Garland

Yankee razor blade case by Reichard & Scheurd, ¼" x 2¼" x 1¼", $100.00 – 150.00.
Courtesy of Dave Garland

Yankee safety razor by Reichard & Scheuber Mfg. Co., New York, 1½" x 2½" x 1¾", $350.00 – 400.00.
Courtesy of Don Perkins

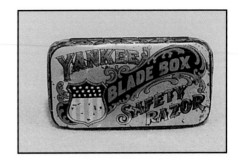

Yankee razor blade case by Reichard & Scheuber Mfg. Co., New York, ¼" x 2¼" x 1¼", $75.00 – 100.00.
Courtesy of Dave Garland

Yankee safety razor by Reichard & Scheuber Mfg. Co., New York, 2½" x 1¾" x 1¼", $350.00 – 400.00.
Courtesy of Don Perkins

Yankee safety razor by Reichard & Scheuber Mfg. Co., New York, 2¼" x 1¼", $450.00 – 500.00.
Courtesy of Don Perkins

SPICE TINS

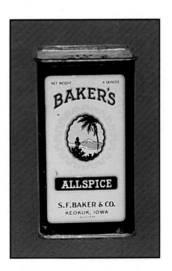

Amocat by West Coast Grocery Co., Tacoma, Washington, 3¼" x 2¼" x 1¼", $100.00 – 150.00.
Courtesy of Alex & Marilyn Znaiden

Baker's by S.F. Baker & Co., Keokuk, Iowa, 4" x 2¼" x 1½", $25.00 – 50.00.
Courtesy of Bob & Sherri Copeland

Bee Brand by McCormick & Co., Baltimore, Maryland, 3½" x 2¼" x 1", $1.00 – 25.00.

Busy Biddy by Davies Strauss-Stauffer Co., left: 3¾" x 2"; right: 3¾" x 2¼" x 1¼", $150.00 – 200.00 each.

Courtesy of Alex & Marilyn Znaiden

College Town by Lef. Kowits Ekias Co., New Brunswick, New Jersey, 3¾" x 2¼" x 1", $150.00 – 200.00.

Courtesy of Alex & Marilyn Znaiden

Daisee by The Herrman Co., Paterson, New Jersey, 3" x 2¼" x 1¼", $100.00 – 150.00.

Courtesy of Alex & Marilyn Znaiden

Dauntless by Hulman & Co., Terre Haute, Indiana, 3½" x 2¼" x 2¼", $100.00 – 150.00.

Courtesy of Mike & Sharon Hunt

Dove Brand by Frank Tea & Spice Co., Cincinnati, Ohio, left: 3¾" x 2", $75.00 – 100.00; right: 3¼" x 2½" x 1¼", $25.00 – 50.00.

Courtesy of Bob & Sherri Copeland

Dove Brand by Frank Tea & Spice Co., Cincinnati, Ohio, 3¾" x 1¼", $25.00 – 50.00.

Courtesy of Tom & Mary Lou Slike

Eagle Brand by Bacon, Stickney & Co. Inc., 3" x 2¼" x 1¼", $75.00 – 100.00.

Courtesy of Alex & Marilyn Znaiden

Elk Lick paper label by Steele & Meridith Co., Springfield, Ohio, 3" x 2½" x 1¼", $25.00 – 50.00.

Courtesy of Bob & Sherri Copeland

Fairfax Hall by Wholesale Grocers Exchange Inc., Richmond, Virginia, 3" x 2¼" x 1¼", $100.00 – 150.00.

Courtesy of Alex & Marilyn Znaiden

Farmers Pride by Hulman & Co., Terre Haute, Indiana, left to right: #1, cardboard with tin top and bottom, 4¾" x 3", $100.00 – 150.00; #2, cardboard with tin top and bottom, 4¼" x 2½", $75.00 – 100.00; #3, 3½" x 2¼" x 1¼", $100.00 – 150.00; #4, cardboard with tin top and bottom, 2½" x 1½", $75.00 – 100.00.

Courtesy of Mike & Sharon Hunt

Fiesta by Field & Start Inc., Utica, New York, 3½" x 2¼" x 1¼", $50.00 – 75.00.

French's Chileo by R.T. French Co., Rochester, New York, 3" x 1", $1.00 – 25.00.

Courtesy of Tom & Mary Lou Slike

Gilt Edge by Moshier Bros. Spice Mills & Chemical Laboratories, Utica, New York, marked S.A. Isley, 11" x 7½" x 7½", $700.00 – 800.00.

Courtesy of Alex & Marilyn Znaiden

Gold Chord by Guyer & Calkins Co., Freeport, Illinois, 3½" x 2¼" x 1¼", $75.00 – 100.00.

Courtesy of Alex & Marilyn Znaiden

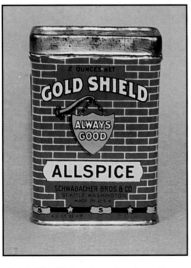

Gold Shield by Scwabacher Bros., & Co., Seattle, Washington, 3¼" x 2¼" x 1¼", $25.00 – 50.00.

Great Bull by Bull Markets Inc., Kingston–Newburgh–Pough-keepsie, New York, 4" x 2¼" x 1", $50.00 – 75.00.

Courtesy of Alex & Marilyn Znaiden

Hale's Leader by Hale Halsell Co. of Oklahoma, 4" x 2", $100.00 – 150.00.

Courtesy of Alex & Marilyn Znaiden

Heekin's by The Heekin Spice Co., Cincinnati, Ohio, 3" x 1¾" x 1¼", $50.00 – 75.00.

Courtesy of Bob & Sherri Copeland

Highland by D.E. Brooks & Co., Newburgh, New York, 3" x 2¼" x 1¼", $75.00 – 100.00.

Courtesy of Alex & Marilyn Znaiden

Honeymoon by D.J. Moore Grocer Co., Sioux City, Iowa, 3" x 2¼" x 1¼", $75.00 – 100.00.

Courtesy of Alex & Marilyn Znaiden

Hotel Belvedere by H.L. Caplan & Co., Baltimore, Maryland, 3½" x 2¼" x 1¼", $150.00 – 200.00.

Courtesy of Alex & Marilyn Znaiden

Ideal Brand by Wilkinson Gaddis & Co., Newark, New Jersey, 3" x 2½" x 1¼", $50.00 – 75.00.

Courtesy of Alex & Marilyn Znaiden

Iris by Haas Baruch & Co., Los Angeles, California, 3¼" x 2¼" x 1¼", $100.00 – 150.00.

Courtesy of Richard & Ann Lehmann

Jackson Park by Frank C. Weber & Co., Chicago, Illinois, 3" x 2¼" x 1¼", $150.00 – 200.00.

Courtesy of Alex & Marilyn Znaiden

Kota'nyi's Hungarian paprika, 3" x 1", $1.00 – 25.00.

Courtesy of Tom & Mary Lou Slike

Lange's by E.A. Lange Medical Co., West Depere, Wisconsin, 3¾" x 2" x 1½", $25.00 – 50.00.

Courtesy of Richard & Ann Lehmann

Maison Royal by Food Trading Corp. of America, New York, New York, 2" x 2½" x 1¼", $1.00 – 25.00.

Marquis by H.G. Smith Ltd., 3½" x 2¼" x ¾", $50.00 – 75.00.

Courtesy of Richard & Ann Lehmann

McConnon's cardboard with tin top and bottom, 4" x 2¼" x 1½", $25.00 – 50.00.

Meteor by Lebanon Wholesale Grocers Co., Lebanon, Missouri, 3¼" x 2¼" x 1¼", $100.00 – 150.00.

Courtesy of Alex & Marilyn Znaiden

Monarch by Consolidated Grocers Corp., Chicago, Illinois, marked Canco, 4½" x 2½" x 1½", $25.00 – 50.00.

Courtesy of Mike & Sharon Hunt

Mother's Pride by Scientific Foods Products Co., 4¼" x 2¼" x 1¼", $50.00 – 75.00.

Courtesy of Mike & Sharon Hunt

National cardboard with tin top and bottom by Geo. Rasmussen Co., 3¾" x 1½", $25.00 – 50.00.

Courtesy of Tom & Mary Lou Slike

Over-Sea by Chitty & Co., Jacksonville, Florida, 2¾" x 2¼" x 1¼", $150.00 – 200.00.

Courtesy of Alex & Marilyn Znaiden

Penn-Harris by Evans-Burtnett Co., Harrisburg, Pennsylvania, 4" x 2", $50.00 – 75.00.

Courtesy of Richard & Ann Lehmann

Pioneer paper label by
Symons Bros. & Co., 3¼" x
2½" x 1¼", $1.00 – 25.00.
Courtesy of Bob & Sherri Copeland

Pocasset by Allen, Slade & Co.
Inc., Fall River, Massachusetts,
4" x 2¼" x 1", $150.00 – 200.00.
Courtesy of Alex & Marilyn Znaiden

Premier by Francis H. Leggett &
Co., New York, New York, 4¼" x
2¼" x 1", $25.00 – 50.00.
Courtesy of Richard & Ann Lehmann

Pumpkin Pie paper label by The
Feilbach Co., Toledo, Ohio, 2½"
x 2¼" x 1¼", $1.00 – 25.00.

Pumpkin Pie by Frank Tea & Spice
Co., Cincinnati, Ohio, 2" x 2½" x
1¼", $1.00 – 25.00.
Courtesy of Tom & Lynne Sankiewicz

Re-Joyce by Joyce-Laughlin Co.,
Peoria, Illinois, 3" x 2¼" x 1¼",
$200.00 – 250.00.
Courtesy of Alex & Marilyn Znaiden

Rose Bud by Bush Grocery Co., Syracuse, New York, 3¼" x 2¼" x 1¼", $75.00 – 100.00.

Courtesy of Alex & Marilyn Znaiden

Roundup by The Roundup Grocery Co., Spokane, Washington, 3¾" x 2¼" x 1¼", $150.00 – 200.00.

Courtesy of Alex & Marilyn Znaiden

S-Bro-Co by Schneider Bros. & Co., Mt. Carmel & Bloomsburg, Pennsylvania, 3" x 2¼" x 1¼", $75.00 – 100.00.

Courtesy of Alex & Marilyn Znaiden

Serv-us by Serv-us Grocery Products Corp., New York, New York, 3¼" x 2¼" x 1¼", $1.00 – 25.00.

Courtesy of Tom & Mary Lou Slike

Snow-Ball by G.E. Howard & Co., Newburgh, New York, 3" x 2¼" x 1¼", $50.00 – 75.00.

Courtesy of Alex & Marilyn Znaiden

Sunbonnet by Indianapolis Fancy Grocery Co., 3½" x 2¼" x 1¼", $100.00 – 150.00.

Courtesy of Alex & Marilyn Znaiden

Sweet Life by Sweet Life Food Corp., Brooklyn, New York, left: 3½" x 2¼" x 1¼"; right; 3" x 2¼" x 1¼", $75.00 – 100.00 each.

Courtesy of Alex & Marilyn Znaiden

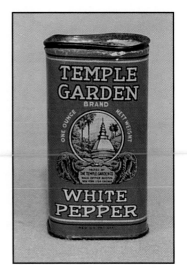

Temple Garden cardboard with tin top and bottom by The Temple Garden Co., Boston–New York–Chicago, 3¼" x 1¾" x 1¼", $25.00 – 50.00.

Courtesy of Bob & Sherri Copeland

Top Knot by The A. Sherman Mfg., Co., Stamford, Connecticut, 3¼" x 2¼" x 1¼", $50.00 – 75.00.

Courtesy of Richard & Ann Lehmann

Turkey Red by Merchants Wholesale Grocery Co., Chicago, Illinois, 3¾" x 2¼" x 1¼", $300.00 – 350.00.

Courtesy of Alex & Marilyn Znaiden

Ward by Weidman Ward & Co., Albany, New York, 3¾" x 2¼" x 1¼", $50.00 – 75.00.

Courtesy of Alex & Marilyn Znaiden

Watkins by J.R. Watkins Medical Co., Winona, Minnesota, 3¼" x 2" x 1¼", $25.00 – 50.00.

Courtesy of Bob & Sherri Copeland

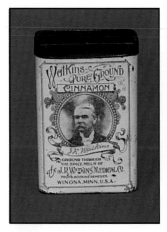

Watkins by J.R. Watkins Medical Co., Winona, Minnesota, 3¼" x 2¼" x 1½", $25.00 – 50.00.

White Goose by Hadley-Taylor Co., Greensboro, North Carolina, 3¼" x 2¼" x 1½", $50.00 – 75.00.

Courtesy of Alex & Marilyn Znaiden

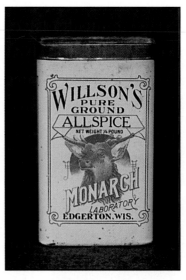

Willson's Monarch, Edgerton, Wisconsin, 3¾" x 2¼" x 1½", $75.00 – 100.00.

Courtesy of Alex & Marilyn Znaiden

Woolson's by Woolson Spice Co., Toledo, Ohio, 3¼" x 1½", $25.00 – 50.00.

Courtesy of Bob & Sherri Copeland

TYPEWRITTER RIBBON TINS

A by Allen Paper Co., Chicago, Illinois, ¾" x 2½", $1.00 – 25.00.

Courtesy of Tom & Mary Lou Slike

A & W by Ault & Wiborg Co., Cincinnati, Ohio, ¾" x 2½" x 2½", $1.00 – 25.00.

Courtesy of Tom & Mary Lou Slike

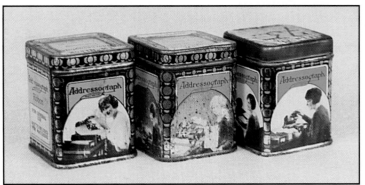

Addressograph by Addressograph Co., Chicago, Illinois, 2" x 1¾" x 1¾", $25.00 – 50.00.

Courtesy of Tom & Mary Lou Slike

Advocate, manufacturer unknown, ¾"
x 2½", $25.00 – 50.00.
Courtesy of Tom & Mary Lou Slike

Allied Flagship by Allied Carbon & Ribbon Mfg. Corp., New York, New York,
¾" x 2½" x 2½", $1.00 – 25.00.

American by H.M. Storms Co., New York, left: ¾" x 2½" x
2½", $100.00 – 150.00; right: ¾" x 2¼", $150.00 – 200.00.
Courtesy of Hoby & Nancy Van Deusen

American Beauty by Nelson Eismann
Co., Chicago, Illinois, ¾" x 2½" x
2½", $25.00 – 50.00.
Courtesy of Tom & Mary Lou Slike

Amity by Keystone Carbon Paper
Mfg. Co., Franklin, Pennsylvania,
¾" x 2¼" x 2¼", $25.00 – 50.00.
Courtesy of Tom & Mary Lou Slike

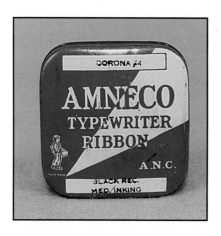

Amneco by American News Co., ¾" x
2½" x 2½", $50.00 – 75.00.
Courtesy of Tom & Mary Lou Slike

Arco by American Ribbon & Carbon Co., Rochester, New York, ¾" x 2½" x 2½", $1.00 – 25.00.
Courtesy of Tom & Mary Lou Slike

Autocrat by Goldsmith Bros., New York, ¾" x 2½", $50.00 – 75.00.
Courtesy of Hoby & Nancy Van Deusen

Bank Note by S.S. Stafford Inc., New York, New York, ¾" x 2½", $1.00 – 25.00.

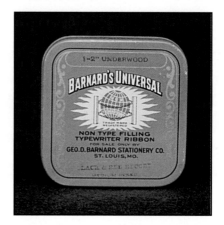

Barnard's Universal by Geo. D. Barnard Stationery Co., St. Louis, Missouri, ¾" x 2½" x 2½", $50.00 – 75.00.
Courtesy of Tom & Mary Lou Slike

Battleship by F.S. Webster Co., Boston, Massachusetts, ¾" x 2½" x 2½", $1.00 – 25.00.

Battleship Brand by F.S. Webster Co. Inc., Boston, Massachusetts, ¾" x 2½" x 2½", $25.00 – 50.00.
Courtesy of Tom & Mary Lou Slike

Beaver by M.B. Cook Co., Chicago, Illinois, ¾" x 2½" x 2½", $25.00 – 50.00 each.
Courtesy of Tom & Mary Lou Slike

Beaver Old Reliable by M.B. Cook Co., Chicago, Illinois, ¾" x 2½" x 2½", $25.00 – 50.00.
Courtesy of Tom & Mary Lou Slike

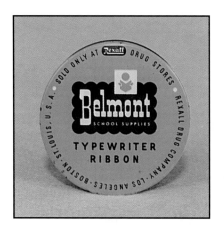

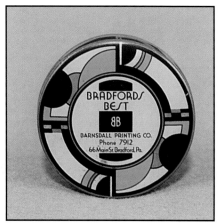

Belmont by Rexall Drug Co., ¾" x 2½", $1.00 – 25.00.
Courtesy of Tom & Mary Lou Slike

Bradfords Best deco stock tin marked Barnsdale Printing Co., Bradford, PA. ¾" x 2½", $50.00 – 75.00.
Courtesy of Tom & Mary Lou Slike

Buck-Skin by F.W. Neely Co., Chicago, Illinois, ¾" x 2½" x 2½", $100.00 – 150.00.

Bucki Supreme by Buckeye Ribbon & Carbon Co., Cleveland, Ohio, ¾" x 2½", $1.00 – 25.00.
Courtesy of Tom & Mary Lou Slike

Bucki Supreme cardboard by Buckeye Ribbon & Carbon Co., Cleveland, Ohio, 1" x 2¼", $1.00 – 25.00.
Courtesy of Tom & Mary Lou Slike

Bucki Supreme by Buckeye Ribbon & Carbon Co., Cleveland, Ohio, ¾" x 2½" x 2½", $1.00 – 25.00.
Courtesy of Tom & Mary Lou Slike

Bundy by Bundy Typewriter Co., ¾" x 2¼", $50.00 – 75.00.

Cadillac Brand by Cadillac Ribbon & Carbon Co., Detroit, Michigan, ¾" x 2½" x 2½", $25.00 – 50.00.
Courtesy of Tom & Mary Lou Slike

Cameo by H.M. Storms Co., Brooklyn, New York, ¾" x 2½", $25.00 – 50.00.
Courtesy of Tom & Mary Lou Slike

Cameo marked Remington, ¾" x 2½", $25.00 – 50.00.
Courtesy of Bob & Sherri Copeland

Cardinal by Miller-Bryant-Pierce, Aurora, Illinois, ¾" x 2½", $25.00 – 5 0.00.

Carter's by Carter's Ink Co., Boston, Massachusetts, ¾" x 2½", $1.00 – 25.00 each.
Courtesy of Tom & Mary Lou Slike

Carter's Cavalier by Carter's Ink Co., Boston, Massachusetts, ¾" x 2½", $1.00 – 25.00.

Carter's Cyclamin by Carter's Ink Co., Boston, Massachusetts, ¾" x 2½", $1.00 – 25.00.

Carter's Buccaneer by Carter's Ink Co., Boston, Massachusetts, ¾" x 2½", $25.00 – 50.00.

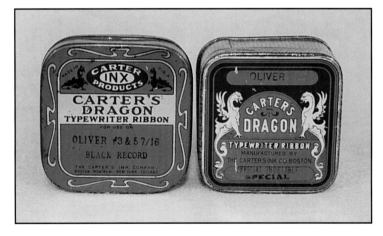

Carter's Director by Carter's Ink Co., Boston, Massachusetts, ¾" x 2¼" x 2½", $1.00 – 25.00.

Carter's Dragon by Carter's Ink Co., Boston, Massachusetts, left: ¾" x 2¼" x 2¼", $25.00 – 50.00; right: 1" x 2¼" x 2¼", $50.00 – 75.00.

Carter's "Five O'Clock" by Carter's Ink Co., ¾" x 2½", $1.00 – 25.00.

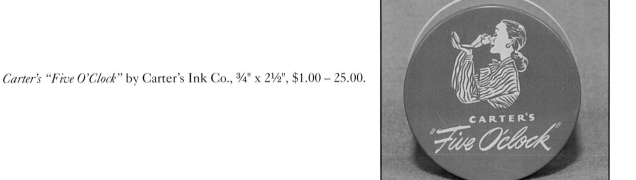

Carter's Guardian by Carter's Ink Co., Boston, Massachusetts, ¾" x 2½", left & center: $25.00 – 50.00 each; right: $50.00 – 75.00.
Courtesy of Tom & Mary Lou Slike

Carter's Golden Arrow by Carter's Ink Co., Boston, Massachusetts, ¾" x 2½", $1.00 – 25.00.
Courtesy of Tom & Mary Lou Slike

Carter's Ideal by Carter's Ink Co., Boston, Massachusetts, ¾" x 2½", $1.00 – 25.00.
Courtesy of Tom & Mary Lou Slike

Carter's Ideal Orchids by Carter's Ink Co., Boston, Massachusetts, ¾" x 2½", $1.00 – 25.00.
Courtesy of Tom & Mary Lou Slike

Carter's Midnight by Carter's Ink Co., Boston, Massachusetts, ¾" x 2½", $25.00 – 50.00.
Courtesy of Tom & Mary Lou Slike

Carter's Midnight by Carter's Ink Co., Boston, Massachusetts, ¾" x 2½", $1.00 – 25.00.

Carter's Midnight Nylon by Carter's Ink Co., ¾" x 2½", $1.00 – 25.00.

Carter's Nylon by Carter's Ink Co., Boston, Massachusetts, ¾" x 2½", $50.00 – 75.00.
Courtesy of Tom & Mary Lou Slike

Carter's Silk extra length by Carter's Ink Co., Boston, Massachusetts, ¾" x 2½", $1.00 – 25.00.
Courtesy of Tom & Mary Lou Slike

Carter's Silver Craft by Carter's Ink Co., Boston, Massachusetts, ¾" x 2½", $1.00 – 25.00.
Courtesy of Tom & Mary Lou Slike

Carter's Valiant by Carter's Ink Co., Boston, Massachusetts, ¾" x 2½", $1.00 – 25.00.

Chancellor stock tin, manufacturer unknown, ¾" x 2½", $100.00 – 150.00.
Courtesy of Hoby Van Deusen

Chieftain by A. Carlisle Co., Reno, Nevada, ¾" x 2½", $200.00 – 250.00.
Courtesy of Hoby & Nancy Van Deusen

Codo Butterfly by Codo Mfg. Corp., ¾" x 2½", $1.00 – 25.00.

Codo Kleen-Rite by Codo Mfg. Corp., Chicago, Illinois, ¾" x 2½", $1.00 – 25.00.
Courtesy of Tom & Mary Lou Slike

Codo Stenocopy by Codo Mfg. Corp., ¾" x 2½" x 2½", $25.00 – 50.00.
Courtesy of Tom & Mary Lou Slike

Codo Super-Fiber by Codo Mfg. Corp., Coraopolis, Pennsylvania, ¾" x 2½", $1.00 – 25.00.
Courtesy of Tom & Mary Lou Slike

Columbia by Columbia Ribbon & Carbon Mfg. Co., Glen Cove, New York, ¾" x 2½", $1.00 – 25.00.
Courtesy of Tom & Mary Lou Slike

Columbia Brand by The Columbia Carbon Co., Dayton, Ohio, ¾" x 2½" x 2½", $1.00 – 25.00.

Columbia Dragon by Columbia Ribbon & Carbon Mfg. Co., Glen Cove, New York, ¾" x 2½", $25.00 – 50.00.
Courtesy of Tom & Mary Lou Slike

Columbia Twins (blue) by Columbia Carbon Co., Dayton, Ohio, ¾" x 2½", $1.00 – 25.00.
Courtesy of Tom & Mary Lou Slike

Columbia Twins (orange) by The Columbia Carbon Co., Dayton, Ohio, ¾" x 2½", $1.00 – 25.00.

Copper Chief by True Mark, ¾" x 2½", $50.00 – 75.00.
Courtesy of Tom & Mary Lou Slike

Crescendo by Peerless Imperial Co. Inc., ¾" x 2½", $75.00 – 100.00.
Courtesy of Hoby & Nancy Van Deusen

Crown by Crown Ribbon & Carbon Mfg. Co., Rochester, New York, ¾" x 2½", $1.00 – 25.00.
Courtesy of Tom & Mary Lou Slike

Crown Brand by Crown Ribbon & Carbon Mfg. Co., Rochester, New York, ¾" x 2" x 2", $1.00 – 25.00.
Courtesy of Tom & Mary Lou Slike

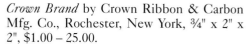

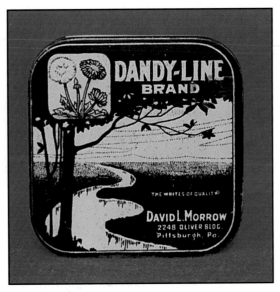

Dandy-Line by David L. Morrow, Pittsburgh, Pennsylvania, ¾" x 2½" x 2½", $150.00 – 200.00.
Courtesy of Hoby & Nancy Van Deusen

Davis, manufacturer unknown, ¾" x 2½", $50.00 – 75.00.
Courtesy of Hoby & Nancy Van Deusen

Degan by Joseph P. Degan Publishing Co., Chicago, Illinois, ¾" x 2½" x 2½", $75.00 – 100.00.
Courtesy of Tom & Mary Lou Slike

Derwood by Underwood-Elliott-Fisher Co., ¾" x 2¼", $1.00 – 25.00.
Courtesy of Tom & Mary Lou Slike

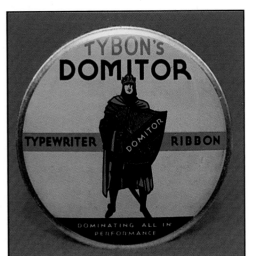

Domitor (Tybon's) by Tybon Corp., Philadelphia, Pennsylvania, ¾" x 2½", $100.00 – 150.00.
Courtesy of Hoby & Nancy Van Deusen

Du-Ra-Bul by Republic-Dodge
Mfg. Co., Brooklyn, New York, ¾" x
2½" x 2½", $25.00 – 50.00.
Courtesy of Tom & Mary Lou Slike

Eagle Brand by Pfeiffer & Brendle, Zurich &
Basel, Switzerland, ¾" x 2¼" x 2¼", $25.00 –
50.00.
Courtesy of Hoby & Nancy Van Deusen

Educational Buyers Association by Miller-Bryant-Pierce, Aurora,
Illinois, ¾" x 2½", $1.00 – 25.00 each.
Courtesy of Tom & Mary Lou Slike

Elk by Miller-Bryant-Pierce, Aurora, Illinois, ¾" x 2½", $1.00 – 25.00.

Empress, manufacturer unknown,
¾" x 2½", $1.00 – 25.00.
Courtesy of Tom & Mary Lou Slike

Ellis by W.L. Ellis Inc., Newark, New Jersey, ¾" x 2½" x 2½", $25.00 – 50.00.
Courtesy of Hoby & Nancy Van Deusen

Empress Nylon, manufacturer unknown, ¾" x 2½", $75.00 – 100.00.

"Everlasting" by American Writing Machine Co., New York, New York, ¾" x 2½" x 2½", $1.00 – 25.00.
Courtesy of Tom & Mary Lou Slike

Everlasting by American Writing Machine Co., New York, New York, ¾" x 2½", $50.00 – 75.00.
Courtesy of Tom & Mary Lou Slike

Fine Service, manufacturer unknown, ¾" x 2½" x 2½", $1.00 – 25.00.
Courtesy of Tom & Mary Lou Slike

Flint Brand by KeeLox Mfg. Co. Inc., Rochester, New York, ¾" x 2½" x 2½", $1.00 – 25.00.
Courtesy of Tom & Mary Lou Slike

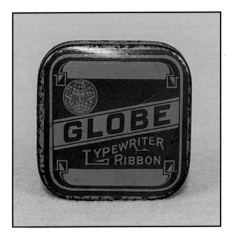

Gibraltar by L.C. Smith, ¾" x 2½", $50.00 – 75.00.
Courtesy of Tom & Mary Lou Slike

Globe by Crown Ribbon & Carbon Co., Rochester, New York, ¾" x 2¼" x 2¼", $25.00 – 50.00.
Courtesy of Tom & Mary Lou Slike

Gold Seal by A.P. Little Inc., Rochester, New York, ¾" x 2½", $1.00 – 25.00.
Courtesy of Tom & Mary Lou Slike

Golden Gopher stock tin, manufacturer unknown, ¾" x 2½", $100.00 – 150.00.
Courtesy of Hoby & Nancy Van Deusen

Government by Mittag & Volger, Park Ridge, New Jersey, ¾" x 2½", $25.00 – 50.00.

H-C-S Brand by Harvard Cooperative Society, Cambridge, Massachusetts, ¾" x 2½" x 2½", $25.00 – 50.00.
Courtesy of Tom & Mary Lou Slike

Hazel Brand by Greylock Ribbon & Carbon Co., New York, New York, ¾" x 2½" x 2½", $25.00 – 50.00.
Courtesy of Tom & Mary Lou Slike

Herald Square by F.W. Woolworth Co., ¾" x 2½" x 2½", $1.00 – 25.00.
Courtesy of Tom & Mary Lou Slike

Hi-Hat by Phillips Process Co. Inc., Rochester, New York, ¾" x 2½", $75.00 – 100.00.
Courtesy of Hoby & Nancy Van Deusen

Highlander, manufacturer unknown, ¾" x 2½", $1.00 – 25.00.
Courtesy of Tom & Mary Lou Slike

Hollyhock by L.W. Holley & Sons Co., Des Moines, Iowa, ¾" x 2½" x 2½", $75.00 – 100.00.
Courtesy of Hoby & Nancy Van Deusen

IBM by International Business Machines, Rochester, New York, ¾" x 2½", $25.00 – 50.00.
Courtesy of Tom & Mary Lou Slike

Indeliba by A.P. Little Inc., Rochester, New York, ¾" x 2½", $1.00 – 25.00.
Courtesy of Tom & Mary Lou Slike

KeeLox Dri Kleen by The KeeLox Mfg. Corp., Rochester, New York, ¾" x 2½", $1.00 – 25.00.
Courtesy of Tom & Mary Lou Slike

KeeLox Oriental by KeeLox Mfg. Co., Rochester, New York, ¾" x 2½", $25.00 – 50.00.
Courtesy of Tom & Mary Lou Slike

KeeLox Wonder Brand by KeeLox Mfg. Corp., Rochester, New York, ¾" x 2½", $1.00 – 25.00.
Courtesy of Tom & Mary Lou Slike

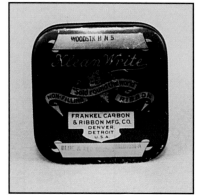

Key Note stock tin, manufacturer unknown, ¾" x 2½", $50.00 – 75.00.
Courtesy of Hoby & Nancy Van Deusen

Klean-Write by Frankel Carbon & Ribbon Mfg. Co., Denver and Detroit, Michigan, ¾" x 2½" x 2½", $25.00 – 50.00.
Courtesy of Tom & Mary Lou Slike

Klean-Write by Frankel Carbon & Ribbon Mfg. Co., Denver and Detroit, ¾" x 2½", $1.00 – 25.00.
Courtesy of Tom & Mary Lou Slike

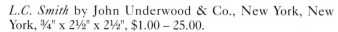

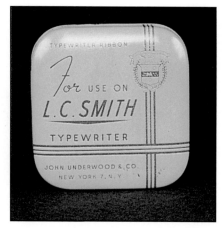

L.C. Smith by John Underwood & Co., New York, New York, ¾" x 2½" x 2½", $1.00 – 25.00.
Courtesy of Tom & Mary Lou Slike

L.C. Smith (horses) by L.C. Smith & Bros., ¾" x 2¼" x 2¼", $50.00 – 75.00.

Lily by Nelson Eismann Co., Chicago and New York, ¾" x 2½", $75.00 – 100.00.
Courtesy of Hoby & Nancy Van Deusen

Mainline by Burroughs Corp., Detroit, Michigan, ¾" x 2½", $1.00 – 25.00.
Courtesy of Tom & Mary Lou Slike

McGregor by McGregor Inc., Washington, D.C., ¾" x 2½", $1.00 – 25.00.

Mercury stock tins, left: ¾" x 2½"; right: ¾" x 2¼", $50.00 – 75.00 each.
Courtesy of Hoby & Nancy Van Deusen

Miller Line by Miller-Bryant-Pierce,
Aurora, Illinois, 2¼" x 1¾" x 1¾",
$25.00 – 50.00.
Courtesy of Tom & Mary Lou Slike

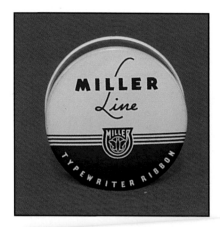

Miller Line by Miller-Bryant-Pierce,
Aurora, Illinois, ¾" x 2½", $1.00 – 25.00.
Courtesy of Tom & Mary Lou Slike

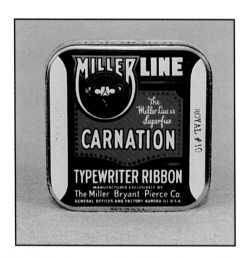

Miller Line Carnation by Miller-Bryant-Pierce
Co., Aurora, Illinois, ¾" x 2½" x 2½", $1.00 –
25.00.
Courtesy of Tom & Mary Lou Slike

National by National Cash Register
Co., Dayton, Ohio, ¾" x 2½", $25.00
– 50.00.
Courtesy of Tom & Mary Lou Slike

No Name Archer-Gazelle marked True-Mark, ¾"
x 2½", $25.00 – 50.00.

No Name Ducks stock tin, ¾" x 2½", $25.00 – 50.00.
Courtesy of Hoby & Nancy Van Deusen

No Name Gazelle stock tin, ¾" x 2½", $1.00 – 25.00.

No Name Pendant stock tins, left: jade; right: ruby; ¾" x 2½", $1.00 – 25.00 each.
Courtesy of Tom & Mary Lou Slike

No Name Race Horses stock tin, ¾" x 2½", $75.00 – 100.00.
Courtesy of Hoby & Nancy Van Deusen

No Name Soldier stock tin, ¾" x 2½" x 2½", $1.00 – 25.00.
Courtesy of Tom & Mary Lou Slike

No Name Spinning Wheel, ¾" x 2½", $25.00 – 50.00.
Courtesy of Tom & Mary Lou Slike

Old Dutch by Neidich Process Co., ¾" x 2¼", $25.00 – 50.00.
Courtesy of Tom & Mary Lou Slike

Old Dutch Line by Old Dutch Carbon &
Ribbon Co., ¾" x 2½", $50.00 – 75.00.
Courtesy of Tom & Mary Lou Slike

Old Dutch Line by Old Dutch Carbon & Ribbon Co., ¾" x 2½" x 2½",
$25.00 – 50.00.
Courtesy of Tom & Mary Lou Slike

Old South by Thorp & Martin
Co., Boston, Massachusetts, 1¾"
x 1¾" x 1¾", $75.00 – 100.00.
Courtesy of Tom & Mary Lou Slike

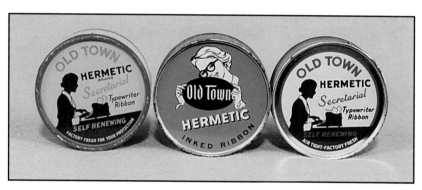

Old Town by Old Town Ribbon & Carbon Co. Inc., left: cardboard, ¾" x
2½", $25.00 – 50.00 each.
Courtesy of Tom & Mary Lou Slike

Old Town by Old Town Ribbon & Carbon
Co. Inc., ¾" x 2½" x 2½", $1.00 – 25.00.

Panama by Manifold Supplies Co., Brooklyn, New York, ¾" x 2½", $1.00 – 25.00.

Panama by Manifold Supplies
Co., Brooklyn, New York, ¾" x
2½", $1.00 – 25.00.

Panama Bronze by Manifold Supplies
Co., Brooklyn, New York, ¾" x 2½" x
2½", $25.00 – 50.00.

Courtesy of Tom & Mary Lou Slike

Panama Bronze Brand by Manifold
Supplies Co., Brooklyn, New York,
¾" x 2½" x 2½", $1.00 – 25.00.

Courtesy of Tom & Mary Lou Slike

Panama Commercial by Manifold Supplies Co., Brooklyn, New York, ¾" x
2½" x 2½", $25.00 – 50.00.

Courtesy of Tom & Mary Lou Slike

Panama Standard by Manifold Supplies
Co., Brooklyn, New York, ¾" x 2½" x 2½",
$1.00 – 25.00.

Pengad by Pengad Companies Inc.,
Bayonne, New Jersey, ¾" x 2½",
$25.00 – 50.00.

Courtesy of Tom & Mary Lou Slike

Penguin by International
Carbon & Ribbon Co.
Inc., Logan, Ohio, ¾" x
2½", $75.00 – 100.00.

Perfex by United States
Manifold Co., Dallas,
Texas, ¾" x 2½" x 2½",
$50.00 – 75.00.

Courtesy of Tom & Mary Lou Slike

Perm-O-Rite by Waters, Burlington, New Jersey, ¾" x 2½" x 2½", $1.00 – 25.00.
Courtesy of Tom & Mary Lou Slike

Pinnacle by Columbia Ribbon & Carbon Mfg. Co., Glen Cove, New York, ¾" x 2½", $1.00 – 25.00.
Courtesy of Tom & Mary Lou Slike

"Pinnacle" by Columbia Ribbon & Carbon Mfg. Co., Glen Cove, New York, ¾" x 2¼" x 2¼", $1.00 – 25.00.
Courtesy of Tom & Mary Lou Slike

Preferred by Aetna Products Co., Hicksville, New York, ¾" x 2½", $1.00 – 25.00.
Courtesy of Tom & Mary Lou Slike

Premier Brand by Smith Premier Typewriter Co., Syracuse, New York, 1¾" x 2" x 1¾", $25.00 – 50.00.
Courtesy of Tom & Mary Lou Slike

Progress by Underwood Corp., Burlington, New Jersey, ¾" x 2½", $1.00 – 25.00.
Courtesy of Tom & Mary Lou Slike

Public Service by Carter's Ink Co., Boston, Massachusetts, ¾" x 2¼" x 2¼", $1.00 – 25.00.
Courtesy of Tom & Mary Lou Slike

Queen by Queen Ribbon & Carbon Co. Inc., Brooklyn, New York, ¾" x 2½", $1.00 – 25.00.
Courtesy of Tom & Mary Lou Slike

Queen Brand by Queen Ribbon & Carbon Co. Inc., Brooklyn, New York, ¾" x 2½" x 2½", $1.00 – 25.00.
Courtesy of Bob & Sherri Copeland

Rainbow by Columbia Ribbon
& Carbon Mfg. Co., Glen
Cove, New York, ¾" x 1¾" x
1¾", $1.00 – 25.00.
Courtesy of Tom & Mary Lou Slike

Rainbow by Columbia Ribbon & Carbon
Mfg. Co., Glen Cove, New York, ¾" x 2½",
$75.00 – 100.00.

Regal by Remington Typewriter Co.,
New York, New York, ¾" x 2½" x 2½",
$1.00 – 25.00.
Courtesy of Tom & Mary Lou Slike

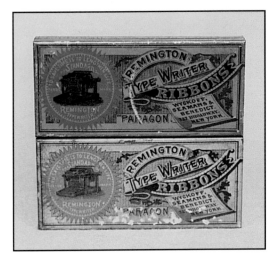

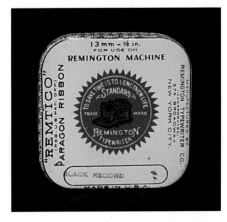

Remington Paragon marked Wyckoff, Seamans,
& Benedect, New York, ½" x 3½" x 1½",
$25.00 – 50.00 each.
Courtesy of Bob & Sherri Copeland

"Remtico" by Remington Typewriter
Co., New York, New York, ¾" x 2½" x
2½", $25.00 – 50.00.
Courtesy of Tom & Mary Lou Slike

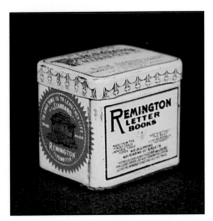

Remtico Paragon by Remington Typewriter Co. Inc.,
New York, 1¾" x 2" x 1¾", $25.00 – 50.00.
Courtesy of Tom & Mary Lou Slike

Royal by Royal Typewriter Co. Inc.,
New York, New York, ¾" x 2½" x 2½",
$25.00 – 50.00.
Courtesy of Tom & Mary Lou Slike

Royal Sheer by Hess-Hawkins Co.,
New York, New York, ¾" x 2" x 2",
$1.00 – 25.00.
Courtesy of Tom & Mary Lou Slike

Roytype Varsity (scottie dog) by Royal Typewriter Co. Inc., New York, ¾" x 2½", $50.00
– 75.00.
Courtesy of Hoby & Nancy Van Deusen

Roytype Park Avenue (hunter) by Royal Typewriter Co. Inc., New York, ¾" x 2½",
$100.00 – 150.00.
Courtesy of Hoby & Nancy Van Deusen

Saint Martin's English tin, manufacturer unknown,
¾" x 2½" x 2½", $50.00 – 75.00.
Courtesy of Hoby & Nancy Van Deusen

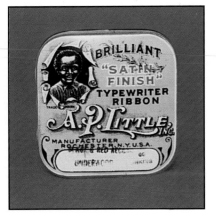

Satin Finish by A.P. Little Inc.,
Rochester, New York, ¾" x 2½" x
2½", $100.00 – 150.00.
Courtesy of Tom & Mary Lou Slike

Satin Finish (Brilliant) by A.P. Little
Inc., Rochester, New York, ¾" x
2½" x 2½", $250.00 – 300.00.
Courtesy of Tom & Mary Lou Slike

Service stock tin, manufacturer unknown,
¾" x 2½", $75.00 – 100.00.
Courtesy of Hoby & Nancy Van Deusen

Silhouette stock tin, ¾" x 2½", $25.00 –
50.00.

Silk Star by F.S. Webster Co., Boston,
Massachusetts, ¾" x 2½", $1.00 – 25.00.

Siltex by Fulton Ribbon & Carbon Co., Pittsburgh,
Pennsylvania, ¾" x 2½" x 2½", $100.00 – 150.00.
Courtesy of Hoby & Nancy Van Deusen

Starlight by Goldsmith Bros., New York, ¾"
x 2½", $50.00 – 75.00.
Courtesy of Hoby & Nancy Van Deusen

Sterling by True-Mark, ¾" x 2½",
$1.00 – 25.00.
Courtesy of Tom & Mary Lou Slike

Stormcrest by The S. Barker's Sons
Co., Cleveland, Ohio, ¾" x 2½",
$25.00 – 50.00.
Courtesy of Tom & Mary Lou Slike

Super Shell by Shell Petroleum Corp., ¾" x 2½"
x 2½", $150.00 – 200.00.
Courtesy of Hoby & Nancy Van Deusen

"Superior" by Great Lakes Carbon Co., Cleveland, Ohio, ¾" x 2½" x 2½", $75.00 – 100.00.
Courtesy of Hoby & Nancy Van Deusen

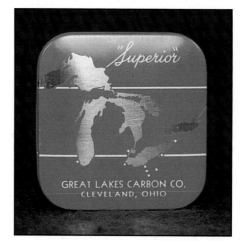

Swallow, manufacturer unknown, ¾" x 2½", $50.00 – 75.00.
Courtesy of Hoby & Nancy Van Deusen

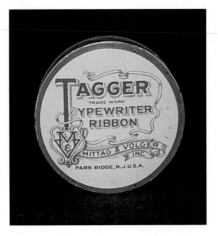

Tagger by Mittag & Volger Inc., Park Ridge, New Jersey, ¾" x 2¼", $1.00 – 25.00.
Courtesy of Tom & Mary Lou Slike

Tagger by Mittag & Volger Inc., Park Ridge, New Jersey, ¾" x 2½", $1.00 – 25.00.
Courtesy of Tom & Mary Lou Slike

Tagger by Mittag & Volger Inc., Park Ridge, New Jersey, ¾" x 2½", $1.00 – 25.00.
Courtesy of Tom & Mary Lou Slike

The Perfect Matched Line by W.M.L. McAdams Inc., Boston, Massachusetts, ¾" x 2½", $200.00 – 250.00.
Courtesy of Hoby & Nancy Van Deusen

Tip Top by Typewriter Equipment Co., San Diego, California, ¾" x 2½", $25.00 – 50.00.
Courtesy of Hoby & Nancy Van Deusen

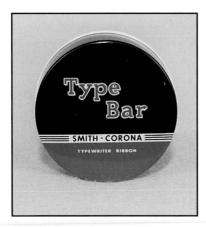

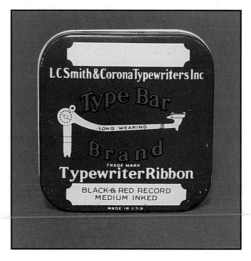

Type Bar by Smith-Corona Inc.,
Syracuse, New York, ¾" x 2½",
$1.00 – 25.00.
Courtesy of Tom & Mary Lou Slike

Type Bar by L.C. Smith & Corona Type-
writers Inc., ¾" x 2½" x 2½", $1.00 – 25.00.

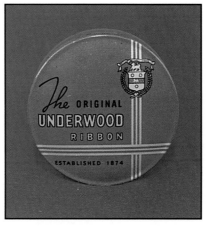

Underwood by John Underwood
Co., Brooklyn, New York, ¾" x
2½", $1.00 – 25.00.
Courtesy of Tom & Mary Lou Slike

Underwood by Underwood Corp.,
¾" x 2½", $1.00 – 25.00.
Courtesy of Tom & Mary Lou Slike

U E F by Underwood-Elliott-Fisher Co., ¾"
x 2½", $1.00 – 25.00.

Van Natta by J.E. Van Natta, Ithaca,
New York, ¾" x 2½" x 2½", $25.00 –
50.00.
Courtesy of Tom & Mary Lou Slike

Viking by Eriksen's Inc., ¾" x 2½" x
2½", $1.00 – 25.00.

Webster by F.S. Webster Co., Boston, Massachusetts, 2¼" x 1¾" x 1¾", $25.00 – 50.00.
Courtesy of Tom & Mary Lou Sike

Webster by F.S. Webster Co., Boston, Massachusetts, ¾" x 2¼" x 2¼", $1.00 – 25.00.

White Gold by Consolidated Ribbon & Carbon Co., Chicago, Illinois, ¾" x 2½", $100.00 – 150.00.
Courtesy of Hoby & Nancy Van Deusen

MISCELLANEOUS TINS

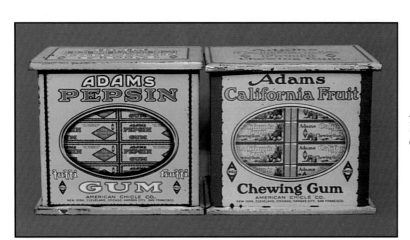

Adams Gum by American Chicle Co., 6" x 6¾" x 4¾", left: $250.00 – 300.00; right: $300.00 – 350.00.
Courtesy of Hoby & Nancy Van Deusen

Aetna Canadian biscuit tin with glass front by Aetna Biscuit Co., Limited, marked Macdonald Mfg. Co., 9¼" x 9½" x 8¾", $250.00 – 300.00.

American Ideal toilet soap tin by California Perfume Co., New York, 1" x 3" x 2½", $100.00 – 150.00.

Courtesy of Bob & Sherri Copeland

Baby's Blessing teething crackers by Johnson Educator Food Co., 2½" x 3", $25.00 – 50.00.

Courtesy of Bob & Sherri Copeland

Bell's insect exterminator, by J.E. Gary & Co., Boston, Massachusetts, 9¾" x 6½" x 5", $100.00 – 150.00.

Courtesy of Alex & Marilyn Znaiden

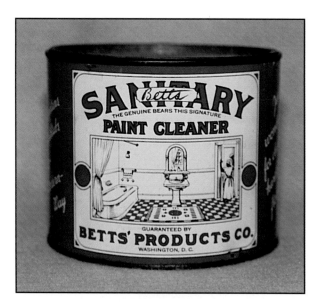

Betts Sanitary paint cleaner by Betts' Products Co., Washington, D.C., 5" x 6", $75.00 – 100.00.

Courtesy of Richard & Ann Lehmann

Black Diamond insect powder by Archibald & Lewis, marked S.A., Ilsley, left: 11½" x 7½" x 7½", $100.00 – 150.00; right: 9¾" x 5¼" x 5¼", $75.00 – 100.00.

Courtesy of Alex & Marilyn Znaiden

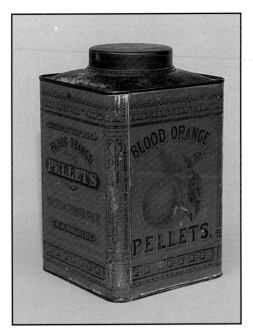

Breethem breath mints by Tennessee Products Corp., Nashville, Tennessee, ¼" x 2¼" x 1½", $1.00 – 25.00.

Blood Orange Pellets by E.J. Hoadley, Hartford, Connecticut, marked Somers Bros., 8" x 5" x 5", $100.00 – 150.00.
Courtesy of Schimpff's Confectionary

Carnation Malted Milk by The Carnation Co., Milwaukee, Wisconsin, and Seattle, Washington, 10½" x 7" x 7", $75.00 – 100.00.

C-I-L blasting caps by Canadian Industries Limited, Montreal, Canada, 1½" x 2½" x 2", $75.00 – 100.00.

Circus Peanuts by Circus Foods Inc., San Francisco, California, dated 1946, 3¼" x 3½", $25.00 – 50.00.

Cottolene by The N.K. Fairbank Co.,
4¾" x 4", $25.00 – 50.00. Note: a larger
size exists with same value.
Courtesy of Bob & Sherri Copeland

Dan-Dee Pretzels by Dan-Dee Pretzel & Potato Chip
Co., Cleveland, Ohio, 10" x 10", $1.00 – 25.00.

Deluxe card tin by Independent Card
Corp., Johnstown, Pennsylvania, ¾" x
2¾" x 3¾", $50.00 – 75.00.
Courtesy of Bob & Sherri Copeland

Diamond Creamery by Diamond Creamery Co.,
Massena, New York, 7" x 6¼", $100.00 – 150.00.
Courtesy of Alex & Marilyn Znaiden

Diamond Creamery by Diamond Creamery Co., Massena, New York, top: 2" x 3½"; bottom: 3¼" x 6¼", $50.00 – 75.00 each.

Courtesy of Hoby & Nancy Van Deusen

Dominant Polish by Dominant Products Co., New York, 5¾" x 3", $1.00 – 25.00.

Courtesy of Hoby & Nancy Van Deusen

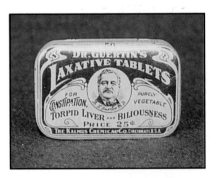

Dr. Guertin's Laxative by The Kalmus Chemical Co., Cincinnati, Ohio, ½" x 2" x 1¼", $25.00 – 50.00.

Courtesy of Bob & Sherri Copeland

Dr. J.D. Kellogg's asthma remedy by Northrop & Lyman Co., Inc., Buffalo, New York, and Toronto, Canada, 5" x 2½" x 1¾", $100.00 – 150.00.

Courtesy of Richard & Ann Lehmann

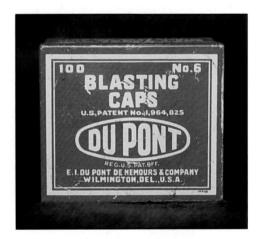

Dupont blasting caps by E.I. Du Pont De Nemours & Co., Wilmington, Delaware, 1½" x 2½" x 2", $25.00 – 50.00.

Courtesy of Richard & Ann Lehmann

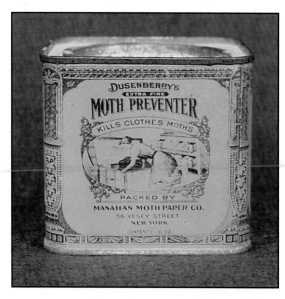

Eclipse Outfit, bicycle repair kit, 1" x 3" x 2½", $100.00 – 150.00.
Courtesy of Grant Smith

Dusenberry's Moth Preventer by Manahan Moth Paper Co., New York, New York, marked Manufacturers Can Co., Harrison, N.J., 3¼" x 3½" x 3½", $75.00 – 100.00.
Courtesy of Tom & Mary Lou Slike

Farmers Pride syrup paper label by Hulman & Co., Terre Haute, Indiana, 4" x 3¼", $50.00 – 75.00.
Courtesy of Mike & Sharon Hunt

Electric Balm by Dr. O.C. Gage, Concord, New Hampshire, ¾" x 2½", $25.00 – 50.00.
Courtesy of Alex & Marilyn Znaiden

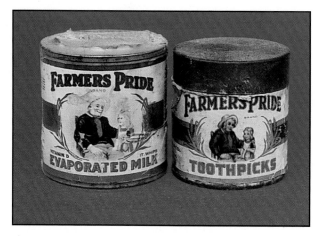

Farmers Pride paper labels by Hulman & Co., Terre Haute, Indiana, left: evaporated milk, 2½" x 2½"; right: toothpicks, 2½" x 2¼", $25.00 – 50.00 each.
Courtesy of Mike & Sharon Hunt

Fly Ded by Midway Chemical Co., Chicago, Illinois, 6" x 3" x 1", $50.00 – 75.00. Note: tin has working bellow for discharge.
Courtesy of Tom & Mary Lou Slike

Fruit Maid jam by Oelerich & Berry Co., Chicago, Illinois, 5¼" x 5½", $50.00 – 75.00.
Courtesy of Mike & Sharon Hunt

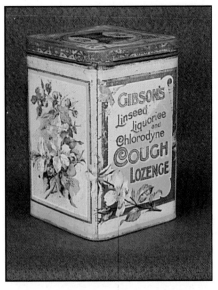

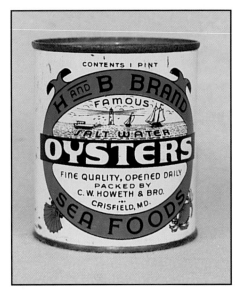

Gibson's Cough Lozenge by Jacob Gibson & Sons, Manchester, England, 9" x 5¾" x 5¾", $100.00 – 150.00.
Courtesy of Tom & Mary Lou Slike

Gold Dust scouring powder cardboard sample by Gold Dust Corp., New York, New York, 3" x 2", $150.00 – 200.00.
Courtesy of Mike & Sharon Hunt

H and B Brand oysters by C.W. Howeth & Bro., Crisfield, Maryland, 3¾" x 3¼", $25.00 – 50.00.
Courtesy of Alex & Marilyn Znaiden

Hartford tire repair kit by The Hartford Rubber Works Co., Brooklyn, New York, ½" x 3" x 1¾", $50.00 – 75.00.

Courtesy of Bob & Sherri Copeland

Hetzel's rubber cement by J.G. Hetzel, Newark, New Jersey, circa 1925, 4½" x 5½", $150.00 – 200.00.

Courtesy of Mike & Sharon Hunt

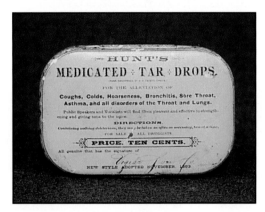

Hunt's Medicated Tar Drops, marked Somers Bros., ½" x 3" x 2", $50.00 – 75.00.

Courtesy of Mike & Sharon Hunt

Imperial Gun Powder paper label by Eureka Powder Works, New Durham, New Hampshire, 5" x 4" x 2", $75.00 – 100.00.

Courtesy of Richard & Ann Lehmann

Icy Point by Alaska Pacific Salmon Co., Seattle, Washington, California 1933, 4¾" x 3", $25.00 – 50.00.

Courtesy of Alex & Marilyn Znaiden

Japanese Pot-Pourri by J.F. Co.,
marked Somers Bros., Brooklyn,
N.Y., 3" x 2¼" x 2¼", $25.00 – 50.00.

Courtesy of Hoby & Nancy Van Deusen

Jayne's Expectorant cold tablets by Dr. D. Jayne & Son,
Philadelphia, Pennsylvania, $25.00 – 50.00.

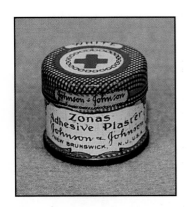

Johnson & Johnson adhesive plaster marked New Brunswick, New
Jersey, ¾" x 1", $1.00 – 25.00.

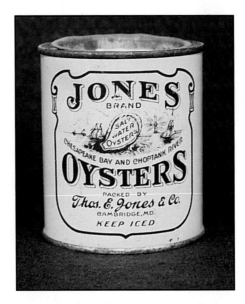

Jones Oyster by Thos. E. Jones & Co.,
Cambridge, Maryland, marked Independent Can Co., Baltimore, MD., 3¾" x
3¼", $50.00 – 75.00.

Courtesy of Alex & Marilyn Znaiden

K Cough Drops by Kibbe Brothers & Co., Springfield, Massachusetts, marked Somers Bros.,
2½" x 2" x 2", $50.00 – 75.00.

Courtesy of Schimpff's Confectionary

Kilflea Powder by Dr. G.W. Clayton, Chicago, Illinois, 4½" x
2¼" x 1¾", $50.00 – 75.00.

Courtesy of Alex & Marilyn Znaiden

Kingan's Reliable lard by Kingan & Co., Indianapolis, Indiana, 5¼" x 5", $50.00 – 75.00.
Courtesy of Alex & Marilyn Znaiden

Layfield Pretzels by Layfield Pretzels Inc., Allentown, Pennsylvania, 7½" x 7½", $1.00 – 25.00.

Liberty Brand by Bettman-Johnson Co., Cincinnati, Ohio, 1¾" x 4½" x 3¼", $50.00 – 75.00.
Courtesy of Bob & Sherri Copeland

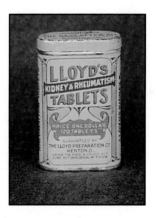

Lloyd's Kidney & Rheumatism Tablets by Lloyd Preparation Co., Kenton, Ohio, 3½" x 2" x 1", $50.00 – 75.00.
Courtesy of Bob & Sherri Copeland

Mentholatum salve by The Mentholatum Co., Buffalo, New York, ½" x 1½", $25.00 – 50.00.

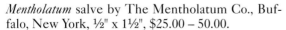

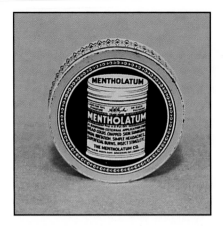

Mentholatum salve by The Mentholatum Co., Buffalo, New York, ¼" x 1¼", $25.00 – 50.00.

Mentholatum salve by The Mentholatum Co., Buffalo, New York, ½" x 1½", $1.00 – 25.00.

Montauk Star Brand female pills by Montauk Chemical Co., 1" x 3" x 1¾", $100.00 – 150.00.

Courtesy of Alex & Marilyn Znaiden

Moss Rose by Elyria Canning Co., Elyria, Ohio, 3¼" x 2¾", $1.00 – 25.00.

Mrs. Rodeback's eczema salve by Rodeback & Son, Toledo, Ohio, 2¼" x 1¼", $25.00 – 50.00.

Courtesy of Bob & Sherri Copeland

Mrs. VanCott's lozenges, marked Tarrytown, New York, ½" x 2¼" x 1¼", $75.00 – 100.00.

Courtesy of Alex & Marilyn Znaiden

Nature's Remedy by Lewis-Howe Co., St. Louis, Missouri, left: 4½" x 2¾" x 1"; right: 3¼" x 2¾" x 1", $1.00 – 25.00 each.
Courtesy of Bob & Sherri Copeland

Natures Remedy by Lewis-Howe Co., St. Louis, Missouri, ½" x 1¾" x 1¼", $1.00 – 25.00.

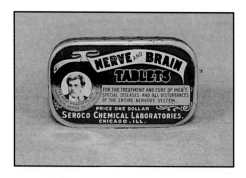

Nerve & Brain Tablets by Seroco Chemical Laboratories, Chicago, Illinois, ½" x 2¾" x 1½", $25.00 – 50.00.
Courtesy of Bob & Sherri Copeland

North Crystal oysters by R.F. Brown Sea Food Co., Lansing, Michigan, 7½" x 6½", $50.00 – 75.00.
Courtesy of Richard & Ann Lehmann

O'Neill's Vegetable Remedy by F.J. O'Neill Medicine Co., St. Louis, Missouri, 4¼" x 2¾" x 1", $1.00 – 25.00.
Courtesy of Bob & Sherri Copeland

Oxien Nazone salve by The Giant Oxie Co.,
Augusta, Maine, ¾" x 1¾", $1.00 – 25.00.

Peerless main spring tin by King & Eise-
le, Buffalo, New York, ¾" x 2½" x 2½",
$50.00 – 75.00.
Courtesy of Tom & Mary Lou Slike

Planters Peanuts by The Planters Co., Wilkes-Barre, Pennsylvania, 9¾" x 8¼", $75.00 – 100.00 each.
Courtesy of Bob & Sherri Copeland

Polly Prim sample paper
label by N.K. Fairbank Co.,
3" x 2", $75.00 – 100.00.
Courtesy of Mike & Sharon Hunt

Popham's asthma medicine
by Williams Mfg. Co.,
Cleveland, Ohio, 4¾" x 2"
x 1¾", $50.00 – 75.00.
Courtesy of Mike & Sharon Hunt

Pounce drafting powder by Keuffel & Esser Co., 5" x 2", $1.00 – 25.00.
Courtesy of Dave Garland

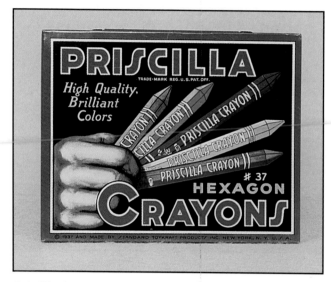

Priscilla Crayons by Standard Toykraft Products Inc., New York, New York, ½" x 5½" x 4½", $25.00 – 50.00.
Courtesy of Tom & Lynne Sankiewicz

Purina fly spray by Ralston Purina Co., St. Louis, Missouri, 10¾" x 8" x 3¼", $25.00 – 50.00.

Courtesy of Hoby & Nancy Van Deusen

Quaker Oats by The Quaker Oats Co., Chicago, Illinois, $75.00 – 100.00.
Courtesy of Grant Smith

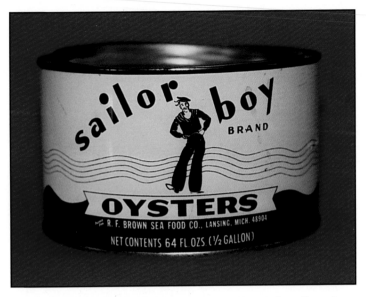

Sailor Boy oysters by R.F. Brown Sea Food Co., Lansing, Michigan, 4" x 6¾", $25.00 – 50.00.

Courtesy of Richard & Ann Lehmann

Savabrush by Schalk Chemical Co., Los Angeles, California, circa 1920, 5" x 3", $50.00 – 75.00.

Courtesy of Tom & Mary Lou Slike

Scholl's Axle-Grease by Independent Oil Co., Mansfield, Ohio, 6½" x 6", $100.00 – 150.00.

Courtesy of Richard & Ann Lehmann

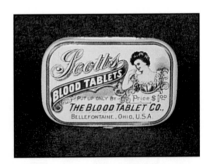

Scott's Blood Tablets by The Blood Tablet Co., Bellefontaine, Ohio, ½" x 3¼" x 2", $50.00 – 75.00.

Silk Hat handkerchief tin by The Silk Hat Handkerchief Co., New York, New York, ½" x 3½" x 2¼", $50.00 – 75.00.

Courtesy of Bob & Sherri Copeland

Squirrel Brand Peanuts by Squirrel Brand Co., Cambridge, Massachusetts, left: 10" x 8", $200.00 – 250.00; right: 9¾" x 8", $100.00 – 150.00.

Courtesy of Alex & Marilyn Znaiden

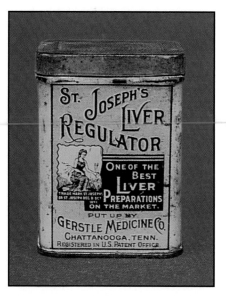

St. Joseph's liver regulator by Gerstle Medicine Co., Chattanooga, Tennessee, 3" x 2¼" x 1¾", $75.00 – 100.00.

Courtesy of Mike & Sharon Hunt

Sun Light axle grease by Monarch Manufacturing Co., Toledo, Ohio, and Council Bluffs, Iowa, 5¼" x 5½", $100.00 – 150.00.

Courtesy of Alex & Marilyn Znaiden

Sunshine Ginger Wafers by Loose-Wiles Biscuit Co., New York, New York, 8¼" x 3", $25.00 – 50.00.

Courtesy of Richard & Ann Lehmann

Taylor's Black Hawk polish by Taylor Mfg. Co., 4½" x 2½", $25.00 – 50.00.

Courtesy of Hoby & Nancy Van Deusen

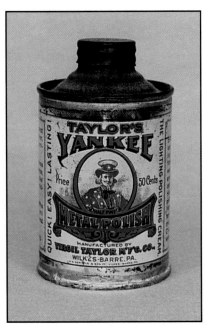

Taylor's Yankee Polish by Virgil Taylor
Manufacturing Co., Wilkes-Barre,
Pennsylvania, 4¼" x 2½", $75.00 –
100.00.

Courtesy of Alex & Marilyn Znaiden

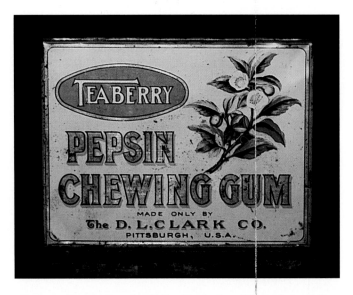

Teaberry Pepsin Gum by D.L. Clark Co., Pittsburgh, 2½" x
6¾" x 5", $200.00 – 250.00.

Courtesy of Richard & Ann Lehmann

"Uneeda Bakers" cheese wafers by National
Biscuit Co., New York, 6½" x 5", $1.00 – 25.00.

Courtesy of Richard & Ann Lehmann

Vantine's Incense by A.A. Vantine & Co., New York, 4" x 2"
x 1¼", $1.00 – 25.00.

Courtesy of Bob & Sherri Copeland

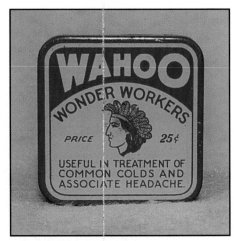

Wahoo by Old Indian Medicine Co.,
Toledo, Ohio, ¼" x 1¾" x 1¾", $1.00 –
25.00.

Courtesy of Tom & Lynne Sankiewicz

Watch Dog Cleanser cardboard with tin top and bottom by E. Myers Lye Corp., St. Louis, Missouri, 4¾" x 3", $75.00 – 100.00.
Courtesy of Richard & Ann Lehmann

Watkins Laxative by J.R. Watkins Co., ¾" x 3" x 2¾", $1.00 – 25.00.

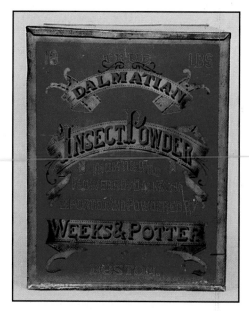

Weeks & Potter insect powder, Boston, Massachusetts, 10¾" x 8¾" x 7½", $100.00 – 150.00.
Courtesy of Alex & Marilyn Znaiden

Western Blasting Caps by Western Cartridge Co., East Alton, Illinois, 1¾" x 2½" x 2¼", $50.00 – 75.00.
Courtesy of Richard & Ann Lehmann

Whalene axle lube by Whalene Co., Cleveland, Ohio, $200.00 – 250.00.
Courtesy of Alex & Marilyn Znaiden

White House peanuts by Dwinell-Wright Co., Boston, Massachusetts, 3" x 3½", $1.00 – 25.00.
Courtesy of Bob & Sherri Copeland

Zanol No-Frost by The American Products Co., Cincinnati, Ohio, ¾" x 2¾", $1.00 – 25.00.

Courtesy of Tom & Mary Lou Slike

Wrigley's Cleaner by Wrigley's Mfg. Co., Philadelphia, Pennsylvania, 4" x 3½", $75.00 – 100.00.

Courtesy of Hoby & Nancy Van Deusen

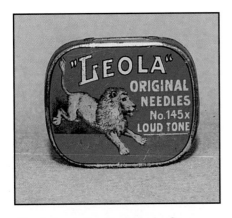

"*Leola*" needle tin made in Germany, ½" x 1¾" x 1¼", $50.00 – 75.00.

Moon Rose tea tin by Hubbard Grocer Co., Charleston, West Virginia, 5" x 2½", $75.00 – 100.00.

Courtesy of Bob & Sherri Copeland

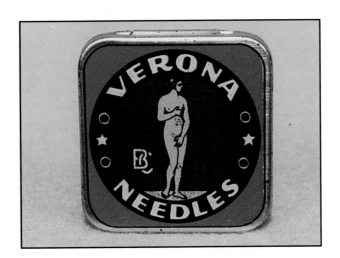

Verona needle tin, ¼" x 1½" x 1½", $25.00 – 50.00.

COLLECTOR BOOKS

Informing Today's Collector

For over two decades we have been keeping collectors informed on trends and values in all fields of antiques and collectibles.

DOLLS, FIGURES & TEDDY BEARS

4707	A Decade of **Barbie** Dolls & Collectibles, 1981–1991, Summers	$19.95
4631	**Barbie** Doll Boom, 1986–1995, Augustyniak	$18.95
2079	**Barbie** Doll Fashion, Volume I, Eames	$24.95
4846	**Barbie** Doll Fashion, Volume II, Eames	$24.95
3957	**Barbie** Exclusives, Rana	$18.95
4632	**Barbie** Exclusives, Book II, Rana	$18.95
4557	**Barbie,** The First 30 Years, Deutsch	$24.95
4847	**Barbie** Years, 1959–1995, 2nd Ed., Olds	$17.95
3310	**Black Dolls,** 1820–1991, Perkins	$17.95
3873	**Black Dolls,** Book II, Perkins	$17.95
3810	**Chatty Cathy Dolls,** Lewis	$15.95
1529	Collector's Encyclopedia of **Barbie** Dolls, DeWein	$19.95
4882	Collector's Encyclopedia of **Barbie** Doll Exclusives and More, Augustyniak	$19.95
2211	Collector's Encyclopedia of **Madame Alexander Dolls,** Smith	$24.95
4863	Collector's Encyclopedia of **Vogue Dolls,** Izen/Stover	$29.95
3967	Collector's Guide to **Trolls,** Peterson	$19.95
4571	**Liddle Kiddles,** Identification & Value Guide, Langford	$18.95
3826	Story of **Barbie,** Westenhouser	$19.95
1513	**Teddy Bears & Steiff** Animals, Mandel	$9.95
1817	**Teddy Bears & Steiff** Animals, 2nd Series, Mandel	$19.95
2084	**Teddy Bears, Annalee's & Steiff** Animals, 3rd Series, Mandel	$19.95
1808	Wonder of **Barbie,** Manos	$9.95
1430	World of **Barbie** Dolls, Manos	$9.95
4880	World of **Raggedy Ann** Collectibles, Avery	$24.95

TOYS, MARBLES & CHRISTMAS COLLECTIBLES

3427	**Advertising Character** Collectibles, Dotz	$17.95
2333	Antique & Collector's **Marbles,** 3rd Ed., Grist	$9.95
3827	Antique & Collector's **Toys,** 1870–1950, Longest	$24.95
3956	Baby Boomer **Games,** Identification & Value Guide, Polizzi	$24.95
4934	**Breyer Animal** Collector's Guide, Identification and Values, Browell	$19.95
3717	**Christmas** Collectibles, 2nd Edition, Whitmyer	$24.95
4976	**Christmas** Ornaments, Lights & Decorations, Johnson	$24.95
4737	**Christmas** Ornaments, Lights & Decorations, Vol. II, Johnson	$24.95
4739	**Christmas** Ornaments, Lights & Decorations, Vol. III, Johnson	$24.95
4649	Classic Plastic **Model Kits,** Polizzi	$24.95
4559	Collectible **Action Figures,** 2nd Ed., Manos	$17.95
3874	Collectible Coca-Cola Toy **Trucks,** deCourtivron	$24.95
2338	Collector's Encyclopedia of **Disneyana,** Longest, Stern	$24.95
4958	Collector's Guide to **Battery Toys,** Hultzman	$19.95
4639	Collector's Guide to **Diecast Toys & Scale Models,** Johnson	$19.95
4651	Collector's Guide to **Tinker Toys,** Strange	$18.95
4566	Collector's Guide to **Tootsietoys,** 2nd Ed., Richter	$19.95
4720	The Golden Age of **Automotive Toys,** 1925–1941, Hutchison/Johnson	$24.95
3436	Grist's Big Book of **Marbles**	$19.95
3970	Grist's Machine-Made & Contemporary **Marbles,** 2nd Ed.	$9.95
4723	**Matchbox** Toys, 1947 to 1996, 2nd Ed., Johnson	$18.95
4871	**McDonald's** Collectibles, Henriques/DuVall	$19.95
1540	**Modern Toys** 1930–1980, Baker	$19.95
3888	**Motorcycle** Toys, Antique & Contemporary, Gentry/Downs	$18.95
4953	Schroeder's Collectible **Toys,** Antique to Modern Price Guide, 4th Ed.	$17.95
1886	Stern's Guide to **Disney** Collectibles	$14.95
2139	Stern's Guide to **Disney** Collectibles, 2nd Series	$14.95
3975	Stern's Guide to **Disney** Collectibles, 3rd Series	$18.95
2028	**Toys,** Antique & Collectible, Longest	$14.95
3979	**Zany Characters** of the Ad World, Lamphier	$16.95

FURNITURE

1457	American **Oak** Furniture, McNerney	$9.95
3716	American **Oak** Furniture, Book II, McNerney	$12.95
1118	Antique **Oak** Furniture, Hill	$7.95
2271	Collector's Encyclopedia of **American** Furniture, Vol. II, Swedberg	$24.95
3720	Collector's Encyclopedia of **American** Furniture, Vol. III, Swedberg	$24.95
3878	Collector's Guide to **Oak** Furniture, George	$12.95
1755	Furniture of the **Depression Era,** Swedberg	$19.95
3906	**Heywood-Wakefield** Modern Furniture, Rouland	$18.95

1885	**Victorian** Furniture, Our American Heritage, McNerney	$9.95
3829	**Victorian** Furniture, Our American Heritage, Book II, McNerney	$9.95

JEWELRY, HATPINS, WATCHES & PURSES

1712	Antique & Collector's **Thimbles** & Accessories, Mathis	$19.95
1748	Antique **Purses,** Revised Second Ed., Holiner	$19.95
1278	Art Nouveau & Art Deco **Jewelry,** Baker	$9.95
4850	Collectible **Costume Jewelry,** Simonds	$24.95
3875	Collecting Antique **Stickpins,** Kerins	$16.95
3722	Collector's Ency. of **Compacts, Carryalls & Face Powder Boxes,** Mueller	$24.95
4854	Collector's Ency. of **Compacts, Carryalls & Face Powder Boxes,** Vol. II	$24.95
4940	**Costume Jewelry,** A Practical Handbook & Value Guide, Rezazadeh	$24.95
1716	Fifty Years of Collectible **Fashion Jewelry,** 1925–1975, Baker	$19.95
1424	**Hatpins** & Hatpin Holders, Baker	$9.95
4570	Ladies' **Compacts,** Gerson	$24.95
1181	100 Years of Collectible **Jewelry,** 1850–1950, Baker	$9.95
4729	**Sewing Tools** & Trinkets, Thompson	$24.95
2348	20th Century Fashionable Plastic **Jewelry,** Baker	$19.95
4878	Vintage & Contemporary **Purse Accessories,** Gerson	$24.95
3830	Vintage **Vanity Bags & Purses,** Gerson	$24.95

INDIANS, GUNS, KNIVES, TOOLS, PRIMITIVES

1868	Antique **Tools,** Our American Heritage, McNerney	$9.95
1426	**Arrowheads** & Projectile Points, Hothem	$7.95
4943	Field Guide to **Flint Arrowheads & Knives** of the North American Indian	$9.95
2279	**Indian Artifacts** of the Midwest, Hothem	$14.95
3885	**Indian Artifacts** of the Midwest, Book II, Hothem	$16.95
4870	**Indian Artifacts** of the Midwest, Book III, Hothem	$18.95
1964	**Indian Axes** & Related Stone Artifacts, Hothem	$14.95
2023	**Keen Kutter** Collectibles, Heuring	$14.95
4724	**Modern Guns,** Identification & Values, 11th Ed., Quertermous	$12.95
2164	**Primitives,** Our American Heritage, McNerney	$9.95
1759	**Primitives,** Our American Heritage, 2nd Series, McNerney	$14.95
4730	Standard **Knife** Collector's Guide, 3rd Ed., Ritchie & Stewart	$12.95

PAPER COLLECTIBLES & BOOKS

4633	**Big Little Books,** Jacobs	$18.95
4710	Collector's Guide to **Children's Books,** Jones	$18.95
1441	Collector's Guide to **Post Cards,** Wood	$9.95
2081	Guide to Collecting **Cookbooks,** Allen	$14.95
2080	Price Guide to **Cookbooks & Recipe Leaflets,** Dickinson	$9.95
3973	**Sheet Music** Reference & Price Guide, 2nd Ed., Pafik & Guiheen	$19.95
4654	**Victorian Trading Cards,** Historical Reference & Value Guide, Cheadle	$19.95
4733	**Whitman Juvenile Books,** Brown	$17.95

GLASSWARE

4561	Collectible **Drinking Glasses,** Chase & Kelly	$17.95
4642	Collectible **Glass Shoes,** Wheatley	$19.95
4937	Coll. **Glassware** from the 40s, 50s & 60s, 4th Ed., Florence	$19.95
1810	Collector's Encyclopedia of **American Art Glass,** Shuman	$29.95
4938	Collector's Encyclopedia of **Depression Glass,** 13th Ed., Florence	$19.95
1961	Collector's Encyclopedia of **Fry Glassware,** Fry Glass Society	$24.95
1664	Collector's Encyclopedia of **Heisey Glass,** 1925–1938, Bredehoft	$24.95
3905	Collector's Encyclopedia of **Milk Glass,** Newbound	$24.95
4936	Collector's Guide to **Candy Containers,** Dezso/Poirier	$19.95
4564	**Crackle Glass,** Weitman	$19.95
4941	**Crackle Glass,** Book II, Weitman	$19.95
2275	**Czechoslovakian Glass** and Collectibles, Barta/Rose	$16.95
4714	**Czechoslovakian Glass** and Collectibles, Book II, Barta/Rose	$16.95
4716	**Elegant Glassware** of the Depression Era, 7th Ed., Florence	$19.95
1380	Encyclopedia of **Pattern Glass,** McClain	$12.95
3981	Ever's Standard **Cut Glass** Value Guide	$12.95
4659	**Fenton Art Glass,** 1907–1939, Whitmyer	$24.95
3725	**Fostoria,** Pressed, Blown & Hand Molded Shapes, Kerr	$24.95
4719	**Fostoria,** Etched, Carved & Cut Designs, Vol. II, Kerr	$24.95
3883	**Fostoria Stemware,** The Crystal for America, Long & Seate	$24.95
4644	**Imperial Carnival Glass,** Burns	$18.95
3886	**Kitchen Glassware** of the Depression Years, 5th Ed., Florence	$19.95

COLLECTOR BOOKS
Informing Today's Collector

4725	Pocket Guide to **Depression Glass**, 10th Ed., Florence	$9.95
5035	Standard Encyclopedia of **Carnival Glass**, 6th Ed., Edwards/Carwile	$24.95
5036	Standard **Carnival Glass** Price Guide, 11th Ed., Edwards/Carwile	$9.95
4875	Standard Encyclopedia of **Opalescent Glass**, 2nd ed., Edwards	$19.95
4731	**Stemware Identification**, Featuring Cordials with Values, Florence	$24.95
3326	**Very Rare Glassware** of the Depression Years, 3rd Series, Florence	$24.95
4732	**Very Rare Glassware** of the Depression Years, 5th Series, Florence	$24.95
4656	**Westmoreland Glass**, Wilson	$24.95

POTTERY

4927	**ABC Plates & Mugs**, Lindsay	$24.95
4929	**American Art Pottery**, Sigafoose	$24.95
4630	**American Limoges**, Limoges	$24.95
1312	**Blue & White Stoneware**, McNerney	$9.95
1958	So. Potteries **Blue Ridge Dinnerware**, 3rd Ed., Newbound	$14.95
1959	**Blue Willow**, 2nd Ed., Gaston	$14.95
4848	Ceramic **Coin Banks**, Stoddard	$19.95
4851	Collectible **Cups & Saucers**, Harran	$18.95
4709	Collectible **Kay Finch**, Biography, Identification & Values, Martinez/Frick	$18.95
1373	Collector's Encyclopedia of **American Dinnerware**, Cunningham	$24.95
4931	Collector's Encyclopedia of **Bauer Pottery**, Chipman	$24.95
3815	Collector's Encyclopedia of **Blue Ridge Dinnerware**, Newbound	$19.95
4932	Collector's Encyclopedia of **Blue Ridge Dinnerware**, Vol. II, Newbound	$24.95
4658	Collector's Encyclopedia of **Brush-McCoy Pottery**, Huxford	$24.95
2272	Collector's Encyclopedia of **California Pottery**, Chipman	$24.95
3811	Collector's Encyclopedia of **Colorado Pottery**, Carlton	$24.95
2133	Collector's Encyclopedia of **Cookie Jars**, Roerig	$24.95
3723	Collector's Encyclopedia of **Cookie Jars**, Book II, Roerig	$24.95
4939	Collector's Encyclopedia of **Cookie Jars**, Book III, Roerig	$24.95
4638	Collector's Encyclopedia of **Dakota Potteries**, Dommel	$24.95
5040	Collector's Encyclopedia of **Fiesta**, 8th Ed., Huxford	$19.95
4718	Collector's Encyclopedia of **Figural Planters & Vases**, Newbound	$19.95
3961	Collector's Encyclopedia of **Early Noritake**, Alden	$24.95
1439	Collector's Encyclopedia of **Flow Blue China**, Gaston	$19.95
3812	Collector's Encyclopedia of **Flow Blue China**, 2nd Ed., Gaston	$24.95
3813	Collector's Encyclopedia of **Hall China**, 2nd Ed., Whitmyer	$24.95
3431	Collector's Encyclopedia of **Homer Laughlin China**, Jasper	$24.95
1276	Collector's Encyclopedia of **Hull Pottery**, Roberts	$19.95
3962	Collector's Encyclopedia of **Lefton China**, DeLozier	$19.95
4855	Collector's Encyclopedia of **Lefton China**, Book II, DeLozier	$19.95
2210	Collector's Encyclopedia of **Limoges Porcelain**, 2nd Ed., Gaston	$24.95
2334	Collector's Encyclopedia of **Majolica Pottery**, Katz-Marks	$19.95
1358	Collector's Encyclopedia of **McCoy Pottery**, Huxford	$19.95
3963	Collector's Encyclopedia of **Metlox Potteries**, Gibbs Jr.	$24.95
3837	Collector's Encyclopedia of **Nippon Porcelain**, Van Patten	$24.95
2089	Collector's Ency. of **Nippon Porcelain**, 2nd Series, Van Patten	$24.95
1665	Collector's Ency. of **Nippon Porcelain**, 3rd Series, Van Patten	$24.95
4712	Collector's Ency. of **Nippon Porcelain**, 4th Series, Van Patten	$24.95
1447	Collector's Encyclopedia of **Noritake**, Van Patten	$19.95
3432	Collector's Encyclopedia of **Noritake**, 2nd Series, Van Patten	$24.95
1037	Collector's Encyclopedia of **Occupied Japan**, 1st Series, Florence	$14.95
1038	Collector's Encyclopedia of **Occupied Japan**, 2nd Series, Florence	$14.95
2088	Collector's Encyclopedia of **Occupied Japan**, 3rd Series, Florence	$14.95
2019	Collector's Encyclopedia of **Occupied Japan**, 4th Series, Florence	$14.95
2335	Collector's Encyclopedia of **Occupied Japan**, 5th Series, Florence	$14.95
4718	Collector's Encyclopedia of **Old Ivory China**, Hillman	$24.95
3964	Collector's Encyclopedia of **Pickard China**, Reed	$24.95
3877	Collector's Encyclopedia of **R.S. Prussia**, 4th Series, Gaston	$24.95
1034	Collector's Encyclopedia of **Roseville Pottery**, Huxford	$19.95
1035	Collector's Encyclopedia of **Roseville Pottery**, 2nd Ed., Huxford	$19.95
4856	Collector's Encyclopeida of **Russel Wright**, 2nd Ed., Kerr	$24.95
4713	Collector's Encyclopedia of **Salt Glaze Stoneware**, Taylor/Lowrance	$24.95
3314	Collector's Encyclopedia of **Van Briggle** Art Pottery, Sasicki	$24.95
4563	Collector's Encyclopedia of **Wall Pockets**, Newbound	$19.95
2111	Collector's Encyclopedia of **Weller Pottery**, Huxford	$29.95
3876	Collector's Guide to **Lu-Ray Pastels**, Meehan	$18.95
3814	Collector's Guide to **Made in Japan** Ceramics, White	$18.95
4646	Collector's Guide to **Made in Japan** Ceramics, Book II, White	$18.95
4565	Collector's Guide to **Rockingham**, The Enduring Ware, Brewer	$14.95
2339	Collector's Guide to **Shawnee Pottery**, Vanderbilt	$19.95
1425	**Cookie Jars**, Westfall	$9.95

3440	**Cookie Jars**, Book II, Westfall	$19.95
4924	Figural & Novelty **Salt & Pepper Shakers**, 2nd Series, Davern	$24.95
2379	Lehner's Ency. of **U.S. Marks** on Pottery, Porcelain & China	$24.95
4722	**McCoy Pottery**, Collector's Reference & Value Guide, Hanson/Nissen	$19.95
3825	**Puriton Pottery**, Morris	$24.95
4726	**Red Wing Art Pottery**, 1920s–1960s, Dollen	$19.95
1670	**Red Wing Collectibles**, DePasquale	$9.95
1440	**Red Wing Stoneware**, DePasquale	$9.95
1632	**Salt & Pepper Shakers**, Guarnaccia	$9.95
1888	**Salt & Pepper Shakers** II, Guarnaccia	$14.95
2220	**Salt & Pepper Shakers** III, Guarnaccia	$14.95
3443	**Salt & Pepper Shakers** IV, Guarnaccia	$18.95
3738	**Shawnee Pottery**, Mangus	$24.95
4629	Turn of the Century **American Dinnerware**, 1880s–1920s, Jasper	$24.95
4572	**Wall Pockets** of the Past, Perkins	$17.95
3327	**Watt Pottery** – Identification & Value Guide, Morris	$19.95

OTHER COLLECTIBLES

4704	Antique & Collectible **Buttons**, Wisniewski	$19.95
2269	Antique **Brass & Copper** Collectibles, Gaston	$16.95
1880	Antique **Iron**, McNerney	$9.95
3872	Antique **Tins**, Dodge	$24.95
4845	Antique **Typewriters & Office Collectibles**, Rehr	$19.95
1714	**Black** Collectibles, Gibbs	$19.95
1128	**Bottle** Pricing Guide, 3rd Ed., Cleveland	$7.95
4636	**Celluloid Collectibles**, Dunn	$14.95
3718	Collectible **Aluminum**, Grist	$16.95
3445	Collectible **Cats**, An Identification & Value Guide, Fyke	$18.95
4560	Collectible **Cats**, An Identification & Value Guide, Book II, Fyke	$19.95
4852	Collectible **Compact Disc** Price Guide 2, Cooper	$17.95
2018	Collector's Encyclopedia of **Granite Ware**, Greguire	$24.95
3430	Collector's Encyclopedia of **Granite Ware**, Book 2, Greguire	$24.95
4705	Collector's Guide to **Antique Radios**, 4th Ed., Bunis	$18.95
3880	Collector's Guide to **Cigarette Lighters**, Flanagan	$17.95
4637	Collector's Guide to **Cigarette Lighers**, Book II, Flanagan	$17.95
4942	Collector's Guide to **Don Winton Designs**, Ellis	$19.95
3966	Collector's Guide to **Inkwells**, Identification & Values, Badders	$18.95
4947	Collector's Guide to **Inkwells**, Book II, Badders	$19.95
4948	Collector's Guide to **Letter Openers**, Grist	$19.95
4862	Collector's Guide to **Toasters** & Accessories, Greguire	$19.95
4652	Collector's Guide to **Transistor Radios**, 2nd Ed., Bunis	$16.95
4653	Collector's Guide to **TV Memorabilia**, 1960s–1970s, Davis/Morgan	$24.95
4864	Collector's Guide to **Wallace Nutting Pictures**, Ivankovich	$18.95
1629	**Doorstops**, Identification & Values, Bertoia	$9.95
4567	Figural **Napkin Rings**, Gottschalk & Whitson	$18.95
4717	Figural **Nodders**, Includes Bobbin' Heads and Swayers, Irtz	$19.95
3968	**Fishing Lure** Collectibles, Murphy/Edmisten	$24.95
4867	**Flea Market Trader**, 11th Ed., Huxford	$9.95
4944	**Flue Covers**, Collector's Value Guide, Meckley	$12.95
4945	**G-Men and FBI Toys** and Collectibles, Whitworth	$18.95
5043	**Garage Sale & Flea Market Annual**, 6th Ed.	$19.95
3819	**General Store Collectibles**, Wilson	$24.95
4643	**Great American West** Collectibles, Wilson	$24.95
2215	Goldstein's **Coca-Cola** Collectibles	$16.95
3884	Huxford's Collectible **Advertising**, 2nd Ed.	$24.95
2216	**Kitchen Antiques**, 1790–1940, McNerney	$14.95
4950	The **Lone Ranger**, Collector's Reference & Value Guide, Felbinger	$18.95
2026	**Railroad** Collectibles, 4th Ed., Baker	$14.95
4949	**Schroeder's Antiques Price Guide**, 16th Ed., Huxford	$12.95
2096	**Silverplated Flatware**, Revised 4th Edition, Hagan	$14.95
1922	Standard **Old Bottle** Price Guide, Sellari	$14.95
4708	**Summers' Guide to Coca-Cola**	$19.95
4952	**Summers' Pocket Guide to Coca-Cola** Identifications	$9.95
3892	**Toy & Miniature Sewing Machines**, Thomas	$18.95
4876	**Toy & Miniature Sewing Machines**, Book II, Thomas	$24.95
3828	Value Guide to **Advertising Memorabilia**, Summers	$18.95
3977	Value Guide to **Gas Station** Memorabilia, Summers & Priddy	$24.95
4877	Vintage **Bar Ware**, Visakay	$24.95
4935	The W.F. Cody **Buffalo Bill** Collector's Guide with Values	$24.95
4879	**Wanted to Buy**, 6th Edition	$9.95

Antique Tins

Identification & Values   Book I

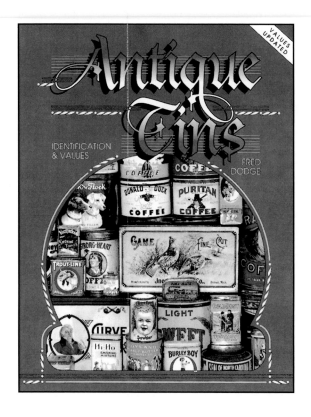

by Fred Dodge

Over 1,500 gorgeous color photos

Countless hours of research

Current price ranges

Condition comparison scale

8$^{1}/_{2}$" x 11, 296 pgs., hardbound, $24.95

This beautiful guide features over 1,500 gorgeous color photos of every type of tin from tobacco & coffee tins to the highly sought after talcum and spice tins, many of which feature beautiful graphic designs. The values in this guide were determined from countless hours of research and input from dealers, collectors, and owners of these tins. The guide provides current price ranges for every tin pictured, information on tin collector's clubs, and a condition comparison scale.

COLLECTOR BOOKS
A Division of Schroeder Publishing Co., Inc.

Schroeder's ANTIQUES Price Guide

. . . is the #1 best-selling antiques & collectibles value guide on the market today, and here's why . . .

Identification & Values Of Over 50,000 Antiques & Collectibles

8½ x 11, 608 Pages, $12.95

• *More than 300 advisors, well-known dealers, and top-notch collectors work together with our editors to bring you accurate information regarding pricing and identification.*

• *More than 45,000 items in almost 500 categories are listed along with hundreds of sharp original photos that illustrate not only the rare and unusual, but the common, popular collectibles as well.*

• *Each large close-up shot shows important details clearly. Every subject is represented with histories and background information, a feature not found in any of our competitors' publications.*

• *Our editors keep abreast of newly developing trends, often adding several new categories a year as the need arises.*

If it merits the interest of today's collector, you'll find it in *Schroeder's*. And you can feel confident that the information we publish is up to date and accurate. Our advisors thoroughly check each category to spot inconsistencies, listings that may not be entirely reflective of market dealings, and lines too vague to be of merit. Only the best of the lot remains for publication.

Without doubt, you'll find
SCHROEDER'S ANTIQUES PRICE GUIDE
the only one to buy for
reliable information and values.

COLLECTOR BOOKS
A Division of Schroeder Publishing Co., Inc.